# Notes on a Beermat

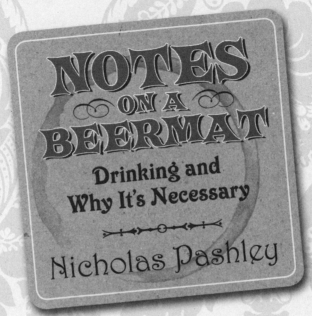

# NOTES ON A BEERMAT

## Drinking and Why It's Necessary

### Nicholas Pashley

Collins

Published by Collins, an imprint of
HarperCollins Publishers Ltd.

Originally published in 2001, in an earlier
version, by Polar Bear Press.

Grateful acknowledgment is made for
permission to reprint the following material:

Page 12: Excerpt from *Ladybird in a Loony Bin*
by Ian Cochrane. Published by Weidenfeld
& Nicolson. Reprinted by permission of the
publisher. Page 52: Excerpt from "Madeira
M'Dear" reproduced by permission of the
Estates of Michael Flanders & Donald Swann
2008. Any use of Flanders & Swann material,
large or small, should be referred to the Estates
at leonberger@donaldswann.co.uk. Reprinted
by permission. Page 67: Excerpt from *Lucky
Jim* by Kingsley Amis. Published by Victor
Gollancz, an imprint of The Orion Publishing
Group. Reprinted by permission. Page 156:
Excerpt from *Up in the Old Hotel* by Joseph
Mitchell. Published by Random House, Inc.
Reprinted by permission.

HarperCollins books may be purchased
for educational, business, or sales
promotional use through our Special
Markets Department.

HarperCollins Publishers Ltd
2 Bloor Street East, 20th Floor
Toronto, Ontario, Canada
M4W 1A8

*www.harpercollins.ca*

Library and Archives Canada Cataloguing
in Publication

Pashley, Nicholas, 1946–
Notes on a beermat : drinking and why it's
necessary / Nicholas Pashley; foreword by
Bill Bryson.

ISBN 978-1-55468-256-0

1. Drinking of alcoholic beverages—Humour.
2. Bars (Drinking establishments)—Humour.
I. Title.

PN6178.C3P383 2008
C818'.5402
C2008-901845-1

WEB 9 8 7 6 5 4 3 2 1

Printed and bound in Canada

Interior design by Sharon Kish

*Notes on a Beermat* is printed on
Ancient Forest Friendly paper,
made with 100% post-consumer waste.

To Anne Pashley, who has been to all these
pubs and more; and in memory of Kitty
Pashley, who liked a good pub into her tenth
decade; Stanley Pashley, who propped up a
bar or two in his time; and my brother John,
who did his share of damage as well.

Ale, ale, glorious ale,
Served up in pewter, it tells its own tale,
Some folk like radishes, some curly kale,
But give I boiled parsnips,
And a great dish of taters,
And a lump of fatty bacon,
And a pint of good ale.

—Traditional English drinking song

## Part II: Drinking in Particular

# Foreword

Though it pains me to say it, I don't believe I have seen Nicholas Pashley sober on more than six or seven occasions. On the other hand, and to be scrupulously fair, that is also the number of occasions on which I have seen Mr. Pashley, and that is where the pain comes in.

Mr. Pashley, as this book joyously attests, is clearly the finest drinking companion anyone could ask for. Unfortunately for me, he lives in Toronto, where he sells books by day and spends his evenings (and, it seems, quite a lot of his days as well) having a grand and amusing time in the city's varied drinking establishments, while I live in New Hampshire, where I spend nine months of the year shovelling snow and the other three months drying out my mittens. Thus, I am able to enjoy his company only on those infrequent occasions when I am on the right side of Lake Ontario.

Still, on the basis of a tragically finite number of such meetings, I can report that he is witty, kind, thoughtful, almost preposterously good-natured, and even smarter than he looks. Now, with this handsomely bound volume, he has produced what is unquestionably the funniest and most enjoyable book on beer drinking written by an English-born Canadian bookseller yet this century.

I joke, of course. This is a truly wonderful book from beginning to end—hugely comic, delightfully acerbic, gloriously discursive, and staggeringly well informed. In short, it is very like an evening with Mr. Pashley himself, but cheaper and with fewer trips to the men's room.

You are in for a singular treat and I envy you for that. Me, I've got some walks to shovel.

—Bill Bryson

# Introduction

**S**o this fellow walks into a bar, right? Then he walks into another bar. And yet another bar. Repeat this action for a very long time. And that's how this book got written.

I don't know if my mother coined it, but it was at her knee that I learned the expression "pub-minded," a pleasing turn of phrase that captures my world view with an uncanny precision. How lucky I was, then, to marry a woman similarly inclined. We met in a pub, of course.

This is a book about drinking. Now, we've seen a number of books about drinking in recent years, most of them telling either sad or inspirational stories about the perils of alcohol and the overcoming thereof. This is not one of those books.

There's no question, of course, that drink is a terrible thing. If I'd never touched a drop I'd have saved myself a lot of money. I'd be driving a fancy car today. On the other hand, I'd know a good deal fewer people, including my wife, so all in all I'm just as happy drinking. Otherwise, I'd be a lonely guy driving a fancy car. (I know—there is an argument that says you never have to be lonely if you have a fancy car. I wouldn't know. I'm a happily married drinking man with a very small car.)

And it's not just about drinking. It's about drinking well and drinking in public. I heard the friend of a friend express bewilderment one evening about why we chose to hang out in pubs when it was much cheaper to drink at home. I suspect this guy's a bit of a piker. For the beer drinker, of course, the pub has draught beer, which you can't get at home unless you live in a frat house. The pub also has that quality of pubness that few of us can achieve at home. Nor would most of us want to, the prime quality of pubness being that anyone is likely to turn up unannounced for a drink.

This friend of a friend is not alone in his disdain for public drinking. Let's be honest about this. I read in the *Toronto Star* a quote from Clay Aiken, who is famous for something. He apparently said, "The only reason people go to bars is to get drunk and have sex. To me, bars are what hell is like." Isn't it good to know that you won't be bothered by Clay Aiken down at the pub?

In his book *The Great Good Place*, Ray Oldenburg writes of the Third Place, a place that is neither home nor work, a place where friends can gather informally, without anyone having to be the host or clean up afterwards, where you can stay for one quick drink or for an evening, depending on your mood or on the social chemistry. Such places can be any of a number of things—a café or a bookstore, for instance—but they are most likely to be a pub, or something like it.

Oldenburg argues that society needs its third places, and that the suburbanization of North America makes third places not only unlikely but practically impossible. The shopping mall does not count. As Stan Rogers sang in "Barrett's Privateers," "God damn the mall!" I think I've got that right.

The need for a third place probably originated in Europe, where people lived multigenerationally in tiny apartments and needed somewhere else to go, if only to get away from the other thirteen people who shared their room. The modern North American, living in splendid suburban isolation in his monster home, has no such need for escape. If you want company, you can invite the people next door in for a drink. Except, of course, that you don't know the people next door. Small wonder we all turn into serial killers. Statistics show that very few pubgoers become serial killers. It's a known fact. They might turn into all sorts of unpleasant things—bores, cadgers, and mutterers, for instance—but seldom serial killers.

As you will discover if you persevere with this book, I live in Toronto. Well, we all have to live somewhere. You'd be surprised where some people live. Within Canada, for some reason, Toronto arouses strong feelings among people who live elsewhere, far stronger feelings than its actual residents ever experience. (A recent mayor reckoned we were living in the greatest city on Earth, but mayors are like that. I'm sure the mayor of Pocatello makes similar claims. It's Mayoral Hyperbole Syndrome, hereafter known as MHS.) Among non-Canadians, Toronto arouses almost no feelings at all. "It's very clean and safe," visitors say, and we beam with pride.

The celebrated cleanliness of Toronto—gradually becoming a thing of the past, thanks to budget cuts—is best exemplified by the oft-told but possibly apocryphal story of the film crew working on a downtown street. Toronto has used tax breaks and what was for a long time an almost worthless dollar to attract American movie-makers to come up here and turn Toronto into New York or another American city. I believe there has been talk of awarding a special Oscar to the cinematographer who most successfully manages to keep the very tall CN Tower out of shots. Anyway, this particular film crew had strewn garbage about to give the street an authentic American look, but then made the mistake of going to lunch. They returned to find that the city had come along and cleaned it all up. Accurate or not, the story reveals a psychological truth about this city.

Toronto used to describe itself as the City That Works, but finally stopped when it had become palpably untrue. Peter Ustinov, of course, has famously described Toronto as "New York run by the Swiss." What makes this line particularly funny is that Torontonians see it as a compliment. If New York is a nice place to visit but you wouldn't want to live there, Toronto's just the opposite. I'm never quite sure how visitors to Toronto fill their time. Actually, I do know, because I'm frequently called upon to give directions to Casa Loma, our authentic rococo castle (built between 1911 and 1914). I mention all of this because in the course of this book you will be subjected to references to Toronto. I feel you should know ahead of time; this book is nothing if not honest.

That said, this isn't a guidebook to drinking in Toronto—or anywhere else, for that matter. It doesn't offer phone numbers, opening hours, or lunchtime specials. Still, if you find a bit of useful information about a pub you might not have discovered otherwise, you're welcome to it with my blessing.

As a young person, still fairly fresh off the boat from England, I was involuntarily relocated to a rugged western suburb called Etobicoke, an Indian name meaning We Planned This Community But We Forgot to Plan a Pub. Faced with the absence of a nearby Anglican church, my parents began attending an odd fundamentalist church that was run exclusively by people from South Bend, Indiana. This church was sound on baseball—Rocky Nelson, who went on to hit a home run in the seventh game of the 1960 World Series, was a parishioner—but death on most other forms of fun, which they called sin. One Sabbath morning a Sunday School teacher informed us—and these words have been etched in my brain ever since—that anybody who drank was a bum. That's what he said: "We know that anyone who drinks is a bum." Surely, I said to myself, he means "has a bum," not "is a bum," though even then I was sophisticated enough to suspect that we all had bums, drinkers and abstainers alike.

I was not a drinker myself at the time, being just a slip of a boy, but most of the adults I knew were drinkers, and they seemed altogether decent people, with not a serial killer among them. Already I was questioning doctrine and I was coming down on the side of fun. And possibly even sin. There I have remained.

People who think the fifties were a joyless period in which the pinnacle of pleasure was a new recipe for anything that included miniature marshmallows should have known my parents. There were no pubs in Etobicoke, so the denizens of that benighted borough drank at one another's homes. And did they drink! On at least one occasion my church organist father left a party in time to go home and shave, go to church and work his magic, then return to the party. An American writer has described my parents' ilk as the Greatest Generation, and I'm tempted to agree, if only on the basis of the parties.

Under the terms of the international regulations that govern the global book trade, it is compulsory in any book about drinking in public to include the words of Doctor Johnson, so I thought I'd get them out of the way early. And here they come now: "There is nothing which has yet been contrived by man by which so much happiness is produced as by a good tavern or inn." Now, I know that such man-made contrivances as indoor plumbing or the tenor saxophone have their supporters, but when it comes to the contriving of happiness, I'm with Johnson all the way.

Not everyone agrees, I know. There are also people who think Kenny G is a jazz musician (I prefer his brother Ali), and people who think that artificial turf is an acceptable playing surface for sporting events. Such people—though I'm reluctant to say it—might not need this book. They may, however, have friends who do, people whose lives might be enriched by this meditation on pleasure. Feel the quality of the paper. Admire the excellent typeface. You don't see value like this every day.

# Part I

# Drinking
# in
# General

# The Impossible Dream:
## Looking for the Perfect Pub

I was thinking about George Orwell one Saturday afternoon as I supped my ale in the Rose and Crown, a theoretically English pub in uptown Toronto. It wasn't that the bartender looked like Orwell or that there were copies of *Animal Farm* everywhere I looked (he didn't and there weren't). Perhaps it was something to do with the 1984-like sensation of seeking pleasure in a place that seemed designed for anything but. The Rose and Crown looked like an accountant's version of an English pub. It seemed more a business plan than a pub.

The notice by the door insisting that customers were not to bring in their own food and/or drink raised the obvious question: what was so bad about the Rose and Crown's food and drink that people were tempted to bring their own? The Rose and Crown is a big pub, a very big pub. And it was disturbingly dark. I'd estimate that two-thirds of the clientele the afternoon I was there were huddled together at the front near the windows, seeking the comfort of daylight.

A singer called Ian Robb wrote a song about the decline of the English pub that you really should get to know. (It can be ordered from www.folk-legacy.com.) It asks the musical question, "What has become of the old Rose & Crown?" In the case of Toronto's Rose and Crown, unfortunately, nothing has become of it. It's exactly as it always was. (I have since learned that novelist Wayne Johnston drinks there, so perhaps I've been a trifle hasty. Or maybe he likes the dark.)

In an essay called "The Moon Under Water," George Orwell—and I knew I'd get back to him eventually—writes about his favourite pub. It has everything he wants in a pub, including draught stout, working fireplaces, and barmaids who call everyone "Dear" (and it has to be "Dear"; "Ducky" won't do at all). Toward the end of this tribute to the perfect pub, Orwell acknowledges that he's made it all up. There is no such place. The Moon Under Water is the pub he dreams of but never finds. Of his ten ideal pub criteria, he knows of a place that offers eight.

Perhaps it's just as well we never find the perfect pub. It is the quest that keeps us going. And, in any case, if we found it, someone would almost certainly wreck it, and what would be the likelihood of future happiness then?

No, it's best as it is, in an imperfect world. Here in Toronto, we haven't been at it for long, so it isn't surprising we haven't created the perfect pub yet. The perfect pub, when it happens, will have taken time. They've had several centuries in England, so it's not surprising that they have more contenders than we have. In London alone, the Dove in Hammersmith and the Nag's Head in Belgravia are pretty darn close to perfect. The New Inn at Waterley

Bottom—and I couldn't make up a name like Waterley Bottom even if I wanted to—is a rural gem, set in a lovely Cotswold valley. The Tan Hill Inn, said to be the highest pub in England, is alone worth the drive to North Yorkshire, but then so is just about everything else in North Yorkshire. The Blue Anchor, in Helston, Cornwall, is an old stone pub that serves its own beer, as it has done for several centuries. And if you haven't seen the Fleece in Bretforton, Worcestershire, please make plans to do so as quickly as possible. Your life to date is practically worthless.

The White Horse, near Priors Dean in Hampshire, is often known as the Pub with No Name, as its sign fell down some decades ago. It is also one of the most difficult pubs to find in all of England, located off a minor road, sheltered from view by a copse of trees. The first time I went there I spotted a local rustic, who was scything down some long vegetation growing by the side of the road. The more I think about it, he can't possibly have been wearing the traditional smock of the agricultural labourer, but that's the way I remember him. I rolled down the car window. "Excuse me," I said, "but would we be going the right direction to find the White Horse?" He looked up from his work and, with the rich, savoury tone of south/southwestern England, explained, "Well, if you're not thursty you might be. But if you're thursty—and by the looks of you, you are—you'll want to turn around." He then gave us impeccable instructions, without which we would never have found the place. When we arrived a few minutes later, the pub's car park was packed. Inaccessibility should never impinge on one's quest for the perfect pub.

The reason I go on about English pubs is that when Toronto finally moved away from the traditional taproom, we instinctively turned to the English pub model. There are, heaven knows, worse models. And we all know what an English pub looks like, which is what the people who brought us our first neo-crypto-quasi-English pubs gave us: flock wallpaper, tin ceilings, dark wood, frosted glass, and staff who said "Cheers" when they served us a drink. (They'd call us "Ducky" if they thought of it.) This model is based on the late Victorian gin palace, which is just one of many English pub styles. None of the above-mentioned great English pubs fits that model. Next time you're in London, check out the Lamb in Lamb's Conduit Street or the Red Lion in Duke of York Street to see the prototypes. It's a perfectly good pub style, but it's far from being the only one.

So what's the formula for a great pub? That's the trick: there isn't one. There are pubs built to a formula—and some are highly successful—but I don't know of a great one or even a very good one. It helps to have a good setting and an ancient building with lots of character. It's imperative to sell good beer that is well maintained.

The key to the great pub is that we feel comfortable in it, which has most to do with the people who run it. This may seem obvious, but there are still people who don't get it. The English novelist Ian Cochrane once wrote of an unsatisfactory pub experience: "The landlord was a very unhelpful unhappy man and didn't agree with drinking in a pub." Some years ago a woman with a similar philosophy ran the Artful Dodger in Toronto.

All great pubs are the handiwork of someone who has a vision of the place he or she would ideally like to drink in. A great pub—like a great restaurant or bookstore—should give the impression that all the important decisions are being made on the premises, not by someone in a suit miles away.

So what would we find in the perfect pub? My perfect pub would almost certainly be different from your perfect pub, but then I'm the guy who's writing the book. (If you want *your* perfect pub, write your own damn book.) My pub, for starters, has no canned music. Orwell notes that one of the charms of the Moon Under Water is that it is always quiet enough to talk. He says he doesn't want a radio in the pub. Radio? Orwell died in 1950, long before the modern sound system was created. Lucky man.

And I'm not convinced that we need a television either. I remember in the early seventies when the old Morrissey Tavern in Toronto got its first television, expressly for the hockey playoffs. It was, we were told, to be used for no other purpose, but eventually, of course, it became part of the furniture. I don't mind bringing in a set for a major occasion. I was surprised in October 1970 to see a television in McSorley's Old Ale House in New York, but it was the World Series, after all. Bushe's Bar in Baltimore, West Cork, one evening suddenly boasted a television so we could all watch Ireland's feisty Sonia O'Sullivan in the World Track and Field Championships; she finished fourth, alas, behind three almost certainly artificially stimulated Chinese women (at least, if the Irish commentators were to be believed).

My wife and I watched the end of a France-Brazil blockbuster in the 1986 World Cup in a bar in Menton, on the French Riviera. As extra time edged slowly toward a penalty kick conclusion, the staff quietly gathered up anything made of glass. When the Brazilians had the ball, we aimed the hex sign at the screen. When the French had the ball, we sang "La Marseillaise." Finally, the French won on penalty kicks, and sixty men fled the bar and drove around honking their horns until they ran out of gas. (Which wasn't for a while; damn the fuel efficiency of those European cars.)

And it isn't just sports. At Christmas in 1967, not having a TV in my little bedsit, I watched the Beatles' *Magical Mystery Tour* in a Camden Town pub. There used to be a big, ugly television in a Toronto pub called the Munster Hall that existed solely, it seemed, to show *Coronation Street* reruns on Sunday afternoons. The rest of the time it sat unused and covered up. Television in a pub—except for special occasions—is anti-social and has no place in my perfect pub.

There is wide disagreement on cellphones in pubs. I admit that I own a cellphone. My wife bought it for me, as it seemed a friendlier way of keeping tabs on me than one of those electronic ankle bracelets they put on convicts on probation and Hollywood bad girls. Occasionally the damn thing has gone off while I've been in a pub, and I think I've had the good grace to apologize for it. There are pubs that ban cellphones. As far as I'm concerned, any pub that inflicts piped music on its customers has no place banning other noisemakers. Quiet pubs, on the other hand, have a point.

The Lewes Arms in Sussex has a zero-tolerance policy on cellphones and warns that use of these devices warrants a penalty of a round of drinks for the house. I haven't seen that extreme sentence inflicted (worse luck), but I have watched a terrier-like barman bustle customers out into the street with their cellphones. The Digby Tap in Sherborne, Dorset, levies a fifty-pence fine for cellphone use, proceeds to charity, which seems not unfair. There seem to be two cellphones for every resident of the UK, so the English are more sensitive to this problem than we are. The otherwise excellent White Horse in west London can sound like a convention of arcade games when it gets busy.

The perfect pub has attentive, friendly bar staff. After I left the Rose and Crown that afternoon I stopped in at the Duke of Kent, just to the south. A woman named Mea was playing the bar like a violin. Serving drinks, chatting with regulars, bestowing a million-dollar smile on all and sundry, she was worth her weight in hops. She might even have been able to brighten up the Rose and Crown, which would be no mean achievement. My wife has accused me of falling in love with any woman who brings me a beer, which is not an unreasonable accusation, but I had a feeling the whole bar—man, woman, and undecided—was in love with Mea. I almost went back to the Rose and Crown to encourage the long-suffering inmates to pay up and move a few doors down, but only a few of them could have got into the crowded Duke of Kent. Tragically, Mea has moved on and can no longer be seen at the Duke of Kent. Things change, as you're no doubt aware.

Like Orwell, I like a fire on a cold day, and God knows we get enough of those. Cold days, I mean. Presumably because we have central heating here, we have very few fireplaces in our pubs, and we're poorer for that. Dora Keogh on the Danforth has a fireplace, if you're interested.

Orwell likes a pub with a garden. We don't go in much for pub gardens here, but we do have patios. I like a patio, but not just any patio. Drinking beer on a city sidewalk holds limited appeal for me, though it's better than not drinking beer at all. My favourite Toronto patio is the rooftop bar at Paupers on Bloor Street. It's a hell of a climb on a hot day, especially as some of us get older, but you're up above the hubbub when you get there. So I might put that rooftop patio on my list.

Now, here's something I resent, as a fellow who goes to pubs on an almost daily basis. I resent not being able to go to a pub on St. Patrick's Day or New Year's Eve just to have a pint or two, as I like to do. No, suddenly the pub is filled with galoots who have their minds—if that isn't too strong a word—set on getting pie-eyed and making as much noise as possible. A pub-minded Irish friend of mine refuses to go into a pub on St. Patrick's Day, citing the unpleasantness of drinking in the aggressive company of so many amateurs.

The pub of my dreams will discourage ritualized drunkenness of this nature, and the bar staff will look askance at customers who dress oddly on October 31. They will not necessarily refuse to serve such people—I'm not an unreasonable man—but they will make it apparent to unduly festive persons that other pubs are more welcoming to their sort. My ideal pub might recognize more offbeat festivals: Stephen Sondheim's birthday (March 22), for instance, or the anniversary of plucky young Marilyn Bell's swim across Lake Ontario (September 9). Such occasions will be marked by the striking of a small bell at the bar and a quiet chorus of "Well done"s from the patrons. If New Year's Eve is your sort of thing, every other bar in town will be catering to your needs. There's nothing wrong with one pub that regards December 31 as John Denver's birthday and nothing more. At midnight, the locals will quietly raise a glass and mutter something about country roads and mountain mamas and such. It'll be very tasteful, and it's not as if we'll actually play the song.

I like to be able to get something to eat in a pub, though usually I don't need a full meal. Too many English pubs—the current term is "gastropubs"—have been ruined by being turned into restaurants that also, grudgingly, serve beer. There are still lots of English pubs that will sell you a sandwich. Just a sandwich. Not with fries, not on a kaiser, just a sandwich: decent cheese on honest bread. The Duke of York in midtown Toronto used to offer a basket of sausage rolls, and I don't think it's an exaggeration to say that those sausage rolls saved lives. Sometimes a few sausage rolls among a small group of people can keep an evening going, especially with a bit of sharp English mustard on the side. Those sausage rolls are gone from the Duke's menu now, which is yet more evidence of a declining quality of life. Sausage rolls would always be available in my perfect pub. And not microwaved, either.

Good beer, of course, is essential. Many great pubs offer only a few draught beer choices, but they're all interesting. Real ale— unpasteurized, cask-conditioned ale served without artificial carbonation—always cheers me up. Here in Toronto, I can think of only a handful or so of pubs that serve real ale. The greatest city in the world, if our ex-mayor is to be believed, and we can boast possibly ten pubs with real ale. The drawback of real ale is that the pub needs someone who knows how to take proper care of beer, but that's what pubs are for. (Just as a bookstore should have someone on the premises who knows something about books.) There is plenty of good beer being made these days throughout the western world, little of which is served in your local pub or mine. Feel free to ask your local publican why not.

The consumption of beer, it goes without saying, leads to the act of micturition—peeing to you or me—and publicans are required by law to provide facilities to accommodate this all-too-human need. I know English pubs from which the drinker has to go out in the rain to reach the toilets. During the colder months—which can include the period from January through December—these are not places you want to linger. For that reason, I prefer paper towels to those infernal hand-drying machines that take roughly ten minutes per hand to work. I don't know what goes on in women's wash-rooms, but my observation is that far fewer men wash their hands before they leave if they have to use the machines.

For reasons of human physiology, women are inclined to come into more personal contact with the facilities so should be able to expect certain levels of comfort and hygiene. The woman with whom I do much of my drinking has been known to judge a pub by the quality of its ladies' room. The first time we visited the New Inn at Waterley Bottom, Anne just about squealed with pleasure at the state of the ladies'.

There are, I know, men who feel that clean toilets only encourage women to go to pubs. The next thing you know the place is serving salads and you're finding lipstick stains on your glass. McSorley's Old Ale House in New York barred women from the premises for decades, relenting only when forced to by a court of law. Even then, the pub drew the line at providing separate micturition facilities for its female customers, which led to some surprised faces in the gents', or what had been the gents'. McSorley's finally got over it and put in a ladies', and nowadays the sexes coexist cheerfully. Though I'm still not sure you can get a decent salad to this day.

My perfect pub is a female-friendly pub and has freshly laundered gingham hand towels in the ladies' loo, or whatever it is women like in there. I'd be grateful, however, if they didn't wear lipstick. It's hell to get off a glass, and it's inclined to kill the head on a pint of beer. Perhaps women with lipstick could be asked to use a straw. If they'll agree to that, they can have as much salad as they like.

And how about children? Traditionally, the English-speaking world has, by and large, banished the tykes from licensed premises on the grounds that drinking is a sin and should not, therefore, be witnessed by the young. This way of thinking is similar to the belief that if we don't tell children about sex it'll never cross their minds. If children were barred so as to give grown-ups a break from their company, I could understand it.

One reason Europeans are more mature about drinking—or so we are told—is that they're exposed to it from infancy and don't regard it as some forbidden fruit. If you believe everything I've read, Bosnia and Herzegovina doesn't even have a minimum drinking age. Yet it is the English who are feared across Europe for their out-of-control drinking, and not just the football supporters either.

I have mixed feelings about children in pubs. The cigarette smoke can't be good for them (though that's becoming less of a problem in most areas), but it does make sense to socialize them early on, to integrate them into the company of adults. If nothing else, watching their elders behave like fools might de-glamorize alcohol for them. If they're going to run around and shout, however, I'd like them to do that outside, and that goes for their parents too.

A non-smoker myself, I'd certainly like a pub that's free of the abominable weed, but I'd be reluctant to tell my friends Alison Owen and Robbie Brown they're not welcome in my pub. The perfect pub offers a forceful yet silent air cleaner, something that may yet be uninvented. I write about smoking elsewhere in this book.

I drink at regular intervals with people of education and breeding, or at least that's what they tell me. When we can hear each other over the music, we frequently have lively discussions on any number of subjects. There are often issues that remain unsettled at the end of the evening because we have no way of looking things up. My perfect pub will have a variety of reference materials: a good dictionary, an all-purpose almanac of some sort, an encyclopedia, a decent anthology of poetry, at least one dictionary of quotations, an atlas, perhaps a film guide, a copy of Strunk and White and a vintage Fowler's, an English-French dictionary, some sort of sports encyclopedia, a fairly recent edition of *Canadian Who's Who,* and a *Brewer's Dictionary of Phrase and Fable.* For the price of a good sound system—which, of course, will not be needed—a pub could offer an arsenal of debate-settling books.

And one last thing: animals. Studies show that the proximity of animals actually lowers human blood pressure and makes people feel better. The best English pubs are filled with dogs and cats. I once knew a pub in West Hampstead in London that held almost as many dogs as people of an evening. The dogs were happy, the customers were happy. This, of course, is strictly forbidden in my jurisdiction, in case people might actually attain some degree of happiness. Technically, animals are barred from pubs for health reasons, which seems pretty bogus to me if you look at some of the people who get in. I went to a west end Toronto pub not all that long ago that at one point in the afternoon boasted four dogs, all cheerfully present with the people who had walked them there. I won't name the pub in question for fear of attracting the local anti-dog activists at the licensing authorities, but I for one will go back to this pub because of its animal friendliness. If I come back as a border collie in my next life, I'll want somewhere congenial to go.

# What a Good Idea:
# The History of Beer

There is an old English music hall song that credits the invention of beer to a man named Charlie Mopp: "God bless Charlie Mopp, the man who invented beer." Although the song makes a fairly convincing case, beer historians remain skeptical. They reckon beer predates Mr. Mopp. They figure beer goes back to early man, or possibly early woman.

Early man was a rough sort of brute, and early woman wasn't much better, though we've been led to believe otherwise by the poster of Raquel Welch in a fur bikini in *One Million Years B.C.* They lived nomadically, without any of what we would consider the necessities: air conditioning, reality television, or modern religious fundamentalists. (One of the reasons early man didn't have religious fundamentalists, incidentally, is that the planet didn't yet exist at that point, according to religious fundamentalists, many of whom believe that the universe was not created until roughly four thousand years after early man had invented beer. But I'm getting ahead of myself.) Their lives were short and mostly bereft of pleasure.

Every now and then, however, something nice happened. Bits of soggy wild barley accidentally came into contact with wind-borne yeasts, and fermented. Primitive, or unnecessarily fastidious, early man might then have said, "Darn, this barley's gone rotten. Better throw it out. Don't want to get sick."

More advanced early man might have replied, "Not so fast, Ogg. Let's have a look at it." The next morning, head pounding, early man might just have decided he had had a good time the night before, what he could remember of it. He might even have woken up with early woman next to him (see the chapter on Drinking and Sex).

Somewhere along the way a bright spark among early man (and it might very well have been early woman) began to think that this fermented barley was a good thing, and that just possibly there might be a way to induce it deliberately rather than wait for one of nature's little accidents. Like fire, fermentation might be created and harnessed. Alas, we don't know the name of the early person who figured this out—it is unlikely to have been Charlie Mopp—but this is very probably a good time to open a beer and drink a toast to the unknown brewer. Cheers.

The era of which we speak is an estimated ten thousand years ago, long before the cable company, airport security, and other modern irritants. To ensure a regular supply of beer, it was necessary to cultivate grain. This, in turn, transformed early man (and the early woman he was now shacked up with after the accidental brewing incident of a couple of paragraphs ago) from the hunter-gatherer to the agriculturalist. Even then, beer was making people smarter.

Another bright spark of prehistory wondered if there was anything else we could make out of grain and yeast, thus inventing bread. Hence the sandwich, the drinker's best friend. Bread, of course, led to variations like cake—which was good—and the kaiser bun, that tasteless, doughy piece of stodge named as revenge upon the Germans for the First World War and served in many pubs to this day to diminish the pleasure of an honest hamburger. (The kaiser bun is mandatory in Ontario bars as a pivotal part of the legislation aimed at curtailing pleasure among the citizenry. Citizens who became accustomed to pleasure might start to see it as their due, which would be inconvenient for the authorities.)

It was beer that gave civilization its kick-start. Without beer, there would have been no agriculture, no science, no Renaissance, no Shakespeare, no Jane Austen, no Mozart, no Charlie Parker, no—well, you get the picture. That said, we might not have liked early beer as much as early man did. When you've never had any beer at all, you're not terribly picky. (Look at the stuff teenagers drink.) The Mesopotamians took germinated barley and made it into partly baked cakes, which were then dumped into a jar of water and left to ferment. (What they almost certainly didn't understand was the role of yeast in the process, but at some point a bit of rogue yeast got into the mixture and turned soggy barley cakes into something wonderful.) The result was a lumpy brew that might, in the classier taverns of the day, be strained through a cloth to make it less chewy. To this day Egyptians make something similar called bouza; oddly enough, they have not found a big export market for this product. Equally oddly, "bouza" is apparently not the source for our word "booze," which entered Middle English from early Dutch.

Apart from being lumpy, early beer lacked the distinctive hops we're used to. We're not quite sure when hops became widely used in the making of beer. Brewers throughout history have used flavouring agents such as herbs, fruit, berries, spices, or honey, and some historians suspect the Hebrews learned to use hops during the Babylonian captivity, in which case the experience wasn't a complete writeoff. Their version of beer was said to alleviate leprosy, which I find altogether plausible. To this day I have yet to see a leper in a pub, and I've been to a few; perhaps you hang out in different places. The ancient Greeks grew hops, but there's not much evidence they used them in beer, which seems uncharacteristically wasteful.

We know that hops were being grown in Bohemia and Bavaria in about the eighth century. The multi-talented Hildegard of Bingen wrote about brewing with hops in the twelfth century, and certainly Flemish brewers were exporting hopped beer into Britain in the early 1400s, to the horror of English traditionalists. Hops, of course, add the bitterness we have come to expect in beer (except drinkers of Molson Golden, who have come to expect almost no taste at all), and they also act as a preservative.

Risk-taking microbreweries these days are known to replace or supplement hops with such oddities as heather, bog myrtle, ginseng, and hemp. As hops are related (by marriage) to cannabis—that other great medicinal herb—we shouldn't be surprised to encounter hemp beer, and indeed you can usually find it on tap in Toronto at C'est What, down on Front Street. It's not bad either, once you get it lit, which is the hard part.

Brewing, until very recently, has always been a local enterprise. The original English alehouses brewed their own beer, as did many private homes. Early commercial breweries sprang up to make beer for local customers, and in parts of Europe that model still works. Until it became a victim of the great metropolis's real estate frenzies and moved out of town, the Young brewery in southwest London used to make its local deliveries by horse-drawn dray. It's cheaper and—given the state of London traffic—no slower than using trucks. It's also good marketing, except when a member of your target demographic steps in a bit of horse exhaust. Pasteurization made beer easier to keep, hence easier to transport, and that led to the rise of mega-brewing. Now, wherever you are in the world, you can enjoy a perfectly bland Carlsberg. No longer need you risk tasting a local beer made for local palates. It's progress, so it must be good.

In any event, over the centuries beer has become less lumpy and more scientific and, until the recent boom of microbreweries, seemed to have reached the end of its evolutionary trail. Companies that had once been run by brewers were now run by accountants and marketing guys. Focus groups were more likely to influence the flavour of beer than the brewmaster. Beer was being dumbed down, brewed to fit an advertising campaign, its flavour downplayed so as not to give offence to a larger market. It almost makes one nostalgic for Mesopotamia.

# Don't Rule Out Miracles:
# How Beer Is Made

Those of us blessed to live in Toronto find it easy to forget that there are other people out there living in other places. I know it seems odd, but it's true. I've seen some of these other places. In the mid-seventies I once undertook a walking tour of Ontario cottage country, thinking I'd throw myself into a body of water whenever I got hot and stop in at local hostelries for refreshments when I got thirsty. A good plan, if a trifle naive.

What I hadn't counted on was there being virtually no bars in cottage country in those days. I had a beer with friends in Orillia, then set off on my walk. I walked to Bobcaygeon, and I found exactly one bar along the way. Hail to thee, blithe Coboconk! I spent some time in that bar, talking to an older guy who had worked on the Avro Arrow and was still bitter about that ill-fated plane. When I hit Bobcaygeon a day or two later and found yet again a town without a bar, I hitchhiked to Lindsay, had a beer, and caught a bus home. On top of there not being any bars, most of the water along the way seemed privately owned, so I managed one swim between

Orillia and Bobcaygeon. All of which taught me to stay close to home. Toronto's not the best drinking town in the world, but at least I know where the bars are.

That said, I'm happy to see that we can learn from others. There's a pair of brothers who opened a brewpub in Halifax back in 1985 and saw it prosper. In 1991 Ron Keefe, one of these brothers, then decided to bring his brewing and pubbing prowess to the Big Smoke and try his luck. And I'm glad he did. The Granite Brewery, on Mount Pleasant south of Eglinton, is the home of some of our best beers. For a time Keefe maintained a second location, which he called Beer Street, taking its name from the Hogarth prints that chronicle life on Gin Lane and Beer Street. Gin Lane is filled with vice, depravity, and poverty, and only the pawnbroker prospers. The residents of Beer Street, on the other hand, enjoy happiness, health, and prosperity. The pawnbroker alone suffers from a want of trade.

The Granite Brewery brews several beers that range from a lightish ale to a fairly hearty stout, with an entertaining raspberry-flavoured ale, an India pale ale, and a noteworthy Peculiar, modelled on Theakston's celebrated Old Peculier. But for me the star of the show is the Best Bitter Special (or dry-hopped, as the locals call it)—I would have called it Special Best Bitter myself, but it's not my brewery—which is their Best Bitter dry-hopped and served as a real ale. Dry-hopping is a process whereby extra hops are added to the cask at the last minute to add aroma and flavour. The first time I had a pint of Keefe's dry-hopped I thought I'd died and gone to heaven, or at least to England. I've been guilty of overlooking Keefe's other beers because, well, who needs anything else? I should note that there are many who swear with equal force by the

Granite's IPA, which is now cask-conditioned, and I'll admit that they have a strong argument.

The forces that for so many years fought any sort of liberalized sale of beer in this province also worked to keep the little guy out of the beer market. Microbreweries were tacitly outlawed, as were brewpubs. The big breweries—which, coincidentally, contributed generously to the local ruling party—succeeded in keeping outsiders outside, where they belonged. Gradual changes in legislation have allowed people who aspire to brew good beer to do so, within limited boundaries. To be fair, this is not just an Ontario problem. Across North America, beer lovers have campaigned to make good beer more readily available, but they have had to fight for that right. If you want to see guns handed out on street corners, Charlton Heston will be delighted to speak on your behalf. In fact, try to shut him up. There is no Charlton Heston equivalent to speak out for beer. Guns good, beer bad.

There have been other, less interesting problems in brewing. Malt, for instance. For years, virtually the only source of malt in these parts was a company called Canada Malting, which produced the malted barley it wanted to produce. If you wanted to use something else in your beer, you had to find your own barley and malt it yourself, which is tough for a small brewery.

Well, here we go. At some point in any book about beer it is essential to discuss the process of brewing. There is no way around it. Frankly, I wish there were. The sad fact is that any description of the brewing process is dull, and I mean gruesomely, gut-wrenchingly dull. Most people will skip over this section, and they're right to do so, although they'll miss the racy bit about the sex life of hops.

The handful of people who actually read it all the way through are people who brew their own beer and they're checking to see if I've got it right.

The mandatory chapter about brewing beer uses a lot of words like "wort," "ullage," "grist," and "sparging." These are the sort of words you might use if you were writing a cheap knock-off of *The Hobbit*: Wort came upon Grist in the forest, sparging his ullage.

Very few people understand the brewing process. People think they will understand it better if they go on a brewery tour. There is nothing wrong with going on a brewery tour—indeed, I encourage it—but please do not think you will understand brewing at the end of it. I've been on brewery tours in all sorts of places, from Munich to Los Angeles, Dublin to Vancouver. I've toured huge, monster beer factories (Anheuser-Busch, L.A.) and tiny local breweries (the Uley Brewery in deepest Gloucestershire). I've even made beer myself, which is probably the only way to begin to understand how it works. Even then, you'll understand it properly only if you grow your own barley and hops, but not many home brewers are prepared to wait that long for their first batch.

What you will see if you tour a brewery is one or two people standing around in rubber boots, looking suspiciously at large copper or stainless steel kettles. The bigger the brewery, the more people standing around. If this is an English brewery, one of the people will almost certainly be called Roger and, if you're lucky, you might hear him say something technical like "Oh arr." If you stay long enough—and there's no reason you should—Roger might draw a small amount of murky fluid from a tap into a glass tube and look at it discouragingly. He will then go for his tea break. This is your cue to move immediately to the tasting room and get as much of the free local product as they're willing to part with.

What you need to know about the brewing process—and honestly, I'm getting to the crunch here—is that rather a lot of malted barley gets boiled up with a smaller amount of hops and (once it's all cooled down a bit) even less yeast in quite a fair bit of water. Depending on how much money the brewer hopes to make from this concoction, you might see less malted barley and more rice and corn syrup. This all gets put into a big container, then transferred to another container and left for a while. Then—and this is the crucial bit—a miracle takes place. Oh, I know, in this secular age we hate to talk about miracles, but sometimes there's no other word for it. At some hard-to-define point this vat of goop becomes beer.

Yes, there are different sorts of hops, some of which have lovely old names like Fuggles and the Hallertau Mittelfrüh, and there are different sorts of barley. The real experts can possibly take a sip of beer and spot whether the brewer used a two-row or a six-row barley, but I can't and you probably can't either. Sometimes, depending on your luck, there are things like bog myrtle in your beer, and some brewers even make beer with chili peppers, which makes you thirsty even while you're drinking. .

If, on your brewery tour, you see the wort in action it might put you off beer forever. It's not pretty. The foamy stuff on the average wort looks more like a rash than a head, but somehow it turns into something quite wonderful. If you have a better word than "miracle" for what transforms something raw and ugly into Fuller's London Pride or Denison's Weissbier, you let me know. The only other word I'll countenance is "alchemy," which I'll accept happily.

So what's in your beer? If you're in Germany—and chances are you're not—your beer contains only water, yeast, hops, and malted grains (usually barley, although wheat, rye, and oats are certainly possible). This is because of the *Reinheitsgebot*, or the beer purity law, of 1516, which decreed what was permissible in Bavarian beer. Interestingly enough, the original *Reinheitsgebot*—contrary to popular opinion—makes no reference to yeast, as proper understanding of what yeast does for beer was still three hundred years away. The *Reinheitsgebot* also set price ceilings for Bavarian beer; defenders of the edict conveniently ignore this part of it. Try to get a *Kopf* of beer in Munich for a *Pfennig* these days.

There is some suggestion that the *Reinheitsgebot* was a self-serving boondoggle passed by Duke Wilhelm IV, who coincidentally held a monopoly on the supply of malt (he was the Canada Malting of his day), but what's the point of being a duke if you can't make people do what you want them to? When the German republic was formed in 1919, the Bavarians refused to join unless the rest of the German states accepted their purity law, which they did, although the law did not apply in East Germany during that interesting era. Given what they pumped into their athletes over the years, it would have been unrealistic to expect the East Germans to quibble over impurities in their beer. Breweries in the former East Germany are now required to hew to the purity laws.

At first glance, this legislation might seem to guarantee a fairly homogeneous beer across the land, which is clearly not the case. There is huge variety (often regional) in the taste and colour of German beers. A Bavarian wheat beer is different from a Berlin wheat beer. On the plus side, the German beer laws keep brewers from cutting corners by using sugar, cornstarch, rice, and other such beer cheapeners, not to mention the sinister batch of chemicals routinely used by modern non-German brewers to add sparkle and clarity and lengthen the shelf life. On the other hand, making hops the only allowable flavouring agent bars all manner of interesting beer flavours that the Belgians and Scandinavians enjoy. Other European countries have argued that the *Reinheitsgebot* exists only to serve as a protection racket for German beers, keeping all sorts of other beers out of the German market.

If you were still awake at this point, I could mention the European debate over the sex life of hops. As you're almost certainly aware, only the female hop is useful in the brewing process. The male hop is charming and witty, but not of much practical use. Nowhere else in nature is this the case. The lager producers of the world use a bottom-fermenting process (you don't have to know this for the exam) in which fertilized female hops create a problem with the clarification of the beer. This problem does not arise with top-fermented beers like the ale family. Lager makers like an unsullied, virginal lady hop, while the brewers of ale are just as happy with a jolly female hop that's been around a bit and has some stories to tell. On the continent the wild male hop has been eradicated, while in sexually permissive England the wild male hop continues to roam free, doing his nasty little deeds wherever he may. And, for my money, long may he do so, though no doubt the commissars of the European Union are plotting ways as we speak to stifle the plucky English male hop.

Some time in the seventies, North Americans began to realize that it was not in fact compulsory to drink beers from huge beer factories, and small breweries started to sprout up. Even in Canada, for heaven's sake. The Granville Island Brewery in Vancouver got the Canadian microbrewery movement going in 1984, and a man called Jim Brickman started the first small Ontario brewery in a good long time with the Brick brewery, just a few months later. Leo Heaps followed along soon after with the Upper Canada Brewery, which got away from the lagers of Granville Island and Brick and into some decent ales.

In the intervening years, microbreweries have come and gone, and the quality of their beers has fluctuated as well. Some of the micros have transcended their micro status, becoming in the process larger regional breweries. Sleeman, for instance, is the brainchild of one John Sleeman, who took his grandfather's brewing recipe and a handsome bottle design and built a company that eventually took on national proportions. Sleeman became successful not through brewing imaginative, flavour-packed beers, but through the traditional, time-tested methods of extensive marketing and taking over other companies. In the late nineties Sleeman bought Upper Canada, closed down the Toronto brewery, and started brewing the Upper Canada beers at its Guelph plant. Beer lovers feared the worst, with justification. More recently it has bought La Brasserie Seigneuriale in Boucherville, the Shaftebury Brewing Company in B.C., and the Maritime Beer Company in Halifax. This is how E.P. Taylor got started on his campaign to conquer the universe. Actually, where it led John Sleeman was to being taken over by Sapporo of Japan.

Canada's first brewpub was the Troller Pub in Horseshoe Bay, outside Vancouver. It remained a brewpub for only a short time, and its founder, John Mitchell, left to help set up Spinnakers in Victoria in 1984, a pub that survives and thrives to this day. (If you want to be technical about it, the Troller's brewery was located in a separate building, hence the Spinnakers claim to be Canada's first actual brewpub. And how many brewmasters can dance on the head of a pin?)

Toronto lagged behind Vancouver in the brewpub revolution, and indeed Canada generally continues to lag behind its southern neighbour. Hell, even Buffalo has more brewpubs than Toronto, and Vancouver offers nothing like the number of brewpubs you'll find in west coast American cities, especially Portland, Oregon. Portland claims to have something like thirty-two brewpubs and microbreweries within the city limits, which is not bad for a city of half a million people. Is it legislation or our entrepreneurial timidity? And how can we get over it?

# The Best Time of Day to Drink

While studies show that most drinking takes place in the evening, the recreational drinker knows that the best time of all is the afternoon, particularly a weekday afternoon. There's something almost blissful about sitting quietly in a pub by daylight, knowing that everyone else in the world is at work. The lunchtime bustle has ended, and the dinnertime bustle is far in the future. The bar manager has not yet turned the lights down to prevent you from reading, and the large groups of people who gather in pubs for the purpose of shouting at each other over the music have not yet arrived.

It was on such an afternoon, many years ago, that I settled in at a barroom table, spreading out my pleasures before me. I had a book, a newspaper, some writing paper. I was what my old auntie used to call "happy as a sandboy," whatever that means. (Extremely happy or carefree, Brother Oxford tells me, suggesting that "sandboy" probably derives from a "boy hawking sand for sale." Why such a boy should be so cheerful beats me, but I was certainly in that ballpark, happiness-wise.)

It couldn't last, of course, although I expected a little more time than I got. I could see—though I was not about to make eye contact—a fellow drinker rising from his table. It was the days of little draught beer glasses, and he clutched three or four of these glasses and brought them over to my table, carefully setting them down in front of him. He gestured toward my book, my newspaper, my writing paper. "You might as well put all that away," he said. "I've got plenty to talk about." And he did. It was, as I recall, a conspiracy theory that had something to do with the automotive industry. People have called me a good listener. If so, this was my finest hour.

It's not always like that, afternoon drinking. Usually it's better. In England, of course, afternoon drinking was until recently actually illegal, at least in pubs. In 1916, David Lloyd George, prime minister of the day, was worried that munitions workers might not get back to work after lunch. So he decreed that pubs should shut during the afternoon. Like income tax, this was intended to be a temporary measure, and so it proved. A mere seventy-five years later, the law was changed. Now publicans may, if they like, open during the afternoon. They are, of course, under no obligation to do so. Shortly after the law had been changed, my wife and I found ourselves in one of our favourite London pubs, the Surprise in Chelsea, getting there moments before three o'clock, the old witching hour. With a drink safely in front of me I asked the barman if the Surprise now stayed open all day. "Naah, guv," he replied, deftly ignoring the fact that his pub was two-thirds filled with people he would soon be evicting, "there's no call for it." It gives me no pleasure to report that the Surprise has since shut its doors forever.

(Late in 2005 it became legal for English pubs—with the permission of the local authorities—to remain open after 11 p.m., and the worrywarts started nattering on about twenty-four-hour-a-day boozefests. The visitor will find little evidence of such debauchery, even in much of Central London, where most pubs might tack on an extra half-hour, maybe an hour on Fridays and Saturdays.)

The Walk to the Ballpark, described elsewhere in these pages, generally takes place on a Friday. Workaholics of my acquaintance complain that it would be easier for them to take part if it happened on a Saturday instead, to which I reply that the whole point of it is to be hanging out in bars while the rest of the world is doing whatever it is it does during the daylight hours. A pub crawl on the weekend is better than no pub crawl at all, but that's about all you can say for it. On a weekday, it is heaven itself.

Urban pubs don't always make it easy for the afternoon drinker. I have found a number of bars in Chicago, for instance, that don't open until 4 p.m. In Toronto, an increasing number of watering holes are also unfriendly to the daytime tippler.

I bring the subject up because many of the pub encounters I discuss in this book took place during the day. Many of those were Saturdays and Sundays, so not really proper daytime drinking, but in daylight hours nonetheless. There are very few bad bars in the afternoon. Needless to say, in the course of one's life one has seen many of these places by evening as well, occasionally with dismay. Still, if you want to know what all these places are like at midnight, you'll need to find a book written by a younger person. I'm assuming these places are filled with packs of young people who have nowhere to be in the morning, and that's good enough for me.

# Is Drinking Strictly Necessary?

**S**trictly speaking, the consumption of alcohol is not essential to the maintenance of human life, although studies reveal that non-drinkers live shorter lives than moderate drinkers. It is possible—with the help of exercise and a sensible diet—to lead (or possibly endure) a long, fruitful life without as much as a sip of alcohol, and there are, in fact, recorded instances of people doing just that. We can only guess at the motivation of such people, but this book takes a live-and-let-live position. This book is open-minded enough to recognize that it takes all sorts to make a world, that one man's meat is another man's poison, and that we should not stand in judgement of others until we've walked 1.609344 kilometres in their shoes. This book has a platitude for all occasions.

If you can believe the figures, 58 percent of Canadian women and 35 percent of Canadian men don't touch the stuff at all, which raises the question of why the rest of us can't get into a midtown pub on a Friday night. It also raises the question of whether this is simply what Canadians tell their doctors. "Drink? Oh no, never touch it." I once read in one of those expensive wine magazines that 80 percent of American homes don't possess a corkscrew. This doesn't mean, of course, that they're not drinking. It doesn't even mean they're not drinking wine. All it means is that they're not drinking wine from corked bottles, unless they're opening those bottles with their teeth.

There are, in fact, many reasons for not drinking, and I've been looking them up. Many people around the world abstain for religious reasons. Islam, of course, is notoriously anti-booze. There are Muslim countries in which drinkers face public lashings, presumably getting in a bit of punishment here on Earth just in case Allah missed it. There are also Christians who disregard—at their peril, I would have thought—the words of St. Paul: "Drink no longer water, but use a little wine for thy stomach's sake." Such heretical Christians regard drinking as a sin. Mormons are dead set against the hooch, as anyone who's ever tried to conduct a pub crawl in Salt Lake City can testify.

Other people say they just don't like the taste, which has always seemed an evasive answer to me. I can name several well-known brands of beer, for instance, that have virtually no taste at all. Don't tell me you don't like the taste of beer until you've had a Kokanee. Some people don't drink because they're afraid of losing control. That's what they say. To my mind they've never been able to make a particularly convincing case for control, but it's their life.

Some people belong to racial or ethnic groups that genetically have trouble processing alcohol; for such people, the pleasure of drinking is outweighed by the hazards. Some people, have specific medical conditions that would be worsened by alcohol.

There are, of course, many non-drinkers who used to be drinkers. These people have quit for any number of reasons. They may have developed worrisome medical conditions from drinking, or their drinking might have become a behavioural problem. Some drinkers become a hazard to themselves and others. Some people go from being sweet-natured sober individuals to quarrelsome monsters when they drink. Once started, some people can't stop until they have consumed everything in sight, plus a few bottles that had been carefully hidden away. Clearly such people should not drink, and we are doing no one any favours by encouraging them to.

As I tried to make clear at the beginning, I'm a tolerant guy, full of love for my fellow creatures (especially when I've had a couple of pints), drinkers and non-drinkers alike. But the people who really bug the bejeezus out of me are the people who don't drink and don't think I should either. I'm slow to anger, but you start taking an axe to my saloon and I'm likely to forget I'm a gentleman.

There's a limit to my tolerance, damn it.

The other people I could live without are the cheerful people who plaster a big, stupid smile on their faces and say things like, "Oh, I don't need silly old alcohol to be happy!" Just because they're able to disregard the inherent painfulness of life doesn't mean the rest of us can. Don't these people read the newspapers?

This, it seems to me, is the issue. We drinkers are perhaps more sensitive souls, or possibly just better informed. Or maybe we live in worse climates. We need a bit of help to get through it all. A non-user of caffeine, I am married to a woman for whom the fancy-pants coffee revolution was a boon. She uses words to describe a cup of coffee that were never before in her vocabulary or mine. She has been known to mock me in the morning, saying, "Just think, this is as good as you're going to feel all day." To her I can say only one word, and that word is "lunchtime."

The world is fraught with peril, as is obvious to most people. Some people drink to forget. Others forget to drink. I don't recommend either extreme. I just think that the occasional tincture of something soothing takes the edge off the planet, cuts the angst just a bit, tones down the *Weltschmerz* a degree or two. I believe we're justified in softening the blows a tad in a world that contains the following:

- ☞ Sweeping global climate change.
- ☞ Devastation of the natural environment.
- ☞ Widespread poverty.
- ☞ Plagues and epidemics, including AIDS, tuberculosis, malaria, Ebola, SARS, bird flu, flesh-eating disease, *Clostridium difficile*, and much more.
- ☞ Céline Dion's career.
- ☞ The end of meaningful democracy in the wake of corporate globalization.

☛ Millions of people who wear the Nike logo without even being paid to do so.

☛ The decline in accessible health care.

☛ The utterly inexplicable popularity of Bud and Bud Light.

☛ Céline Dion's husband and child.

☛ Hatred and intolerance, except where aimed at pop stars.

☛ Drug cartels (because cartels are a bad thing).

☛ Céline Dion's houses.

☛ Political corruption.

☛ Movies starring Arnold Schwarzenegger or Bruce Willis.

☛ Movies with soundtracks that feature Céline Dion.

☛ Violence of the strong against the weak.

☛ The growing toxicity of our food and water.

☛ The designated hitter rule.

☛ A so far unused frozen Céline Dion embryo.

I could go on, but you see what I mean. Tough people can live in this world, somehow, without the buffering qualities of alcohol. We more sensitive folk cannot. If alcohol had not existed, the international drug companies would have come up with something even more expensive. And we can only imagine the side effects.

# Beer and I:
# A Match Made in Heaven

**W**inston Churchill once said, "Most people hate the taste of beer—to begin with. It is, however, a prejudice that many have been able to overcome." I managed it. In fact, I managed it fairly early on. If there was any resistance at the beginning, I don't actually remember it. I had the occasional glass of beer at home, and from time to time the more roguish friends of my parents laid one on for me.

My first beer in a public place happened on October 1, 1965, and it was John Diefenbaker's fault. Younger readers may not recall our thirteenth prime minister, the Man from Prince Albert, but he cut quite a figure in his day. Dief the Chief took the rap for a lot of things—occasionally unfairly—but there is no letting him off on this one. He is on the hook for my life of squalor. To paraphrase W.C. Fields, it was John Diefenbaker who drove me to drink, and I forgot to thank him for it.

I was a fresh-faced young university student at the time, a pup of nineteen. If this seems rather old to be enjoying one's first public drink, please remember that in those days one was required to be at least forty to drink legally in the province of Ontario, on top of having a letter from one's mother and a form authorized by a doctor and a clergyperson. Even then, a Toronto taproom waiter could still refuse to serve you on the slightest whim. It is difficult now to comprehend the kind of power a beverage room waiter wielded in those dark times. A tall friend of mine came close to eviction from the Embassy Tavern one afternoon for slouching. This is absolutely true.

In any case, on October 1, 1965, I left Hart House Theatre at the University of Toronto and strolled northward up Philosopher's Walk on my way to the subway. I had been rehearsing a production of Shaw's *Heartbreak House*, directed by the wonderful Robert Gill, who had directed the likes of Kate Reid and Donald Sutherland, so was used to actors who were better than me. I had never seen a man use a cigarette holder before, so society's taboos were tumbling all around me. For what it's worth, Herbert Whittaker in *The Globe and Mail* thought I showed promise in the small role of the craven yet pragmatic burglar, but this was only October 1 and we were still a week or so from opening.

There was a parking lot in front of Varsity Arena through which I had to pass on my way home, and this particular evening people were gathered. Inside the arena John Diefenbaker was addressing a crowd of cheering Tories. It was the former prime minister's last hurrah in his final election as Tory leader, and he was spitting fire inside. Loudspeakers carried his message to an overflow crowd outside.

Passing through, I encountered a young fellow of my age in debate with an older man, a Tory. I don't recall the specifics of their discussion, but I joined in on the side of my contemporary, until finally the older man, clearly giving up on my generation, went back to listening to the Chief. The young guy turned to me and suggested a celebratory beer. There seemed no good reason not to, and I followed him to the Embassy Tavern. It was everything I hoped it would be—noisy, smoky, and as decadent as Toronto was likely to be in 1965. A waiter in white shirt and black pants dropped four glasses of draught beer on our table at fifteen cents per, and no questions were asked about our age. I felt a long way from Etobicoke. Even as I left, I couldn't wait to come back.

Where the Embassy once stood, rich guys now come to buy suits from Harry Rosen. I wept the night the Embassy closed down. A year later I sat in the Morrissey Tavern, drinking with John, one of the long-time Embassy waiters. He had come downtown that day and found himself walking past the old place. As he stood there, a group of men—U of T grads, as it turned out—came along, looking for their old haunt. It was gone, but there was John, one of the great waiters of the era. By the time I ran into him at the Morrissey, he'd had a few with these guys and he was feeling nostalgic.

I remember three waiters from the Embassy Tavern. Mike and Cliff were biggish guys. You didn't mess around with Mike or Cliff because they could tear you apart. You didn't mess around with John because you didn't want to disappoint him. He was a taproom philosopher with plenty to say, almost all of it worth listening to. Even in retirement.

The beer we drank in the Embassy was swill, and there was no choice, not on draught. They regularly changed brands, but it all tasted pretty much the same. You ordered draught and you drank what they brought you. We were young and drinking beer; we didn't care what it was. By 1969 I was living in England and working behind the bar at the Argyll Arms, one of the prettiest pubs in London. To this day there is still not a plaque outside, even though I tack one up every time I'm in the area. By this time I was drinking English ale and enjoying it, but I was still missing out on the good stuff. I was drinking Double Diamond, for Pete's sake. It was better than the Canadian swill I was used to, but that's not saying a lot. My cat pees better than that.

Young people drink lousy beer, or what a friend of mine calls "training beer." It's just one of those facts of life. If they get through youth without killing themselves, some of them will go on to develop a bit of taste. Now I like a good hearty ale, something with a nice balance of malt and hops, something with a surprising aftertaste. Nowadays I don't often drink with the intention of getting drunk; that's for kids. If nothing else, grown-ups don't have time for hangovers. Give me a good conversation and a nice beery buzz, and I'm happy as a clam.

I like the taste of good beer, and I like the way it feels in my mouth. I like the way you can feel the first swallow of the day slide down the gullet. I wish every day could be the first time again—you never forget the first time—and that old John Diefenbaker was back again, ranting in a losing cause at Varsity Arena.

# The More I Drink, the Better I Look: Drinking and Sex

Yes, I might have known you'd head directly to this chapter, you mucky reader, you. I'll try to make it worth your while.

I think I've made it clear that I enjoy reading in pubs. Other people, on the other hand, go to licensed premises with darker, more basic drives in mind. The seventies, of course, were famous for singles bars, places people went to with no higher purpose than to find sexual partners. I didn't have the clothes for singles bars, and I was always too shy in any case. While North Americans from coast to coast were out there having it off, I was sitting in Toronto's Morrissey Tavern, reading a book.

Not that chances didn't crop up. One night in the early seventies, I found myself at the El Mocambo with a glass of beer in front of me. (Funny, isn't it, the way we talk about "finding ourselves" in bars, as if we'd had no intention whatever of actually stepping inside such a place.) This particular evening I had in fact gone to a party, which led to a group of people going to the El Mocambo to hear some band or other. I found myself (here we go again) sitting next to a young woman I had not previously met, a woman with a reputation of being formidable. During a quiet spell, she leaned toward me and said, "I only came out tonight because I thought I might find a good lay. [Pinteresque pause.] I guess I didn't."

In the intervening years, I have thought of many amusing responses to this line, some of which might have led to heaven-knows-what. I might not have been a good lay, but she wouldn't have found that out until it was too late, would she? They do say that sex is like golf, in that you can enjoy it without necessarily being very good at it.

At the time, I didn't know quite what to say. The girls I had known in high school were notable precisely for *not* saying things like that, so I was out of my depth. You can see what's coming. I blew it. Sex is like *Jeopardy!*: you've got to be quick on the buzzer. I didn't have my hand on the buzzer, or anything else.

When you think about it, I probably didn't have to say much. "Oh yeah?" might have done the trick. Practically any form of human speech might have done it. "That's what you think," for instance. I would not have been the first guy to get lucky as a result of a chance encounter at the El Mocambo, or the last—just look at the Rolling Stones—and who knows where it might have led? Mutual disappointment, outbreaks of lying, and that overall funk of shabbiness, in all likelihood, but that's what makes the world go round.

Early humans lived short, arduous lives, leaving little behind them for their time on the planet. Keeping the species going was touch and go. As discussed elsewhere in this book, the Mesopotamians invented beer, whereupon civilization really got going. After a couple of beers, other Mesopotamians started to look pretty good, and procreation really took off. You could argue (and I know how you get after a couple of pints) that humanity might not be here at all if not for beer.

The bond between alcohol and sex is historic. People who drink are more likely to multiply. Look at the Irish. There's never been a shortage of Irish people. (This may be a Catholic issue. Historically, the Catholic countries have managed to keep their populations up without having to evangelize. It's the non-drinking Protestants who need converts to maintain their numbers. Fair enough, the Inquisition wasn't Catholicism's finest hour, but these days they're fairly well behaved.)

Teetotallers, on the other hand, are usually too busy making sure that other people don't have fun to have any themselves. One teetotaller is never going to look suddenly wonderful to another teetotaller. And there are teetotallers who don't approve of dancing, either. How that gene has survived down the centuries is a mystery to the evolutionists. If Darwin was right, non-dancing teetotallers should have been bred out of the species some time around the Phoenicians.

In 1969 I met a woman at a Bavarian brewery, and we wound up living together for two years. A few years later, in a Toronto bar, I met the woman who was to become my wife. We courted at another Toronto bar, and our first destination after tying the knot at City Hall was yet another Toronto bar. Interestingly enough, our marriage has outlasted all three bars, although two of them now exist in other forms.

The second of those three bars—the Morrissey Tavern on Yonge

Street—was not an obviously romantic haunt. There were no cozy little tables with candles. One of the long-time waiters was so slow and desultory in his duties that people sometimes fell in love just for something to do while they waited for another beer. I know of at least four other long-term couples whose relationships gestated at the Morrissey, and I'll draw a discreet veil over some of the shorter-term alliances that sprang up as well. There are people alive today who wouldn't have existed if not for the Morrissey Tavern.

That the Morrissey could be destroyed to build yet another tire-some condominium block is an indictment on us all. It should have been treated as a sacred place, rather like a hospital. Oh, hang on—they're shutting down hospitals too, aren't they?

Mind you, it's a fine line we walk when we drink, if we have sex on our minds. Not that this has ever happened to any of us, but the medical professionals warn of the danger of diminished performance, particularly in the male of the species. To be blunt about this, by the time you've got her drunk enough to find you palatable, you may be too far gone to deliver the goods. The porter in *Macbeth* speaks of drink: ". . . it provokes the desire but it takes away the performance. Therefore much drink may be said to be an equivocator with lechery: it makes him and it mars him; it sets him on and it takes him off; it persuades him and disheartens him, makes him stand to and not stand to . . ."

Aristotle, of course, thought the problem might arise (or not) because the "lower parts" need to be heated, while wine natu-rally travels upward, producing heat higher up and withdrawing it farther down. All right, do you have a better explanation? If caught in this predicament, you might try saying, "Hang on, I think I'm having an Aristotelian moment." I can't imagine what good that could possibly do you, but she might be impressed with the classical reference.

The only other advice I can think of comes from the cad in the Michael Flanders/Donald Swann song "(Have Some) Madeira, M'Dear." (Now there's a song you don't hear played in pubs; it might be a useful warning for maidens whose natural defences collapse a bit after a couple of tequila sunrises.) The cad, in attempting to seduce a sweet young thing by plying her with fortified wine, warns her against the evils of gin, adding as an afterthought, "Besides, it's inclined to affect m' prowess."

Nevertheless, as long as intoxicating beverages are served, the preservation of humankind seems guaranteed, and I'll drink to that.

# Play that Funky Music, Barkeep

I have friends who feel that researching a book of this sort is a doddle, a piece of cake, a walk in the park. Going about town, sitting in pubs—what's so tough about that? Still, I am reminded of the words often attributed to the English actor Ernest Thesiger, who, when asked about his experiences in the trenches of the First World War, replied, "My dear, the noise! And the people!" In my case, the people weren't so bad, but, my dear, the noise!

In *McCarthy's Bar*, Pete McCarthy notes that Van Morrison music always appears to be playing in every pub in Ireland, as if there were some sort of government quota in effect. Here, it's more likely to be Sting. My legal advisors have been working around the clock on our behalf, and they have concluded—to my shock—that there is no actual legislation that requires licensed premises to play every song you've ever heard by Sting over their sound systems much of the day. Bizarre as it may seem, they do this of their own accord. The government inspector who comes around to check for

mouse fewmets in the kitchen does not then slap a health warning on a bar for the insufficient playing time of "Every Breath You
Take." "You've been warned before," this inspector does not say to a
trembling publican. "You've got five minutes to make those guys at
the bar listen to "Roxanne," or I'm shutting this joint down."

My crack legal team assures me that, not only do bar owners
not have to play *Sting's Greatest Hits* several times a day, but they
are under no legal requirement to play any music at all. I'm going
to give you a moment to absorb that bit of news. No legal requirement: they're doing it to annoy you.

There was once, in more innocent times, a Toronto pub that
didn't play music: Paupers Pub on Bloor Street. I parted
with a fair bit of cash while sitting in that lovely, quiet
room. Its sister establishment, the Madison, also maintained a music-free area for some years, allowing the
traditional sounds of human conversation to create a
convivial environment. And, you know, it worked!
It's all in the past now, of course, like something you're
not sure if you dreamed or if it was real. It was as if they
had responded to some government directive to make their
customers listen to music they had not asked for. Even outdoor
patios are no longer safe. Paupers has in recent years sullied its
idyllic rooftop deck with aural claptrap.

Pub owners all seem to be worried that we will think we're not
enjoying ourselves if we're not tapping our toes to idiotic music,
much of it pitched at people who are too young to be in pubs anyway. (These same pub owners also believe it's important to dim
the lights soon after six o'clock, whether or not there are paying

customers reading at the time. There is a fear that a young person or two will look in and recoil with horror at the sight of some old geezer quietly reading. ("Look out, Jason—this place isn't for us! And let's make sure we tell all our friends as well!") There is also the question of whether the music in pubs is there for the entertainment of the staff or the customers. Well, it's not much of a question, really, is it?

It's no accident that it is for the most part music lovers who hate enforced music in pubs (or, indeed, other public places). I used to drink with Tom Monohan, then principal bassist of the Toronto Symphony, a large man who kept the Duke of York quiet for years. He's dead now, unfortunately, and the music has crept in. Music lovers can't help listening to music, even if it's music they hate. Ironically, the music is there for the people who are more or less indifferent to music, people who don't really notice what's being played. (Which is why pubs occasionally forget to turn the damn stuff on; the only people who have noticed are the least likely to complain.) Anyone who has ever played piano in a lounge or restaurant will testify that most nights someone will come up to request a song you've just played. They didn't really hear it while you were playing it, but they absorbed just enough to remind them that they like the song and wouldn't mind hearing it some time. Let's get the piano player to play it for us.

The relegation of music to background din is offensive to music lovers, as is the notion of inflicting unwelcome music upon others. A subway station near my home plays loud classical music through its halls with the clear intention of discouraging troublesome teenagers from lingering. And it seems to work. I have to conclude that pubs that make me listen to Sting or any number of other pop stars are actively trying to discourage me from spending my time and money with them, and it also works. I like reading in pubs, but I'd get cranky very quickly if a member of the staff handed me the latest Danielle Steel when I arrived and told me that was what I'd be reading today.

There are two principal reasons I spend so much time in pubs, apart from the draught beer. As mentioned, I like reading in pubs, and I like talking to friends in pubs. Neither of these activities is enhanced by the presence in the air of the Eagles singing "Hotel California." Indeed, both are hampered. I can't imagine any form of human endeavour that is improved by listening to "Hotel California." Defenders of canned music argue that it enables pub-goers to converse without being overheard, which is obvious nonsense. Everyone simply talks louder to be heard over the bloody Eagles, at which point some bright young spark on the bar staff usually cranks the music up higher because they can no longer hear it.

According to the director of music at Eton College (not to be confused with the venerable down market Eton House on the Danforth), George Bernard Shaw once arrived at a restaurant and was asked by the manager what he would like the band to play. "Dominoes," said the music-loving Shaw. This story comes from a fine guide to English pubs, called *The Quiet Pint*. The editors of this excellent book have located a host of pubs that—apart from any other distinguishing features—don't have piped music. Many of the great pubs of Britain, including a number of personal favourites, are in this guide, which clocks in at over 550 pages in length. It is sad that a corresponding guide for Toronto might occupy one photocopied page. Even fancy-pants hotel bars are not always immune to this blight.

The guide to quiet British pubs (heartily endorsed by an organization called Pipedown, a campaign to rid Britain of unwanted music) was necessary because most pubs play enforced music. I can date some of my trips to England by which songs were being played in practically every pub in the country. One trip was the "Bette Davis Eyes" trip, while another belonged to "Baker Street." "Baker Street," you may recall, was the song that became popular because it had a recurring saxophone solo. It was played exactly the same way each time it recurred—that's what Top Forty pop music is all about—but it gave an otherwise dull song a touch of sophistication. I wanted to cry out, "Are you people aware that you can buy whole records of saxophone music, all of them more interesting than this?" It would have been true at the time: Kenny G had yet to burst onto the scene.

Would it make a difference if pubs played the sort of music I like? Hard to say, because it's never been tried. I've spent a chunk of my life in pubs and bars, and I don't think I've ever heard a John Dowland lute piece, or a William Byrd mass, or a Stephen Sondheim show tune. (All right, I sat on a pub patio outside London in 1999 and heard bits of *Sweeney Todd* being played from a nearby house, but that doesn't count.) Once, in a Chicago brewpub, I heard a song by Wesla Whitfield—one of my favourite singers—but that's a total of once in many thousands of man-pub-hours. There's a bar called Tosca in San Francisco that includes opera arias on its jukebox, but it's a long commute from my place. There's a pub called the Hand in Hand in Brighton, on England's south coast, that was playing Mozart horn concerti the first time I was there. You get occasional jazz if you know where to look, and sporadic blues, but for the most part it's the Eagles, Sting, Whitney Houston, Sheryl Crow, Rod Stewart, Oasis, and the rest of them. You've heard it all a thousand times, and here it comes again. Have people no boredom threshold at all?

I'm a pro-choice kind of guy, especially when it comes to listening to the whiney boys and yowling girls of the contemporary pop scene. My choice would be no thanks. In fact, the musicians we drinking folk have to listen to make me feel very pro-abortion, retroactively if necessary. I have a piano-playing cousin who feels strongly about music in pubs, and I have spent many hours with him in New York, helping him in his quest to find the perfect Gotham drinking spot. Well, that's what family's for. There are no quiet bars in New York—even the lobby of the august Algonquin Hotel inflicts easy listening on its customers—but many of them have jukeboxes. And many of those jukeboxes actually offer a few jazz selections. So our standard procedure now is to head straight for the jukebox, feed it a few bucks so that we get at least our choice of music, and only then get the bartender pouring Michael's Guinness. One of the pleasant by-products of this practice is that it really annoys the staff to have to listen to grown-up music. Michael reckons it's good for them, and maybe it is. (My wife and I were once thanked by the bouncer of a bar in Washington, D.C., for playing self-protective intelligent music, rather than the stuff he was generally exposed to. Which raises another point. In recent years lawmakers have expressed concern about the amount of cigarette smoke inflicted upon bar staff in that shrinking number of jurisdictions that still permit smoking. Has anyone done a study of the effect of listening to non-stop Greatest Hits of the Eighties and Nineties on bar staff? Think about that.)

Cousin Michael, being a jazz guy, claims that he never liked rock 'n' roll, even in the sixties. I did. I was not always squaresville, daddio. I saw the Beatles live. I saw Hendrix live, on a bill with Pink Floyd. I saw the Stones in London, in their first gig after they got home from Altamont. I saw the Grateful Dead in a Lower East Side theatre, doing a benefit for the Hell's Angels. I was out there, man. I've met Mike Stoller, who co-wrote "(You Ain't Nothin' but a) Hound Dog." I even have an interesting theory about Little Eva, which I will tell you some time after a few pints. So I have some credentials. (Admittedly, I've kind of lost track since the end of the sixties. I've never been able to tell Peter Frampton from Peter Gabriel, for instance, not that I care.)

But there comes a time when you've heard it all. The rock music era has now lasted roughly as long as the Classical era of Mozart and Haydn. In an age with no way of broadcasting music, an age when to hear music you either had to make it yourself or be in the same room as a musician, people wearied of the Classical sound in about fifty years. No one would have given rock 'n' roll five decades. One of the early practitioners of rock in about 1956 suggested the sound had a good six months left; after all, it had already outlasted the mambo. Can we not put it painlessly to rest?

So which songs do I particularly not want to hear in a pub? It's a very long list, but there are a few clear choices. I've mentioned

"Hotel California." How about "Horse With No Name," arguably the worst pop song since "Sugar Shack"? One way to guarantee that your songs don't get turned into elevator music is to make sure they have no discernible tune at all, and that nameless horse managed it. In recent years I've been extremely annoyed by a Sheryl Crow song that I assume—because the words get repeated far too often—is called "If It Makes You Happy." This song does not make me happy, not in the least. It asks the question: "Why the hell are you so sad?" I am sad because I am being made to listen to Sheryl Crow for what must be the thousandth time. Sheryl Crow is, to my mind, a guarantee of lifetime employment for Dr. Kevorkian. For Lance Armstrong to have endured Sheryl Crow and testicular cancer in one lifetime seems cruel.

There's also a famous song, presumably by some famous band, probably called "More Than a Feeling." This is a song I hear in pubs all the time and wonder why. Likewise "Play That Funky Music, White Boy," another Dr. Kevorkian favourite. How about "Witchy Woman," which might be by the Eagles again? "What a Fool Believes." "Rikki Don't Lose That Number." "I Can't Go For That (No Can Do)." "Whoa Ho Ho, Listen to the Music." "Doan Chew Wan Me Baybay, Doan Chew Wan Me Oh-oh-oh-oh." "You're My Wonderwa-a-a-all." The list is endless. This is all stuff that saps the will to live, and few of us need more will-sapping in our lives.

I recognize that my selection of the worst songs will not be the same as yours. A late friend of mine had in his younger years enjoyed some sort of romantic encounter—and I'm putting the best possible light on "romantic"—against the backdrop of "MacArthur Park," and would never hear a word against what was possibly the worst song ever recorded. The only good thing I can think of about "MacArthur Park" is that it is so bad that no bar in North America would dream of playing it today, and as I write these words I imagine some vindictive publican reaching for his *Greatest Hits of Richard Harris* CD.

And even as I write these words I remember that I heard not that long ago a song I hoped had been buried along with so much other dross of the sixties. There is almost nothing I disliked about the sixties, but I'll make a very big exception in the case of a song that annoyed the hell out me then and did so again more recently. It was the one and only hit for a guy called Peter Sarstedt, and I assume it was called "Where Do You Go To, My Lovely." Remember that one? He wanted to see inside her head, yes he did, yes he did. Her loveliness went on and on, as did the song, yes it did, yes it did. Do I ever want to hear that song again? No I don't, no I don't. I'm not a violent man, but even today I think I'd cheerfully deliver a blow to Peter Sarstedt. I expect it's been done a time or two already.

The one piece of music I would unreservedly encourage the publicans of the world to play is a solo piano work by John Cage, a 1952 composition called *4′33″*. In this work a pianist, armed with a stopwatch, very pointedly does not play the piano for exactly four minutes and thirty-three seconds. I see no reason why this piece could not be played (or not be not played, if you see my point) on other instruments. I picture a two-CD set of *4′33″* arranged for horns, strings, electric guitar, the Javanese gamelan, and mixed-voice choir. The pop divas—Barbra Streisand, Céline Dion, Whitney Houston, and their awful like—could perform *4′33″* without taking a breath. Roberta Flack could perform *4′33″* very, very slowly, so it would take about twelve minutes. And when the young person in a pub asks why there's no music playing, the bartender will shush him. "We're listening to John Cage, man," he will say. "It's the eighth cut on the second CD—4′33″ arranged for Hawaiian guitar. Amazing, man."

In 1950 a man named Jack Newman bought a Toronto bar on Dundas Street East. He also bought a jukebox and filled it with his own jazz records. All these years later, you can drink in that same bar—though it was touch-and-go for a while when the city decided it needed the land for its Yonge-Dundas redevelopment—and play that same jukebox at practically 1950 prices. The drinking's a bit pricier than in 1950, but there isn't much Mr. Newman can do about that.

The Imperial Public Library is the upstairs bar of the two Imperial pubs, and that's where you'll find the jukebox. Photographs of jazz greats and somewhat undressed (yet tasteful) women of the jazz era decorate the walls, and old books sit on shelves, hence the name of the bar. Occasionally the bar is quiet, which is nice, and the rest of the time you're listening to altogether decent jazz, which is also nice. Mr. Newman—helped by his sons—is still rotating the choices from time to time, and long may he do so.

The Imperial is at the edge of the Ryerson campus, so you may be surrounded by irrepressible university students, and sometimes the pub hosts literary readings when the jazz will be replaced by the tones of poets and novelists. It still beats the hell out of the Doobie Brothers. Or Peter Bloody Sarstedt.

# Losing the Will to Live:
# Surviving the Hangover

**F**or a population of a titch over five million, the Finns make a fair impact on the planet. They produce hockey players, orchestra conductors, opera singers, and Formula One racing car drivers way out of proportion to their size. Given that there are so few of them, it's not surprising that we don't meet more Finns.

In the summer of 1968 I met Finns for the first time. It helped that I was in northern Europe, which brought me closer to the source. Studies have revealed that in the summer of 1968, some 23 percent of the world's population was hitchhiking in Europe, and I was one of those people. We were all pretty dusty from spending our days at the sides of roads watching cars zip by (European drivers drive as quickly as they can), and we hauled great heavy knapsacks around. There was one exception, and I hitchhiked with her one day from Frankfurt to Hannover. She was a lovely young woman in a flimsy summer dress, carrying only a tiny purse. She was a Finn.

The number one male hitchhiker's fantasy entails being picked up by an oversexed blonde in a convertible, but meeting up with a vision of Finnish loveliness in a summer dress is not a bad second. I will draw a discreet veil over what happened between us, only because nothing at all happened between us. Are you kidding? If something had happened I'd be writing a chapter about it. Anyway, she had nothing at all to do with hangovers, but I thought it would be nice to let her make a cameo appearance in the book. And she did make me think about how little I knew of Finland.

I met my second Finn two or three days later. I had by now arrived in Lübeck, a handsome old town that had been painstakingly restored after the war. Lübeck, it turns out, is the marzipan capital of the world, which I didn't know at the time. It is also now home to what is apparently the best Irish pub in Germany, which shows you how crazy the world is. I'm fairly sure there were no Irish pubs in Lübeck in 1968, but nevertheless it looked very nice that morning, and I thought I'd get to know it a bit better by tasting the local beer. As I quietly drank my beer, I listened in on a political discussion between the bartender and the bar's only other customer. It stinks now, but for a spell in the late sixties my German wasn't at all bad, especially when I was drinking beer. More evidence that beer makes you smarter.

Pashley's Third Rule of Drinking (and don't ask me what the first two are) is: never argue with the bartender. But it was 1968 and we young people were convinced we had the right to our opinions, so I joined in on the side of the other customer. Who turned out to be another Finn. He had spent the summer working in Germany but was now on his way back to Finland, where beer at the time was practically illegal. He had enjoyed a jolly summer of drinking German beer and was embarking on a full day of the same before he caught his ferry back to Helsinki.

(Had I known then what I know now, I'd have asked him about sahti, the great beer of Finland, beloved of home brewers. According to Michael Jackson, sahti is generally made from equal parts rye and barley and seasoned with juniper berries. It gets fermented with baker's yeast for a week in wooden pails and is filtered through juniper twigs and straw. Apparently, it is frequently brewed in the sauna and often gets consumed there, which doesn't surprise me a bit. At last word there was one commercial brewer of sahti and, to buy the stuff, you had to purchase a voucher at a government liquor store then take said voucher to a producer, the only one of which was located some two hundred miles northwest of Helsinki. No wonder many Finns simply make their own. Or just drink vodka.)

Despite their government's stand on alcohol—which makes Canada look quite sinful—the Finns like their beer. The early Finns even had a god of beer and barley, who went by the name of Pekko. The Finn I met in Lübeck was clearly a worshipper, possibly even a Pekko-head. He asked me—and all this went on in German, so if I seem a bit sketchy on the details, that's why—if I was familiar with the concept of *ein Stiefel Bier*. *Ein Stiefel* is a boot, not to be confused with *Das Boot*, which is a movie about a submarine. *Ein Stiefel Bier* is a practice whereby a large quantity of beer is poured into a big glass boot and then consumed. Well, you can see where this is going. I blame the Finn.

My new friend and I made it our project to have *ein Stiefel Bier*, the most important component of which involved finding a bar that had the requisite glass boot. Lübeck, I can tell you, has a number of bars, but not many of them—in 1968, at least—boasted the *Stiefel*. "*Guten Tag*," we greeted any number of Prussian barkeeps, "*Haben Sie ein Stiefel Bier?*" "*Ach, nein*," they replied sadly. It seemed impolite—especially since they were all so nice—simply to walk on, so we stopped for a beer or two anyway.

By the time we found what we were looking for, we no longer needed it. But have it we did anyway. My, those big glass boots hold a lot of beer. And at what point my Finnish friend thought schnapps chasers were in order I cannot say. I know that at some point he set out for his ferry to Finland, and I somehow hitchhiked up to another ferry terminal at Puttgarden.

The other end of my ferry ride was a place called Rødbyhavn, which is Danish for Nowheresville, Denmark. It was a ferry terminal and nothing else, so another troupe of dusty hitchhikers stood about waiting for the next ferry to arrive. By chance, I met up with a pair of young Irish women. By now it was dark and chilly, and the Irish women offered me some of their native whiskey as a warming agent. It seemed to work, though in retrospect I recall the age-old wisdom: Beer on whiskey makes you feel frisky; whiskey on beer makes you feel queer. And queer—queer in the old-fashioned sense, at any rate—is what I quite distinctly felt some hours later as I rode with the Irish women in someone's truck through the landscape of southern Denmark.

I awoke the next morning alone in a Danish field. I assume it was morning. It certainly felt like it. No part of me was functioning in anything like a normal way. Standing up was an adventure, and I didn't achieve it in my first few attempts. My normal aversion to death was suspended. I had had hangovers before and I've had them since, but this was the sort of experience that has turned strong men into abstainers, if only temporarily. I felt like the hero of Kingsley Amis's *Lucky Jim:* "His mouth had been used as a latrine by some small creature of the night, and then as its mausoleum." Alas, there was no running water in this field to combat the dehydration, no raw eggs to do whatever raw eggs are supposed to do for you. Nothing, in short, to promote the will to live.

Fifteen yards away, up a short incline, lay the road to somewhere else in Denmark. It had to be better than where I was. To its credit, wherever I was was a quiet part of Denmark, but in the long term I required somewhere a trifle more sophisticated, at least to the point of offering large quantities of water. It was several hours before I had recovered sufficiently to make my way to the road and be able to stand long enough to hitch a ride to Copenhagen. Once there, I holed up in the youth hostel for a couple of abstemious days, cursing the Finn who had brought me to this state. Oddly enough, I have never attached much blame to the Irish women who had put me over the edge with their grain tea, but then I wouldn't, would I?

There are many theories about hangovers, most of them not worth much. The ancient Greeks apparently believed that if you wore a garland of parsley on your head while you were out on the razzle you wouldn't get a hangover the next morning. That seems highly unlikely, but—like you, I imagine—I haven't tried it. Many of the places I frequent would almost certainly refuse to serve a customer with a garland of parsley on his head, even a regular.

One medieval hangover cure entailed consuming a raw eel and bitter almonds, but I can't imagine what sort of ethnic neighbourhood you'd have to live in to have easy access to raw eels. The Assyrians of yesteryear made a paste of ground swallow's beak and myrrh, and I've seen somewhere a recipe for fried canary that's supposed to be useful. Hungover cowboys, I am told, used to fix up a brew of dried rabbit droppings, which was probably about as pleasant as it sounds.

The hangover can be prevented, of course, by just saying no to intoxicating beverages. Many people do it every day. But not me, and probably not you either. And most of us drinking folk are smart enough to call it an evening before it comes to destruction on that scale. Every now and then, however, circumstances seem to dictate just the teensiest bit of excess. Where did I recently encounter the following exchange? Q. Do you ever drink to excess? A. I'll drink to anything.

The hangover might possibly be prevented by avoiding Finns, but I can recall hangovers after evenings that included no known Finns at all. Drinking lots of water or fruit juice along with the alcohol will definitely help, though you'll pee all night. A couple of Aspirin before retiring might help, unless it attacks your stomach lining, in which case you'll wake up with a sore gut instead of a sore head. Depends which you prefer, really. Cheap red wine is a sure guarantee of a hangover, as is widespread mixing of alcohols. And those alcohol-sugar-coffee concoctions can do untold damage: the alcohol makes you drunk, the sugar makes you sick, and the coffee makes sure you stay awake to enjoy every moment of it.

Vitamin $B_1$ is said to be a good preventive measure, and no less authoritative a source than the *Quarterly Journal of Alcohol Studies*—and I hope your subscription's up to date—recommends taking Vitamin $B_6$ before, during, and after a drinking session. The alternative health people, who tend not to drink much in my observation, swear by something called milk thistle. For best results, unfortunately, you need to take this stuff daily for a week before you go out on the bender. Most of us aren't that well prepared.

If the hangover has caught you by surprise and it's too late for milk thistle, what then? Plenty of fluids. Water, fruit juice, or sports drinks. You're dehydrated, buster, and you've got to replace them fluids. A professor at the University of Sunderland says that when we drink a pint of beer we pee a pint and a third of fluid. I know it feels that way, but this guy says it's true. So if you drink six pints, you lose two whole pints of bodily fluid; no wonder you feel rotten afterwards. Coffee, like alcohol, is a diuretic, so it should be avoided in the treatment of your hangover.

Modern science leans away from the old greasy breakfast cure. (The time for oily food is before you start drinking; it lines your stomach.) A mixture of lemon juice, maple syrup, and cayenne pepper in hot water is supposed to help. Pineapple juice is apparently good for the stomach. A doctor in the UK has recently sung the praises of artichokes for the morning after. The Russians—who should know something about hangovers—swear by cabbage juice with something fizzy in it. For the Ukrainians, there's nothing like a cup of chilled sauerkraut, which is rich in potassium, natural salts, and magnesium. Northern Europeans recommend a breakfast of marinated fish, while a New England bar called Friendly's boasts a hangover cure that comprises a bowl of clam chowder, followed by a beefburger, then a chocolate pancake. I think I'd rather take the pledge and be done with it.

The list of hangover cures is practically endless: cucumber juice, orange pop with a chocolate milk chaser, bananas, pickle juice, coconut, hot baths, tomatoes, or a quail's egg in a cup of warm sake. Paul McCartney apparently blends a mixture of carrot, beet, celery, and parsley juices, and he's a billionaire so he should know.

There are those who practise even harsher measures than pickle juice for hangovers. The Scandinavians, for instance, are likely to jump into an icy lake, but it's worth remembering the allegedly high Scandinavian suicide rate. I suspect this method leads to hungover Swedes who are now also extremely cold. I don't see it myself.

Another traditional cure is the drinking of a glass of bitters. There are a number of such herbal concoctions, all of which combine an unspeakable taste with a strong alcohol content. Fernet-Branca is probably the best known, though Kingsley Amis favoured Underberg. He compared the effect on the system to throwing a cricket ball into an empty bathtub; in North America we can substitute a baseball. The bad taste is the gastric equivalent of the

Swedish icy lake, as well as making you feel that it must be good for you, while the alcohol actually does the job.

Because of the alcohol, drinking bitters is really no different from taking a hair (or, as Cyril Connolly preferred, a tuft) of the dog that bit you. Amis points out that the breed is not important; it doesn't have to be the same form of alcohol that brought you to this dire state. The danger here is what a friend has called the compound-complex hangover. By taking on another drink you ease the current pain, but you may be setting yourself up for something even bigger. One drink should suffice. Then consider going back to bed, if that's an option.

The American drug companies, needless to say, are working round the clock to develop an anti-hangover pill. There are fortunes to be made here. It is said that America loses $148 billion a year in poor performance and days missed owing to hangovers. I don't know how they come up with numbers like this, but I read it in a respectable newspaper so it must be true. A team of researchers from the University of California, San Francisco, believes that a cure to the hangover lies in creating a pill that blocks the release of something called cytokines. These are molecules that are released by white blood cells to fight viruses and the like. As I understand it, the body gets hit by all this alcohol (strictly speaking, the congeners in the alcohol, but there won't be a quiz at the end of this chapter) and thinks it's getting the flu, so it sends out these cytokines to fight it. Knowing the drug companies, we won't be able to afford this pill when they finally invent it, so keep drinking water and taking the milk thistle. And avoid Finns.

# The Silliest Conversation
# I've Ever Had in a Bar

Those who know me might quibble with my choice of Silliest Conversation in a Bar, choosing instead any number of conversations that I myself have initiated or even serious conversations that I have turned silly. Let them quibble. They weren't present for this one, and anyway it's my book.

And I'm not talking about the time a bunch of us were gathered in the Embassy Tavern some time in the mid-1970s. We knew from the newspapers that Elton John was in town recording, and there was, at a nearby table, a man who looked a lot like Elton John. This was just before Toronto had proper drinking places, but even so the Embassy seemed an unlikely spot to encounter a major recording artist. But still.

We were intrigued. Was it or was it not Elton John? The realists among us insisted that Elton John would not be drinking in a place like the Embassy, while others were reluctant to disbelieve the evidence of their eyes. This was before Mr. John had adopted the really bizarre attire that would have made him readily recognizable anywhere. At any rate, our group was unsure. Finally, one of us—Patrick Lee, by name—volunteered to go over and ask. We did not discourage him. Patrick approached the table of the solitary drinker and exchanged a few words. He returned, poker-faced, to our table.

Well, we said, what did he say?

No, said Patrick, it's not him.

How do you know? we asked.

He said so, said Patrick.

He said he's not Elton John?

That's right.

Did he say it in an English accent?

Patrick paused. Yes, he admitted.

To this day we have no idea if we were drinking in close proximity to Elton John. Nor do we really care, if the truth be told. But you'd like to know, wouldn't you?

Anyway, that's not the conversation I had in mind. This one is.

It was an afternoon, I remember that much. A day of the week, very possibly ending in "y." Very likely in or about 1974, and almost certainly in Toronto. I found myself at a bar called the Young Station, no longer with us, in the building that is now the Brass Rail. I am given to understand that if you go into this place today, young women will undress in front of you, which never in my experience happened when it was the Young Station. I don't get to the Brass Rail much, my limited knowledge of this sort of place informing me that the beer selection is invariably very poor, and overpriced too. And those young women can be very distracting if you're trying to read.

The Young Station was an odd sort of bar. By night it offered very loud rock bands, while by day it served up very cheap beer. The Young Station brought a new twist to drinking in those distant days. Most bars of that era served beer in tiny glasses cleverly designed to look bigger than they were. The Young Station served beer in glasses designed to look smaller than they actually were. This had the interesting effect of encouraging consumption on an industrial scale, and it worked. If getting people very drunk indeed was its goal, the Young Station succeeded brilliantly. Its motto might have been: A buzz for a buck, drunk for two bucks, falling down for three.

The cheap beer attracted a mixed clientele, with only a desire to get drunk cheap in common. Most of its daytime customers were obviously people with only a passing familiarity with the work ethic, though others did much of their work within its walls. A dealer in illicit substances I knew from high school (I knew the dealer, you understand, not the illicit substances) kept regular office hours at the Young Station. There was an older man, always well turned out, who I was absolutely sure was a remittance man of some sort. And it was in the Young Station one characteristic winter day that my friend Russ Hughes referred to Toronto as "this snow-soaked shithole of a city," a splendidly alliterative characterization I quote frequently.

As I then lived around the corner, I got to the Young Station more frequently perhaps than I should. You never knew what was going to happen. One day I sat next to four university boys who had just finished for the year and who celebrated by ordering a hundred glasses of beer. The ringleader told me he had always wanted to order a hundred draught beers, and he did it. They arrived in some splendour, four trays full of beer. Eventually, of course, I had to help them out, and I did my best.

I have every confidence that there was some fairly silly conversation that afternoon, but I don't remember any of it. No, the conversation I had in mind was a different afternoon, albeit in the same bar. I was sitting by myself at a Formica-topped table, quietly reading. At the next table sat a man I didn't know. Like many men who sit alone in bars, he had nothing to read, apparently happy to stare ahead and think his thoughts. Me, I don't have enough thoughts to see me through a whole afternoon in the pub, so I like to bring along a book. We had not spoken or acknowledged each other's existence.

Two men in turbans came in. They walked past us, paused while they considered sitting in our section of the bar, then moved on. When these men were out of earshot, the fellow at the next table leaned toward me.

"Them Pakis bug you?" he asked.

I hesitated, considering the implications of my answer. Was I willing to get into a fight about this? "No," I replied.

He paused slightly, apparently having decided we had both stepped out of a Harold Pinter play, then he said, "Yeah, me neither."

I returned to my book, we both took a sip from our beers, and we never exchanged another word.

# Who Owns Your Pub?

**B**y law, English pubs have to sport a notice over the entrance advising the public of the identity of the licensee. While this is interesting information, it is seldom that the licensee of a pub is also the owner. Until quite recently, most English pubs were owned by breweries, most of them regional. Driving through England in 1980 you would be aware of travelling through an area dominated by Morland's pubs, then Morrell's pubs, then, as you approached Wiltshire, Wadworth's pubs. If you wanted to drink Donnington's beers, you went to northern Gloucestershire and kept your eyes open.

The breweries generally leased their pubs out to tenants, most of whom stayed for many years and stamped their own personalities on the pubs. They bought their beer from the breweries to which they were tied and—for the most part—lived in relative harmony with both their brewery and their customers. It was a system that worked for a very long time. There were also pubs that were independently owned, with no tie to any brewery, free to sell whatever beer they chose. These were called free houses and were generally seen as a good thing. They were such a good thing that many pubs lied and called themselves free houses when they were not. I know: imagine that.

In the 1990s the British government—in a well-intentioned move that was intended to protect the smaller breweries that were getting slammed by the big guys—passed legislation that limited the number of pubs a brewery could own, and also forced pub owners to allow their tenants to sell guest beers. The bigger companies had to either divest themselves of some of their pubs or get out of brewing. It is the nature of big companies that they don't like becoming smaller companies, and the new legislation guaranteed full employment for a number of corporate lawyers. The upshot is that a lot of English pubs are now owned by what is called "pubcos," companies that don't make beer but own lots of pubs. These companies are constantly buying and selling pubs and generally making drinkers nervous. While they are not owned by breweries, most of these pubcos have deals with big brewers, so the beer selection is likely to be unsurprising.

One of the more interesting of these companies is the rapidly expanding J.D. Wetherspoon chain, which predictably has nothing to do with anybody called Wetherspoon. Most of its pubs have been placed in buildings that were not originally pubs, some quite imaginatively. There is no music in these pubs and they offer food all day—both pretty radical concepts in the UK.

Other chains have come and gone. Back in the late seventies, a fellow called David Bruce, laid off by one of the big breweries, got the idea of opening his own pubs. He started with a pub in

Southwark that was being closed down as economically unfea-
sible by one of the big guys. Bruce installed brewing equipment,
redecorated, and gave the place a cute new name: the Goose and
Firkin. Soon he was opening more brewpubs in slightly unfashion-
able areas: the Frog and Firkin, the Pheasant and Firkin, and—in a
fire-damaged railway station—the Phoenix and Firkin. Eventually,
of course, he sold the company and his concept got watered down
and finally disappeared altogether.

The Firkin name has been adopted by a Toronto company that
at last count boasts thirty pubs in Ontario and a number of others
elsewhere, mostly in suburban locations. Their boast reads: "Firkin
is now, and always intends to be the largest and most dominant
English Pub chain in North America. Over the next few years,
Firkin foresees having over 1,000 pubs in development." God
knows the Firkin pubs have been a godsend for people in out-of-
the-way places and for thirsty people just passing through those
places, though there is something formulaic about the pubs. There
are few surprises at the Firkin pubs (though it was sometimes surprising how loud the music used to be at the Ferret and Firkin in
Toronto); on the plus side, Anne used to swear by their hamburgers,
despite the kaiser buns.

Perhaps the biggest success in Toronto's pub scene is that of
David and Isabel Manore, proprietors of the Madison and Paupers,
two midtown pubs that cater both to students and to residents of
the hip Annex area. The Madison started life as a basement pub
in an old house on Madison Avenue, inspired by the success of the
nearby Duke of York. Eventually, the Manores took over the ground
floor, then the second and third floors of the house. By the 1990s

they had bought the house next door and made their no-longer-little pub even bigger. At full tilt, when they have everything open, including three levels of patios and decks in the back, the Manores can accommodate almost two thousand people. That's the full roster of all the teams in Major League Baseball and the National Hockey League, plus the original Broadway cast of Sondheim's *Follies*. Given the proximity of several frat houses, they frequently accomplish this goal.

In the mid-eighties the Manores took over what had been a bank on Bloor Street and turned it into Paupers, complete with a quiet little room in what had been the vault. In 1999 they opened a twenty-room "boutique hotel" just north of the Madison, possibly to be convenient for those people who meet other people at the Madison and feel a sudden need to become closer, and in 2000 they opened a villa in Puerto Vallarta, Mexico. Something tells me that David and Isabel have done well.

They didn't succeed by being dopey business people, of course. From the start, they have been on the premises, keeping an eye on things, though presumably they have to spend more of their time in Mexico these days. To their credit, their staff includes a number of people who have been there forever, which suggests that the Manores are not dreadful to work for; bartenders and waiters are inclined to be nomadic.

That said, however, one could possibly take issue with the small notice in the menu that observes that, just in case you were tempted to be stroppy about this, a pint of beer is deemed to comprise approximately eighteen ounces of beer in a twenty-ounce glass. Readers of *The Globe and Mail* will be familiar with the injunction of Junius, who reminds us every day: The subject who is truly loyal to the Chief Magistrate will neither advise nor submit to arbitrary measures. As my friend Robbie Brown has noted, if an eighteen-ounce pint is not an arbitrary measure, I don't know what is. Mind you, it's only a 10 percent ripoff, and who could bicker with that? Oops, I think I just did. And one could argue that a pub capable of housing two thousand people could afford to be a tad more adventurous in its choice of beers.

(And it's not just the Madison, by any means. The world is full of pubs that boast eighteen taps, twenty taps, twenty-two taps. But you go inside and it's always the same beer. Now I know that in supermarkets and big chain bookstores—or big chain anything—suppliers pay to have their products available. The more they pay, the better the placement. This practice is legal in most retail endeavours, and it may be legal in bars and pubs in some jurisdictions. I don't think it's legal in the province of Ontario, where I live, and I'm not suggesting that any under-the-table payments are being made. Who'd be crazy enough to jeopardize their licence? No, I have to assume that a lot of publicans simply lack the imagination to offer their customers a meaningful variety.)

But back to the Madison. I've had some good times within those walls. One night Anne and I met up with a guy who claimed to have worked with Neil Young. We drank far too much and sang along as he played the Madison's old piano. You can't put a price tag on that. Well, you probably can, but I've long since lost the Visa receipt. And I've gone there a time or two on Christmas Day. The Manores were the ones who broke the old taboo on serving drinks at Christmas. English themselves, they knew about pubs being open on Christmas Eve and the day itself. In Toronto, pubs historically closed early on Christmas Eve and never dreamed of opening on the big day. But this is a biggish town and there are people without friends or family to go to—not to mention a few people who actually do have friends and family and like to go to a pub anyway—who appreciate a place to go. (Not to mention the many people who don't celebrate Christmas.) As one who has traditionally worked on Christmas Eve, I know I like to have a pint after work. And there are usually enough bar staff who—gypsies themselves—are just as happy to work. Still, just in case, it's worth tipping a bit extra, okay?

Then there are the Dukes: York, Gloucester, Kent, Westminster, and Richmond. Sounds like one of those history plays from Shakespeare. What word of York, good brother Gloucester? Ah, good Lord of Kent, he is gone—i'faith!—with Westminster to do battle with the knave Richmond. It seems a loose federation of pubs. Westminster caters to the TSE 300, Richmond to downtown shoppers, Gloucester to the raffish Yonge Street set, Kent to a crew of uptown regulars, and York to the midtown mix of practically everything, but particularly the university. A few years ago the Duke of York underwent a major renovation, which included adding a third floor. And the place looks great. It looks like a million bucks, which the rumour mill suggests would about cover the bill, but regulars guess that most of it was made up pretty quickly by attracting large groups.

That's where the money is these days: getting in a gang of sixty lawyers, or a hundred teaching assistants, or what have you. It's good for the bottom line, but it's tough for the regulars, who sometimes can't get in the door without a reservation. Still, at some point it kind of stops being a pub. To my old mind, a proper pub does not need a crew of greeters at the main entrance helping people find a table or redirecting a team of regulars to this week's destination because their regular table is overrun by yet another group booking. A proper pub does not have a "Please Wait to Be Seated" sign at the front door.

No one ever said the pub life was a democratic one. Drinking men and women are ever at the mercy of their publican, the despot who can discontinue your favourite ale, take sausage rolls off the menu, or inflict Led Zeppelin upon you with impunity. The drinker is, of course, free to vote with his or her feet. We can take our business elsewhere, which is not always an easy option.

Sometimes we have no choice but to take our business elsewhere. The bar in which I courted the Evergreen Bride has long since been reduced to a pile of rubble on a building site, en route to becoming yet another block of condominiums, or is that condominia? The bar in which I drank my first public beer is now an upmarket menswear emporium. And on and on.

In late 2000 (early 2001 for North American viewers) *Coronation Street* ran a storyline in which the Rover's Return—the quintessential cozy backstreet pub—was on the brink of being sold to a pubco with plans to tart the place up and rename it the Boozy Newt. This was more than the traditionalists could stand, and the perennially earnest Ken Barlow uttered a speech that brought tears to this pubgoer's eyes:

"The world is full of nasty theme pubs with flashy decor and thumping sound systems, without this place being taken over as well. It's history and tradition within these walls, and it can't be replaced once it's lost."

In the next episode, Fred Elliott, the doughy butcher, reminded us, "It's the punters who decide what they want from a pub, not these so-called experts, these market researchers with their ruddy clipboards."

It is not fine speeches, however, that save pubs. Sometimes it takes cash, and in this case it took three of the regulars to put in a bid to buy the pub themselves, offering what Fred called "the last stand against the evil tide of fancy food and foreign beer." A grateful nation rose to its feet in applause.

The idea of a drinkers' cooperative is not confined to soap operas. There was a pub called the King's Arms in Toronto's trendy Yorkville area that became endangered when its owner decided to sell up and return to England. What to do? A quintet of regulars raised the money and bought the place. (Not that it's still there, of course.) One day you're a familiar face at the bar, next day you're the guv'nor. Who owns your pub? Maybe you do.

# It's Supposed to Have Flavour:
# Tasting Beer

According to something called Impact Databank, the two big-gest selling-beers on planet Earth are Bud and Bud Light. Between them, these two anemic beverages accounted for slightly more than 6 per cent of all the beer consumed by *homo* otherwise *sapiens* in 1999. Given that many of us drank absolutely no Bud or Bud Light in 1999, and given that it isn't even available in the Czech Republic, where they drink a lot of beer, you have to assume that somebody somewhere is drinking an awful lot of the stuff. As has been said, people who drink Bud Light don't like the taste of beer; they just enjoy peeing a lot.

All the beers on the global top ten list are predictably bland, brewed for people who don't want to be surprised by a sudden burst of flavour. Anheuser-Busch didn't get where it is today by overesti-mating the public's palate. Yet there are people out there who really do like the taste of beer, people who like to be surprised, people who like a bit of variety. Some of these people even attend beer tastings. A few years ago, the idea of beer tastings would have been laughed at. It's beer, for Pete's sake. It tastes like beer—what did you expect? If pressed to describe one's beer, the words "suds" and "foam" sprang to mind.

Nowadays, the beer experts can be as over-the-top as the wine guys. The *Good Beer Guide*, published by the Campaign for Real Ale, describes beers in terms like: "A refreshing, copper-amber session bitter with a well-defined citrus hop aroma and taste, and a nutty, malty background ending dry"; or "A strong golden beer reminiscent of hot cross buns. Fruity, malty and sweet with butterscotch notes"; or "The intense roast flavour is backed by coffee, chocolate and liquorice, and hints of spice and smoke." Other beers are redolent of "cooked vegetables," "a glorious blackberry bouquet," and "a hint of sulphur leading to a pleasant crisp apple finish." If I'd talked about beer like that in the taprooms of my youth, I'd have been out on the street by the time I got to the butterscotch.

Very few of us—this humble reporter included—have palates as finely tuned as the authors of the above descriptions, but there's nothing to stop us from getting better at identifying beer flavours. The beer experts—the likes of the late Michael Jackson, Roger Protz, and Canada's own Stephen Beaumont—aren't feeding us a lot of bull about tasting beer. If they say they're tasting hot cross buns, they're tasting hot cross buns. The point is that there are many interesting whiffs and flavours attached to a good beer, and it's part of the fun to spot at least some of them. Drinkers brought up on the Buds of this world haven't even come to grips with the smell and taste of hops, let alone liquorice and blackberries.

Beer is just as worthy of flowery talk as wine. Beer probably came first, after all, and brewing is a more sophisticated process, not to mention that beer doesn't need a bunch of peasants trampling the barley in their bare feet. Best of all, no one at beer tastings expects you to spit it out after you've tasted it, which makes beer tastings a lot jollier than wine tastings.

I like wine too, but you have to admit some of those people are a bit serious about it. I am reminded of the wine bore who was holding forth at a restaurant one evening, sipping wines and declaring at high volume what the grape was, which end of the vineyard it had come from, and what vintage it was. A man at a nearby table could endure it no longer, and finally passed a wine glass to his neighbour. The wine bore held it up to the light and declared it a Chardonnay, probably New World. In due course he sipped from the glass. Quickly he spat it out, crying, "This is piss!"

"I know what it is," said the man at the nearby table, "but how old am I?"

South African novelist André Brink tells the story of an attempt to produce wine in Zimbabwe, a country generally perceived as too hot for wine. Somewhere near Victoria Falls a vineyard was planted. In time, the grapes were ready for harvesting, and they were duly turned into wine. When the process was complete, the wine bottled, aged, and labelled, a French expert was invited to come and give it his blessing. He came, he went through the tasting ritual, and he raised a glass to his lips. The locals held their breath as he swished the wine around his taste buds. When at last he spoke, he asked where the wine had been made.

"Right here, Monsieur," the winemaker said, gesturing. "Just across the road."

The expert frowned and thought for a moment. "Eet does not travel well."

Apart from the spitting business, beer tasting is much like its wine equivalent. Pour your beer into a nice clean glass. It's worth pointing out that detergent residue can kill the head on a beer, so wash your beer glasses separately from the rest of your dishes. (Oh sure, beer tasting is supposed to be so relaxed, and suddenly I'm coming on with all sorts of rules. I'm just trying to make it nice for you.) Now take a look at your beer. Hold it up. Like the colour? Are there things floating in it? Occasionally there are supposed to be things floating in it, but it's worth asking at this point. Now take a good sniff. If you can't smell anything, you're not likely to taste much either. Can you smell the hops? No? Maybe the next one will be better.

Now taste the beer. Let it hit the taste buds right up front and then further along. Are you getting one taste at the start, followed by something different as it passes through? Excellent! That's just what good beer should do. Now, this is important—don't spit it out. Swallow it. Unless it's really awful. If you have reason to believe that you've just allowed some mass-produced abomination into your mouth—your body is a temple, remember—then feel free to spit it out, perhaps in the direction of the person who has played this sinister trick on you.

A lot of drinkers pick a beer they like at the age of about twenty and stick with it for life, which is like eating the same dinner every night or listening to the same band every day. (As I write these words, I've been married to the same woman for thirty years, so I'm definitely not taking this analogy any further. I may be daft, but I'm not stupid.)

Beer comes in many colours and many flavours, and limiting yourself to one kind of beer seems an act of masochism. You won't always like the beers you taste, but try to see what the brewer was getting at. Sometimes a beer will strike you as funny, just as music can be funny. Brewers often have a sense of humour, and they'll brew a beer with chili peppers or ginseng, just to see what happens. It's okay to laugh at your beer. Hell, drinking beer's supposed to be fun, so lighten up. There is no set taste of beer. Predictability is boring. And even if you haven't developed the keen palate of the experts, there's no reason you can't have a darn good time. Elsewhere I note that sex and golf are two activities you can enjoy without displaying great skill; tasting beer is another. Mind you, the better you get . . .

There's no reason you couldn't substitute good beer for wine at mealtimes. The general rule of thumb is to substitute a lager where you would otherwise serve a white wine, and offer an ale of substance instead of a red. There are fruit beers that complement a dessert, and a good barley wine—if you can get one—is just as good (and often just about as strong) as a glass of port afterwards.

Beer tasting on a large scale is called a beer festival, and I recommend it highly. Early every August beer lovers descend on London for the Great British Beer Festival and the chance to taste more than three hundred British draught beers and a growing number of imports as well. Friends, you've never seen so many casks of beer in one place. If you have to wonder whether this is a wonderful sight, you're reading the wrong book. The Great American Beer Festival in Denver is even bigger (though the samples, at a mere ounce apiece, are smaller).

Beer festivals are to be found in many parts of the world, even Toronto. August brings Toronto's Festival of Beer to old Fort York and, though it's not the Great British Beer Festival, it's better than no beer festival at all. And in my experience it doesn't even rain (jinx alert!). At the 2000 festival I saw a man whose party piece was drinking beer while standing on his head. Imagine how drunk you'd have to be to think that was a good idea. So go along, try a few new beers, and remember to comment on the cooked vegetable quality of the beer. The others will be impressed. If they're not, try standing on your head.

# To Your Health:
# Relax, It's Good for You

The temperance movement that arose in the latter half of the nineteenth century succeeded in persuading a good many people that alcohol was a kind of poison, and we've lived with that slur ever since. If it brings you pleasure, it must be bad for you. Only in the last few years have we heard any encouraging words from the scientific community, but some of them have been mighty encouraging indeed.

There's alcohol, of course, and there's alcohol. Red wine has had plenty of good press in the last few years, after people started to ask why, if red meat, alcohol, tobacco, cream sauces, and the like were so unhealthy, French people didn't die at thirty. This was a very good question. By all rational reckoning, the French should have become extinct long ago, yet here they were indulging in everything that could be considered toxic and living long, apparently healthy lives, engaging in physical activity no more strenuous than watching the Tour de France whiz by once a year. And don't tell me that boules is the perfect aerobic exercise.

The fellows and gals in the white coats went away to study the phenomenon of French longevity and came back giving credit to red wine, which sent burgundy sales soaring through the roof, where they have remained ever since. En masse, women—traditional drinkers of white wine but more health-conscious than men—switched to red. Party-givers found themselves completely out of red wine within half an hour, with cases of white untouched. Subsequent studies have suggested that, in general, the health benefits of red wine stem largely from the alcohol, not from some magical quality of red wine, though red wine is richer in antioxidants than white. In other words, alcohol is good for you.

(The red wine boom was similar to the yogurt boom of the sixties, when it was discovered that yogurt-chugging residents of the Caucasus routinely lived to the age of 106. Typically, of course, very few of these ancient people actually had birth certificates, and it was later suggested that it only felt like 106 years. Living in the Caucasus on a diet of yogurt will do that to you.)

The original healthy beverage was beer. Made of the same ingredients as bread, beer was considered an exemplary, almost medicinal drink until the temperance zealots came along. When William of Orange left the Lowlands to take the British throne in 1688, he brought gin with him. William taxed beer to support his military activities in Ireland, driving up the price of beer and making gin more popular with the masses. By 1740 there were nine thousand gin shops in London (compared with the present seven thousand pubs in that now much larger metropolis). Hogarth's engravings of Gin Lane and Beer Street demonstrate the social perils of gin and the life-enhancing qualities of beer. Gin came by the moniker "mother's ruin" honestly.

Beer (and, all right, wine too) put us on the map as a species. If you didn't drink beer you had to drink water, and water was a hazard. The brewing of beer called for the boiling of water, a measure that saved lives. There are not many references in the Scriptures, for instance, to people drinking water. You will remember that I quoted St. Paul a few chapters ago, but it bears repeating here: "Drink no longer water, but use a little wine for thy stomach's sake." I'm not a doctor and neither was St. Paul, but he was clearly on the right track. Water was the ticket to cholera and other unpleasant diseases. The life expectancy of the early teetotaller was dismally low. Early man, whom you may recall from forty-odd pages ago, was not clever enough to keep his water supply pure, so he needed beer. Columbus crossed the Atlantic with wine, not water, and he had the capital of Ohio named after him.

There is a school of thought that says that Europeans learned to make beer and wine to avoid raw water, while the Asians learned to make tea. This kept both groups healthy but gave Europeans a genetic disposition toward alcohol that Asians do not share. (It is also possible, of course, that the Asians—not genetically disposed to alcohol—gravitated to tea because it suited them better. Apparently, more than 40 percent of Asians lack the gene that turns alcohol first into acetaldehyde, then into acetic acid, while virtually all people of European origins can turn this little trick every day without thinking twice about it. Whether they preferred tea because they lack the gene or they lack the gene because they didn't develop it through centuries of drinking beer and wine is unknown.)

According to this theory, European society from the Iron Age lived in a state of at least a mild buzz until the Victorian era, when modern engineering brought clean water to the public at large. Coincidentally—or not—the temperance movement arose at the same time. For the first time it was possible for westerners to live an alcohol-free life and not perish. (Fair enough, tea and coffee had made their way to Europe by this time as well.) Alcohol became an indulgence rather than a fact of life. Ironically, we seem to be moving backwards again. A diet of beer rather than E. coli–infested water could have saved lives in Walkerton, Ontario, in the late 1990s. Now that our water is not quite so safe again, we need ways of treating it to render it harmless. Turning it into alcohol seems to work.

For years we read of studies proving that alcohol was bad for us. A pregnant woman today who takes as much as a sip of wine will be shunned and scolded, yet there can be few members of my generation whose mothers did not drink throughout their pregnancies. (In their defence, our mothers didn't know they were doing wrong. I'm not actually endorsing drinking while pregnant.)

Fortunately, in the last few years the people who do studies of this sort have been coming out on the side of the drinking person. It's amazing the sort of thing these people will study, and wouldn't you love to see their funding proposals? Ten years ago, researchers at the University of Western Ontario established that a stirred martini was healthier than a shaken one. "Let me get this straight, Smithers. You need a research grant for a case of gin, a bottle of vermouth, and a couple of jars of olives?"

"Any chance we could have some swizzle sticks as well?"

A Japanese study revealed that drinking can be good for the brain cells. The National Institute for Longevity Sciences did IQ tests on two thousand people between the ages of forty and seventy-nine. Men who drank moderately scored 3.3 points higher than those who didn't drink, while female drinkers scored 2.5 points higher than their abstaining counterparts. It didn't matter what sort of alcohol they drank. Researchers acknowledged that the results did not take into account the possibility that people who drink are just naturally more intelligent than those who don't, and I couldn't possibly comment.

Around the same time, the 2000 International Chemical Congress of Pacific Basin Societies—and, given what conventions are like, who's to say they weren't hitting the sauce a mite themselves?—took aboard a study done by Canadian and American researchers that showed that the antioxidants in beer can reduce the risk of cataracts and heart disease. Ale lovers will be pleased to learn that dark ales and stouts have more antioxidants than lighter beers, so are particularly healthy. The study involved giving hamsters the equivalent of two beers a day, and the results were very good indeed. At least for diabetic hamsters. The Canadian input into this study seems to have been the same guys who were involved in the martini study mentioned above, which tells you practically everything you need to know about the University of Western Ontario. Let's just say there's no difficulty getting volunteers for alcohol-related scientific studies at Western. (And what exactly is the equivalent of two beers for a hamster, anyway? What's that in hamster pints?)

The more of these studies you read, the more you think doctors should be prescribing beer. In fact, my mother, in girlhood, was diagnosed as anemic and was made to drink Guinness. It was only at eighty-nine, when her Guinness input had declined, that her health degenerated. Until recently it was common for new mothers to be prescribed stout—rich in iron—as an aid to nursing. You tell me that an infant breastfed from a stout-sipping mother is not going to be a happy baby.

Beer contains the B vitamins—niacin, riboflavin, pyridoxine, and folate, to name but four impressive-sounding ingredients—which provide protection against cardiovascular disease and some cancers. The hop—a little pharmacy all in itself—contains antioxidants that fight cancers of the gastrointestinal tract, breast cancer, and thyroid cancer. Hops also reduce the risk of kidney stones and osteoporosis.

Beer is low in sodium but rich in potassium, magnesium, zinc, and copper. (I used to wonder why I always set off the metal detectors in airports, until I realized that my body, which I had thought of as a temple, was in fact a warehouse for semi-precious metals.) Beer's low alcohol content makes it a wholesome, excellent source of these nutrients. Beer lowers cholesterol levels and is a good source of fibre. It's a wonder we don't drink it for breakfast, as in fact many Germans do.

Another recent study even reveals that there's no such thing as a beer belly. There's nothing in beer that inherently makes you fat (beer contains fewer calories than milk or fruit juice). If beer drinkers get fat, it's because beer is an excellent appetite stimulant. Beer drinkers—like wine drinkers—are likely to eat three meals a day. (And they're less likely than wine drinkers to be dining at *nouvelle cuisine* restaurants; when beer drinkers have their appetites stimulated, they're more inclined to order a mess of wings.) And, as we know, beer helps out with the regularity, if you get my drift.

And here's one for the womenfolk. Sadly, women's stomachs produce half as much dehydrogenase—an enzyme that helps metabolize alcohol—as men's. This, along with other unfair factors, makes women less able to tolerate alcohol than men. At least until menopause. As men grow older, they become less tolerant of brother booze, whereas women become more so. Eventually, we all become more or less equal in the eyes of Bacchus, which is as it should be.

All of this good news comes to us a bit grudgingly. The authorities don't want to unleash an orgy of pie-eyed health seekers on a binge, and they're not about to let Guinness go back to using its old slogan: Guinness is good for you. They're scared to death that some dope, desperate for riboflavin, is going to overindulge, wreck his car, and sue them. The threat of litigation makes cowards of us all.

Then there's our traditional notion that medicine by its very nature tastes bad. If it tastes good, it can't be doing us any good. Honestly, we are so auto-repressive. Just look at the fuss over the recent studies that point out the healthy qualities of cannabis. The authorities, unable to deny the usefulness of the reefer, are now attempting to create a medicinal form of cannabis that will not have any psychoactive effect on the user. Let's not let those terminal cancer patients get a little high along with their painkillers. After all, someone might invent a cure next week and we'll end up with a bunch of healthy people with a taste for a spliff at lunchtime.

And I hate to say it, but all these studies pack the word "moderation" into their accounts as many times as they can. We find that moderate drinkers live longer than heavy drinkers, but also longer than abstainers. Predictably, no one can agree on what constitutes moderation. The American definition is lower than the German definition. The British definition changed in 1995, allowing drinkers more of what they fancy. Drinkers in the UK get to have four more bottles of beer a week than Americans, and it's often better beer as well. The Canadian figures are, alas, the same as the American: fourteen "standard" drinks a week for men, nine for women. Mind you, early in 2008 one of the people who had been given the responsibility of figuring out these numbers in the UK admitted that they had just made it all up in the first place. It was guesswork.

If you're going to be moderate—and it would be irresponsible of me to suggest otherwise—there's a good argument for improving the quality of what you drink. As the Unibroue folk of Quebec say, *Boire Moins, Boire Mieux*: Drink Less, Drink Better. (Given that their beers tend toward the head-crashingly strong, this is good advice anyway.)

To your very good health.

# Life's a Drag:
# Drinking and Smoking

Some people can practise a variety of vices at the same time: drinking, smoking, caffeine, adultery, gambling, butterscotch sundaes, you name it. I admire people who can do this, but I'm not one of them. When it comes to vice, some people are generalists. I'm a specialist. Besides, butterscotch sundaes don't go with beer.

I tried smoking for a while once, but it didn't take. Smoking's like the piano: if you don't take it up when you're a kid, you'll never be really good at it. But I was in a play once in which I had to smoke a cigar, and I practised on cigarettes so I'd look natural. (What I didn't realize until the big cigar craze of the 1990s is that hardly anybody looks natural smoking a cigar. Studies show that a full 99 percent of human beings look like utter weenies with cigars in their mouths.) We were doing this play at a tiny theatre where even sitting in the back row was no guarantee of avoiding actors' spittle. I've had romantic relationships that were less intimate than this theatre.

Everything was going fine on opening night until we hit the cigar scene. Another actor and I were seated downstage, inches away from the audience, puffing on our stogies. Slowly we realized we could no longer see the back row. A minute or so later we couldn't see the front row, and we were practically in the front row. The only evidence of an audience was a few strangled coughs in the murky haze. It looked like old movies of London. Not only did the audience miss most of the cigar scene, they missed several scenes immediately afterwards as the fog slowly lifted. It was a confusing enough play even when you could see it, so we scrapped the cigars and I stopped practising smoking. It didn't seem to make me seem louche or dashing or bohemian or any of those attractive traits that used to be associated with smoking. I wasn't getting lucky without cigarettes, but I wasn't getting any luckier with them, so I stopped.

And it's just as well, really, because smokers today are a much put-upon class of people. This has happened in a short time. Remember smoking on airplanes? There's a theory that since most airlines banned smoking they no longer circulate the air as often as they formerly had to, so we're still no better off in terms of air quality. At least the crappy air in airplanes doesn't smell like cigarettes any more. Remember smoking at work? Young folks today don't believe that not long ago people routinely smoked at their desks. How much productivity has been lost to cigarette breaks? Mind you, as comic Dave Broadfoot has noted, there's no healthier group of people today than smokers: look at all the fresh air they get. A visiting Russian dignitary, being driven through the streets of Ottawa a few years ago, commented on the liberal Canadian practice of allowing prostitutes to gather outside government buildings. Actually, he was told, these were not prostitutes but government office workers on their smoke breaks.

People used to smoke anywhere they liked. They smoked at the movies, they smoked at hockey games, they smoked through their dinners at fancy restaurants. Bit by bit, the total freedom of smokers has been curtailed. If California is still the benchmark of how the rest of us will be living in a few years, smokers are in big trouble. There's even a part of Los Angeles that's threatening to ban people from smoking in their own homes. I don't know if the firefighters' union is lobbying against this measure. Their jobs are in jeopardy.

California has introduced no end of wacky trends that the rest of us gradually catch up on—Chardonnay, artichokes, voodoo economics, tofu, and liposuction, to name a few—so we shouldn't be too quick to mock its anti-tobacco stance. It was California that first banned smoking in bars. This measure has met with only partial compliance, possibly depending on the habits of the local police chief, but you can see which way things are going.

Emboldened by California's position, many other jurisdictions are attempting similar approaches. Vancouver, sharing not only a coastline but a fault line with California, has banned smoking practically everywhere. The city of Toronto tried it in the late nineties but didn't really carry it off. Being essentially decent people, we don't like to come across as too heavy-handed here in Toronto. I recall a debate that went on in the early eighties about how far strippers should be permitted to go. At that time they were going about as far as they could go, as Oscar Hammerstein II wrote in *Oklahoma!*, and a few city burghers felt this was a trifle too far. This was Toronto, for Pete's sake. So legislation was passed that ruled that strippers should keep one item of clothing on at all times. We all knew which item that was and what it was meant to conceal, but nobody liked to spell it out too concretely in official legal documents that schoolchildren could stumble upon.

Strippers are a cagey bunch, and they quickly saw a loophole. According to the newspapers, they obeyed the law to the letter, usually choosing a headband as their one item of clothing. The city fathers and mothers sputtered in rage. "That's not what we meant and you know it!" they cried, quickly putting together another law that made it very clear indeed what they meant, though they blushed as they picked the words. (In the end, a higher court threw the legislation out altogether, turning Toronto into the sin capital it is today.)

So they hoped that Torontonians, being civilized people, would see the sense of curtailing smoking in pubs and bars. Just in case, however, they passed a law decreeing that a certain percentage of a bar or restaurant had to be designated non-smoking, and that the area in question should have its own source of ventilation. For the first few days, we were treated to the sight of local publicans skating around the issue. Bartenders developed a mantra whereby they explained to their customers that they were no longer permitted to smoke and that they could be fined large sums of money for doing so, but as long as they knew that and were determined to take that risk they might as well have an ashtray rather than wreck the furniture.

It was all the pub community talked about. Smokers insisted they'd never give up. Publicans predicted doom if they were forced by anti-smoking totalitarians to send their customers out into the cold. Dozens of pubs would be shut by Christmas if this law was enforced. Even Smokeless Joe—the publican who never had permitted smoking in his establishment—probably worried that his unique status was in jeopardy.

As days passed, it gradually became clear that the city was not actually going to do anything about the situation. Defiant smokers were not being tossed into the hoosegow. Publicans nervously kept changing their non-smoking areas. One day the bar area was non-smoking, next day it was the back part of the room, the day after it was somewhere else. But nothing seemed to happen.

The only publicans who could afford to provide separate ventilation for non-smoking areas already had pubs so large that they could easily designate entire floors non-smoking. They were all right. The city backed off, for the time being. But, they cautioned darkly, they would be back.

The debate continued. There was for a time legislation that distinguished between bars and restaurants; bar patrons could smoke, but not their restaurant counterparts. The distinction had nothing to do with, say, the quality of food offered in any given establishment. Quality control doesn't figure greatly in any legislation that I'm familiar with. No, the distinction was that children could enter restaurants but not bars, so proprietors were forced to decide whether they preferred to part with their smoking clientele or to bar families with young 'uns from entering. People who had been bringing their kids to the pub for years were suddenly turned away at the door.

Interestingly, when England was contemplating a smoking ban they came up with a similar idea, in that smoking would be banned in any place that offered prepared food. This led to publicans declaring that they would be closing their kitchens, sacking the cook, and serving nothing but crisps and nuts (potato chips to us, and, well, nuts to you). Eventually the government took a different path and banned smoking in pubs and restaurants altogether.

Which is what Toronto had already done in 2004. Its initial attempt in 1997 had failed for a number of reasons, among which was the spectacularly loony decision to activate the ban on January 1. January in these parts can be a frosty place, and suddenly sending people outdoors to smoke seemed harsh. The 2004 law came into effect on June 1, which was considerably smarter. Smokers had the summer to adjust to going outside, and by the time the snow fell they were more or less used to it.

Publicans predicted catastrophe, and indeed many reported a decline in business when fall arrived. How much of this was due to the smoking ban and how much to the hockey lockout of that winter is impossible to guess. I spoke to the owner of what is very much not a sports bar and he said that to his surprise his takings that fall were actually up from the year before. (When England went non-smoking in the summer of 2007, there were similar dire predictions, followed in many cases by lower sales. We'll never know the actual immediate effect of the ban because England in 2007 suffered the wettest summer in living memory. A number of pubs indeed shut in July of that year, for the very good reason that they were underwater.)

Toronto got tougher in 2006, banning separately ventilated smoking rooms and placing stricter restrictions on patio smoking. Henceforth there would be no smoking on patios with awnings.

Even patio umbrellas that touched each other now constituted an enclosed space, for heaven's sake.

It's all part of a global trend, of course. We expected the west coast to go smoke-free, but New York City? Ireland? More recently even Italy, France, and Germany have turned on their smokers. One German publican bashed holes in the wall of his bar so smokers could stick their heads and an arm out and smoke legally. I don't think that would wash in Toronto. Apart from anything else, it's just too cold for holes in the wall.

Back when smoking was legal, I knew people who refused to go to pubs because of the smoke. They were allergic, they hated the smell, and so on. Have these people rushed back to the pubs now that the air is fresh and healthy? I'm sure a few have, but the majority, I fear, have not. Having won the battle for clean air in pubs, they could have stepped up and supported their local pub. They could have shown the flag, but by and large they have not.

Now, I like a smoke-free pub myself. I don't like coming home and watching my wife wrinkle her lovely nose and say, "I don't need to ask where you've been" before taking my clothes out back and burning them. She loathes cigarette smoke—she's never had as much as a puff in her life, she won't even eat smoked salmon—but she acknowledged that it was part of pub life. Interestingly, she never minded anywhere near as much the cigarette smoke of people she liked.

My concern about the anti-smoking lobby is the element of pious social control that attaches itself to it. Once these people have rid the world of the curse of tobacco, they'll be after us drinkers next, just you watch. In my perfect world—coming soon to a universe near you—smokers will see the error of their ways, realize that they're poisoning and bankrupting themselves and making the world a much smellier place, and will stop of their own accord. God knows where American politicians will get their funding from, but that's not my lookout. Meanwhile, of course, the tobacco companies continue to target each new generation that comes along, guaranteeing themselves millions of new users for decades to come.

In the last couple of years we have looked on as cultural life in Canada threatens to shut down completely because the federal government will no longer permit cigarette companies to sponsor jazz festivals, golf tournaments, and the like. Our streets will fall silent, famous golfers and tennis players will shun us, because the tobacco pushers have been shown the door. Cultural czars plead with the feds to let music and theatre thrive again. The government winds up looking like the villain and the tobacco people get to look like saints. Heck, I've been to events sponsored by cigarette companies and nothing bad has happened to me. I haven't suddenly developed some lethal habit. Maybe these companies should be allowed back in.

But let's think for a moment. Why do tobacco companies sponsor jazz festivals? Is it because they love jazz and want us to be happy? Is it because they feel guilty about the huge profits they make from giving people cancer and emphysema? No. It's because they're banned from advertising on television and radio and in magazines. Surely the solution to this problem is not to let the tobacco people back in, but to ban other corporations from advertising on television and radio and in magazines. We can all think of products we'd prefer not to see advertised on television. And what about the quality of the advertising? I've never eaten McCain's Pizza Pockets, and I'm not about to start. It's not that they taste bad—they may taste terrific, but I'll never know—but that their commercials are obnoxious and have been for years.

Would I feel better about McCain's if I attended the McCain's Pizza Pocket Theatre Festival? You bet I would. And how about the Norwich Union Tennis Championship? Count me in! Just get them off the air. I'm sure you have plenty of commercials you hate, commercials that would justify, say, a five-year ban from the airwaves. Corporations would be lining up to sponsor jazz festivals. Better they should be spending their money in a useful way rather than becoming enablers for yet another tacky reality television show.

What's the worst thing that could happen? Owing to a shortage of advertising revenues, we might end up with a little less television. The thing is, most of us would never know because we'd be out at a play or a concert or a golf tournament. There you are: with one only very slightly draconian measure, the world is made a better place. Glad I could help.

# The Very Fat Men
# Who Water the Workers' Beer

Just because beer is the beverage of the toiling classes, we should not assume that brewery moguls are champions of the working stiffs who make them rich. They are business people, after all, and they like to hang out with their own sort. Adolphus Busch, the man who invented Budweiser—or at least the American Budweiser, not its vastly superior Czech counterpart—didn't even like beer. This will not surprise anyone who has tasted it. He referred to it as "that slop," which is about right. He was the first man to pasteurize beer, which is not a nice thing to do to beer. Unless it's Budweiser, in which case, who cares? They call it the king of beers, but it's a pretty minor monarchy, if you ask me, something on the order of, say, Albania's ex-king Zog.

Our own E.P. Taylor, a card-carrying magnate if ever there was one, became one of the villains of British brewing history. The owner of Northern Dancer, Taylor was a better judge of horseflesh than beer. He felt that everyone in the world should be drinking Carling Black Label, perhaps because he owned the brewery. Once he had convinced many Canadians to drink the stuff, he began to think more globally. England, for instance. They drank a lot of beer in England, Taylor noticed, but they weren't drinking Black Label. This might have been related to the difficulty of finding it in English pubs, Taylor was told, the great majority of English pubs at the time being owned by breweries. A pub that was owned by, say, the Shepherd Neame brewery would stock the beers produced by that company.

The other problem, of course, was that the English still hadn't had their brains sucked out, and they continued to prefer their traditional ale over bland, fizzy, Canadian lager. Never mind about that, thought Taylor, these people haven't seen big-time North American advertising. They'll drink lager by the time I'm through, he said, twirling his imaginary moustache and picturing the poor beer drinker tied helplessly to the railway tracks.

The key was getting the pubs, and the solution was to buy the breweries that owned them. From 1960 to 1967, Taylor and the companies he controlled bought up some 273 British breweries, closing down almost all of them and keeping the pubs. By the end, Bass Charrington controlled a fifth of British brewing and eleven thousand pubs. The destruction of the rich British brewing heritage was under way, and it was a Canadian who put the boot in. And why? Carling bloody Black Label.

Taylor, of course, had learned his vile techniques on his home turf. He started with the Brading's Brewery, but a small Ontario brewery was not enough for a man of Taylor's ambitions. In 1930 he bought up nine breweries, including the Carling Brewery, and by 1952 he had scooped up nearly thirty breweries, most in Ontario and Quebec. Most of these breweries were simply shut down. Taylor was less interested in diversifying his portfolio than in shutting down the competition. Thus was consumer choice limited to an ever-shrinking selection of beers that started to taste more and more alike.

An English music hall performer of the thirties named Paddy Ryan wrote a song about beer moguls that contained the proud boast, "I'm the man, the very fat man, that waters the workers' beer." Now, I'm sure that the majority of brewery owners are decent folk—and in some cases not even terribly fat—who want only to make good beer and make an honest living doing so. There are, however, exceptions.

One of the great brewing families—all right, let's say one of the most interesting brewing families—is the Coors family of Golden, Colorado. I recall living in Brooklyn in 1971 with a woman I had met at the Löwenbräu brewery in Munich. The times being what they were, we were heading out for the coast in a driveaway car— do they still have driveaway cars?—making stops in Colorado and Arizona. A friend said he envied me going to Colorado, the home of Coors beer. In those days Coors was available only in the western states and had a cult following elsewhere, presumably for the reason that we miss what we can't have. As a beer lover, he told me, I was going to love Coors.

Over the years I have learned to be suspicious of beers that are advertised on the basis of the pure mountain water with which they are brewed. I still remember my first Kokanee Glacier Pilsner. I mean, I like pure mountain water as much as anyone, but I'm old-fashioned enough to think they should put some malt and hops in with it if they're going to call it beer. I don't recall encountering much of either in my first, disappointing taste of Coors.

In those politically intense days I don't think I knew anything about the wacky Coors family. Like the beer, the news about their interesting positions on race, unions, homosexuality, women's equality, and so much more had not filtered back to New York in 1971. I recommend to you Dan Baum's book *Citizen Coors: An American Dynasty*.

The original Adolph Coors fled Bismarck's Prussia in 1869 and stowed away on a ship bound for Baltimore, an uncharacteristic act of freeloading that haunted him all his life. In 1873 he started his own brewery in Colorado and was a millionaire by 1890. Always a self-reliant breed that refused to borrow money or be beholden to anyone, the Coors family survived Prohibition, ever more suspicious of government. Well, when I say the family survived, I don't actually mean old Adolph, who threw himself off a ledge on the sixth floor of the Cavalier Hotel in Virginia Beach, Virginia, in 1929, seeing no end in sight to Prohibition.

Old Adolph was probably the sanest of the Coorses, a man who wanted to make good, unpasteurized beer for local sale without outside interference. His son, Adolph II, played around with the notion of making an extra-strong beer, opting instead to make his father's beer even lighter than it had been. Watering the workers' beer, as it were. The family invented the aluminum beer can, but loathed advertising almost as much as it hated unions. The Coorses hated anyone telling them how to run their business, and they became early adopters of a Hollywood actor by the name of Reagan. They wound up being boycotted by labour, women, gays, blacks, Hispanics, and environmentalists, and pretended they didn't care. Many of them were born-again Christians, although only one of them seems to have had any problem with the dichotomy of making beer and Christian fundamentalism. Adolph's was not the last family suicide, and his grandson was brutally murdered in a botched kidnapping. Another scion was blackballed from the family for marrying without his father's permission. It's a saga. The beer might be watered down, but the story is full-blooded. The Coors family carries on its old ways. In 2004 Pete Coors, great-grandson of old Adolph, ran as a Republican (if there were a party to the right of the Republicans, he would have run for them) in the Colorado senatorial race, supporting the Bush campaign to enshrine anti-gay-marriage legislation in the constitution. The boycotts came back, and Coors lost anyway.

Nowadays, Coors is just another big beer company, the family more on the sidelines. It's a more efficient company now, with a big advertising budget, and there are still a lot of Americans who refuse to touch it. And not just because they don't think it's good.

And what about Molson, that proudly Canadian brewer, maker of a beer actually called Canadian? (I can't think of a beer called American or English or Irish or pretty much anything of that sort. Mind you, we have Canada Day, which is also unusual. Other national days have slightly more imaginative names.) Once Molson's great rival Labatt wound up in the hands of the massive Belgian company InBev, Molson wrapped itself in the Maple Leaf. To demonstrate its patriotic fervour, Molson in 2000 launched a hugely successful television commercial in which a plaid-shirted regular guy pointed out the differences between himself and Americans, ending with the cry, "My name is Joe and I AM CANADIAN!" Which, coincidentally, was the name of the brand he was flogging. Within months of the ad's appearance, the actor who played Joe had moved to Hollywood to further his career and Molson sold the fabled Montreal Canadiens to a businessman from Colorado. In 2004 Molson announced a merger with (you guessed it) Coors, also from Colorado. My name is Joe and I have dual citizenship.

Even Guinness is not above corporate beastliness. The company that built up such goodwill with its long-standing Guinness Is Good for You campaign (eventually quashed by the anti-beer lobby) and the imaginative use of toucans in its marketing turns out to be no better than the rest. In 2001 it called in the lawyers on Hart Robinson, a small Ontario brewery, and issued a cease-and-desist order. The brewery's crime lay in naming one of its beers Dragon's Breath, in direct contravention of the Because We Say So Act. Why is it wrong to name a beer Dragon's Breath? Because Guinness says so. Because Guinness brews something called Dragon Stout in Jamaica. Anyone who confuses Canada with Jamaica needs the help of more than lawyers. I've had Dragon's Breath and Dragon Stout, and I think I could tell the difference in a blindfold test.

Dragon's Breath had been available in Ontario since at least 1992, without—as far as anyone can tell—damaging the domestic Jamaican market. Yet, unable to afford a suitful of legal help to combat the Irish-Jamaican juggernaut, Hart Robinson was forced to take a pleasing, hoppy pale ale off the market. My latest *Good Beer Guide* lists no fewer than twelve British beers with the word "dragon" in their name, from Dragon Fire to Dragonslayer. There's

even a Welsh brewery that makes a strong (but not hoppy) bitter called Dragon's Breath, which rings a bell. I trust the suits of
Guinness are in full cry there as well, unless they've decided that
northern Wales is even less like Jamaica than Canada.

Accustomed to near-monopoly in its native Ireland, Guinness
seems to think it a natural state. It's teetering on the edge of not
being good for us.

# I'm Just a Barmaid Connoisseur: Bar Staff

I once worked in a pub with a woman named Mary. Mary was a terrific barmaid—bright, pretty, friendly, and omnicompetent. This was in England, before decimalization, and we had a handsome but very basic cash register, so you had to be quick with figures: what's 1/10 plus 2/4 plus 11d plus 2/6? Mary's customers loved her, so we were all surprised when the manager fired her. Apparently, Mary was too friendly and down-market. The manager—a very stupid man—wanted to make the place a little tonier, less chummy, and he replaced Mary with a hapless young woman from Leicester who couldn't add.

I think about Mary sometimes when I see bar staff at work. Like taxi drivers, booksellers, and major league shortstops, some are better than others. If you ever take cabs, you know that sometimes you can tell as soon as you get in that you're going to have to work hard for this ride home: "You need to turn left here . . . no, left . . . no, here! . . . oh, for God's sake, if you'd put down the cellphone for a

. . . please turn left . . . please . . ." Other times you get in and relax and enjoy the ride.

It's the same with bar staff. A good bartender or server can add immeasurably to your drinking experience, and should be remembered in your tipping thoughts. Different bars, of course, call for different kinds of people. There's a man named Harold who for countless decades graced the rooftop bar at what used to be the Park Plaza Hotel in Toronto. I say "graced" very deliberately, because Harold had the style and class you want in a pricey hotel bar, along with an unhurried friendliness. It's easy for people in Harold's shoes to become supercilious and pompous, two words you would never use of Harold, a local legend who has been immortalized in novels.

Harold's elegance might have been misplaced at, say, the rather more earthy Grossman's Tavern, which is why one values the brash, wise-cracking Dawn. One afternoon, as a group of us were leaving Grossman's, Dawn called out to us, "Sure, go somewhere else and get ripped off for your beer. You'll be back!" If she did that at an upscale hotel bar, her career would be a short one, but she's universally admired at Grossman's. I've written elsewhere in this book about John, the philosopher-waiter at the old Embassy Tavern. John ruled not through fear but through some strong, quiet moral force. (I had a cat like that once.) There was a waiter called Tommy at the Morrissey Tavern who had a similar quality. I saw Tommy use physical force a couple of times, but it was definitely his approach of last resort.

Today's drinking scene seems to call for less physical strength, or perhaps I'm just drinking in classier places. It's also possible that I don't stay up as late as I used to, so I've left before the violence kicks in. I once saw a waiter at the late, not terribly lamented, Young Station deal with a difficult customer by taking about a seventy-foot run and blindsiding the guy with a blow that levelled him, with not much chance for a replay any time soon. You hang out in bars, you see just about everything.

The Duke of York used to have a server called Olga, a slender Irish woman from County Antrim who made her customers feel the world was a better place. Well, that and the beer. I never saw Olga punch anybody, and I'm not sure if I'm glad about that or not. She eventually went back to Ireland and took a suitcase full of hearts with her. More recently, the Duke was home (he's been seen lately at the House on Parliament) to a fellow from Timmins, Ontario, who does a bit of wrestling on the side. Dale doesn't look particularly menacing—in fact, he seems a damn nice guy, and I suspect he probably is beneath that damn nice exterior—but he's clearly capable of dropping a troublesome drunk. I'm a peace-loving guy, I am, but part of me wouldn't mind seeing Dale twist a troublemaker into a knot. I can even think of one or two candidates.

Sometimes you get to know people outside their working hours. I once played golf with a guy called Ed who slung beer at the old Red Lion (as opposed to the new Red Lion). Ed was an interesting man, of at least part-Aboriginal roots, from the far north somewhere, who got up early and played golf five days a week, then downed numerous beers before going into work, where he hauled pitchers of the stuff to the softball teams that gathered at the Lion. In the off-season he travelled to places like India or South America. Interesting guy.

The guys who run the Graduate Students' Union Pub on the University of Toronto campus are an odd duo. Harry is gay and acerbic, with a taste for art and tattoos. When he's behind the bar, you're likely to be bombarded with high-volume music of what might be the techno variety, as if I'd know. Ed, on the other hand, is straight and married, taciturn and middle of the road, with a taste for easy listening music. Like his namesake from the old Red Lion, Ed would rather be golfing than serving you a beer, though he's usually pretty gracious about it once he gets to know you. Ed listens patiently when Harry comes up with a new design concept. Between them, they make the place work.

Bar staff, of course, do more than smile and serve you beer. One day I ventured into Paupers Pub on my way home, as I occasionally do. There's a spot at one end of the bar I particularly like, with its own little lamp so guys like me can read even after they turn the lights down to make it atmospheric. Walking in, I saw the seat was free. It was my lucky day. As I took off my coat, Patrick—the server whose Subway Game is recounted in these pages—called me down to the other end of the bar. There was something he needed to talk to me about. Reluctantly, I abandoned my favourite spot and went over to where Patrick waited. "It's all right," he said quietly, "there's nothing I need to talk about. I just don't think you want to get too close to the guy you were about to sit beside." Patrick was right.

Next to the ideal seat with the little lamp sat the most tiresome human on the planet, a loudmouth and a bore, and I was saved from a fate almost indistinguishable from death.

Many of us male persons are criticized for apparently falling in love with any woman who brings us beer, though it's not necessarily justified. I can think of at least two or three women who have brought me beer without invoking Cupid's arrow, but why dwell on the negatives? There used to be a server—we called them waitresses in those days without a second thought—at the old Sticky Wicket who had it all: talent, looks, people skills, you name it. The Sticky Wicket was a hard bar to leave when she was in charge. Back in the golden age when people occasionally had long lunches and the world was a better place altogether, a small group of us gathered for a pint and a bite to eat. Lunch concluded, we settled up and prepared to leave, whereupon one of us suggested one more pint. We had that and settled up again, and yet another pint was proposed, motion carried. One of our number dredged through his pockets and located exactly the price of a pint, tax included. He sadly reported to our near-divine waitress that he lacked the funds for a tip. She looked at him kindly and said, "That's all right. You always tip too much anyway." I vaguely recall that we all proposed to her on the spot.

I used to fall in love with Olga every Friday night at the Duke of York. A place called Kilgour's on Bloor Street had a succession of splendid female beerslingers, though in more recent times they seem to have gone very masculine. Paupers Pub had a terrific, funny server named Claire who was on the list to be a contestant on *Jeopardy!* before she sadly succumbed to cancer. Down at the Graduate Students' Union Pub, Ed's wife, Michelle, a lively anthropologist, used to tend the bar on Fridays, and beer sales soared. She certainly sold a fair bit of it to me.

The late David Parry used to sing a song by English songwriter Keith Marsden called "Greasy Mack." The narrator of this fine song is aware of his reputation. He's always seen in pubs, so people think him a sot. He is accused of every perversion going, but without cause. He's no good at the standard male hobbies of philately, collecting vintage wines, or growing potted plants. No, he's "just a barmaid connoisseur." It's not such a bad thing to be.

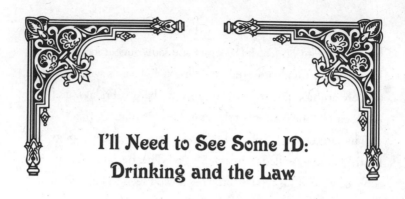

# I'll Need to See Some ID:
# Drinking and the Law

Some chapters ago we discussed the origins of beer. You may recall early man (or early woman) . . . damn, let's just say early person. Early person tasted a bit of soggy barley that had come into contact with a bit of windborne yeast and fermented. Early person got a buzz, and saw that it was good. You can bet that within a month some other early person had introduced legislation governing the permissible strength of fermented soggy barley, the hours of the day during which fermented barley could be ingested, the minimum age of fermented barley consumers, the required signage in premises that provided fermented barley, and in what circumstances fermented barley users could legally operate fire.

Well, it's human nature, isn't it? If you don't pass a law, somebody somewhere is going to get away with something, and then how will you feel? And there's something about alcohol that brings out the legislator in people. Not the people who are enjoying it, of course, but the other people.

Growing up with Ontario's frequently odd drinking laws, I

often wondered where these curious bits of legislation could possibly have come from. I mean, it was against the law to drink standing up. Who thought of that? When they were sitting around inventing laws, did someone get up and say, "Look, why don't we make it illegal to drink standing up? That'll fox them." And did the others say, "Excellent idea, George. They'll be scratching their heads over this one." Had there been a problem with standing drinkers? Had someone felt driven to cry out, "Why won't they just sit down?"

And it wasn't even drinking. You couldn't stand up with a drink in your hand, whether you drank from it or not. I suppose we should have been grateful that they hadn't thought to regulate which hand we drank with. "I'm sorry, pal, but you've been drinking left-handed again. I'm gonna have to ask you to leave."

The first clue I got to the origins of drinking in Ontario came when I went to Scotland for the first time. It was like coming home. I'm sure there are very nice pubs in Scotland (and I have since found a number of them), but the first two or three I encountered reminded me of Ontario taprooms. They had the look of rooms that couldn't be wrecked, because there was nothing breakable in them. And they could be hosed down after an evening's drinking. You could fight, bleed, throw up, wet yourself, and there'd be no evidence of it the next morning. Well, not in the pub.

There can't be many Ontario towns whose telephone books don't have pages of names starting with the letters "Mac" or "Mc." The English might have owned much of Canada, but it was the Scots who lived here and did the work. Canada was no colder than Scotland, after all. And Scotland—like the Ontario I started drinking in—was made up of exactly two groups of people: people who drank too much, and people who drank too little. And the people who drank too little got to write the laws that governed the people who drank too much. You could characterize these people as joyless, except that some of their laws demonstrate a wry sense of humour.

I remember at one time in Ontario you were permitted to drink outdoors on your property only as long as no one could see you doing so. Many areas—and I know the Toronto suburb of Etobicoke was one—had legislation limiting the height of fences and hedges. So you could drink outdoors in your backyard in Etobicoke only if you had short neighbours who lived in bungalows.

And it isn't just Ontario, of course. There is hardly anywhere on the planet that doesn't have some wonky drinking laws. Until recently, practically every pub in the UK had to close between 3 p.m. and 5:30 p.m., and hardly anyone could remember why. In Pennsylvania you can't buy a six-pack of beer. Beer can be sold only in cases of twenty-four, and don't bother asking them to explain it. The state of Georgia passed a law, at the end of Prohibition, that defined beer as having a maximum strength of 6 percent alcohol by volume. (South Carolina was 5 percent.) Early in 2001 a group of adventurous beer drinkers sought to have this law overturned so that they could enjoy the occasional strong beer, but the state's wise, all-knowing legislators—presumably fearful that outbursts of fun might break out—left the comfort of their interns and turned out to defeat this radical measure.

The granddaddy of heavy-handed alcohol legislation—and I'm ignoring the Muslim world here—was Prohibition. Canadians didn't suffer nearly as badly as Americans from this scourge of right-eousness. Between 1920 and 1933, no American touched as much as a drop of alcohol. Ha ha—just joking! It has been estimated that by 1922 there were more speakeasies in America than there had been legal bars in 1920. It was Prohibition that succeeded in organizing crime in the USA. Before 1920 crime had been chaotic, but the Volstead Act offered an incentive to criminals who were organized. Millions of dollars were made by people we would char-acterize today as gangsters, although they might have seen them-selves as businessmen providing a popular service. The authorities spent millions of other dollars in a futile attempt to uphold the law. The murder rate soared, and no doubt a few people succumbed to unregulated rotgut liquor. And nobody stopped drinking.

The proliferation of lawyers in the postwar era has made the drinking world a minefield. Early in 2001 an Ontario woman was awarded a large sum of money after she sued her employer for let-ting her drink and drive following a company Christmas party. Her boss had offered to call her husband to take her home, had offered a taxi ride. He had not, however, hog-tied the woman, delivered a fire-and-brimstone sermon, and personally made sure she got home safely, so he was on the hook when the woman—having gone off to a pub for yet more drinks—crashed her car some time later. We are not sure what percentage of the damages was claimed by her lawyer.

Not that I want to sound critical of lawyers. A lawyer can be a wonderful thing. Just ask Mo Vaughn. Early in 1998, Mo Vaughn— a robust first baseperson for the Boston Red Sox—left a Rhode Island strip club and, on his way home, somehow drove into a car parked off the highway and rolled his pickup truck. Investigating officers testified that Vaughn failed eight sobriety tests at the scene. On his third attempt to recite the alphabet, he managed only A-B-D-C-H-L-M, which suggests a willingness to pitch in but not much more.

All this would seem to indicate a verdict of guilty, but you'd be underestimating the skills of Vaughn's lawyer, one Kevin Reddington. This latter-day Cicero posited that his client might not have been drunk, all evidence to the contrary. His alphabet problems might have been caused by his having been (a) sleepy, (b) dazed by his recent accident (which he had caused, don't forget), or (c) unstable because he had gained weight in the off-season.

The judge—who I'm betting was a Red Sox fan—ruled in favour of the defendant, and Vaughn was acquitted. My point here is that a lawyer who can turn weight gain into a legal defence is worth remembering next time you're facing charges in Massachusetts. The name is Reddington, Kevin Reddington.

The issue of drinking and driving is a sensitive one. One of the reasons I live in the heart of a city is that I'm always a cab ride from home. I don't want to drink and drive. I'd rather have a few pints and then go through the merry fun of explaining where I live to a cab driver who's talking on his cellphone. It's part of a good night out.

There are, as we know, people who do drink and drive. I did it on occasion when I was young and even more stupid than I am now, so I'm not going to take a pious tone about it. I have before me a brochure I picked up in an English pub, called "Dying for a Drink?" That's the name of the brochure, by the way. The pub was called the Royal Oak. Published by the Department of the Environment, Transport and the Regions and dated July 2000, this brochure tells me a lot. Among other things, it tells me that it was printed on paper that is 75 percent post-consumer waste, 5 percent pre-consumer, and 20 percent TCF pulp. I'm not sure what any of that stuff is, but I'm certainly not putting the brochure in my mouth.

The purpose of "Dying for a Drink?" is to make us think twice about drinking and driving in Britain, and it's full of common sense and interesting information, including a reference to how much alcohol can remain in your bloodstream the morning after a night on the ale. You could get busted driving to work. Lucky thing I walk.

One of the interesting facts is this: "Nearly one in seven of all deaths on the road involve drivers who are over the legal limit." Well, for starters, there's that weasel word: "involve." If the Department of the Environment, Transport and the Regions means "are caused by" why doesn't it say so? Apparently, in the UK, if a sober driver with a drunk passenger is "involved" in an accident it is automatically treated as a drink-related incident. You can't be too careful with statistics.

But even if one British road fatality in seven is actually caused by drunk drivers—which is a bad thing, no question—we're left with the daunting fact that 86 percent of British road fatalities are caused by sober people. What's being done about them?

I have another brochure on my desk. Actually, I've got a lot of stuff on my desk, including possibly a cat or two, but it's the brochure that's at the top of the pile. It comes from the Ontario government and it's called "Break the Law Pay the Price." Personally, I'd have put a comma in there somewhere, but the Ontario government laid off the punctuation guy in a cost-cutting drive. (I gather he lasted longer than the water inspection guy.)

According to "BTLPTP," "Drinking drivers are responsible for one-quarter of all people killed on Ontario roads." In other words, only 75 percent of Ontario traffic fatalities are the work of sober people. Either we have more drunks in Ontario, or our sober people are better drivers than Britain's.

Now, despite the damning evidence in these brochures that sober people are causing carnage on our roads, the people who know what's good for us are busy trying to lower the legal blood alcohol limit. Early in 2001 the Quebec government announced that it was lowering the limit from eighty milligrams to fifty, throwing in a complete drinking ban for professional drivers—cabbies, bus drivers, and the like. This last measure was a reaction to—well, nothing at all. Were drunk ambulance drivers creating havoc on the roads of Quebec? No. But it gave the government of Quebec the appearance of having taken a strong stand on something. Predictably, the Ontario government immediately made noises about following suit.

The lowering of the blood alcohol limit is a canard, or—as we say in English-speaking Canada—a duck. Is there any evidence that drivers with sixty or seventy milligrams of alcohol in their bloodstream are doing untold damage on our roads? Nope. The police don't seem to think so, and they're out there more than I am. "Break the Law Pay the Price" notes, "Most drinking drivers killed in crashes had blood alcohol levels almost double the legal limit."

Exactly. Problem drunk drivers have more than fifty milligrams before they set out in the evening. They have fifty milligrams with their breakfast. They're guys like Richard Sawyer McLeod of Alberta, who back in 2001 rang up his seventeenth drunk driving conviction to go along with eighteen raps of driving while disqualified. Mr. McLeod has not had a valid driver's licence since 1967, but he keeps on driving anyway, except when he's in jail. Guys like Richard Sawyer McLeod drive home from court. Lowering the limit thirty points will not make a difference to McLeod and his ilk. All it will do is get law-abiding people into trouble. Tougher enforcement in England has led to countless idyllic country pubs going under because their respectable customers are afraid to go out at night for fear of being a few milligrams over the line. These are members of the non-criminal classes who just don't want to be arrested, who don't want to pay more for their insurance.

The anti-booze crusaders are indifferent to their plight. When they get the limit lowered to fifty milligrams, they will begin their campaign for twenty milligrams, then no milligrams at all. The issue is not driving, it is drinking, and their goal is zero tolerance. I don't know—I was brought up to believe that tolerance is a good thing. These people succeed because they have so much time to attend meetings. While the rest of us are sitting in pubs, they're holding meetings.

And where does it end? In 1999 a California man—and why is it so often California?—was pulled over by the police for driving too slowly. He failed a sobriety test and was charged with Driving Under the Influence, although a subsequent urine test showed that he had no alcohol or drugs in his system. Taufui Piutau—for that is the man's mellifluous name—acknowledged that he had been drinking kava tea, and possibly eight to ten cups of it, with his church friends. Although California law is vague on how many milligrams of kava kava you're allowed in your bloodstream, the DA's office carried on with the prosecution of Mr. Piutau, which cost the father of four his job with Federal Express.

Nearly fifteen months later, the case ground to a halt with a mistrial, a hung jury unable to reach unanimity, though ten of the twelve jurors favoured acquittal. A grumpy District Attorney grudgingly acknowledged that the state would probably not pursue the matter further. Mr. Piutau's lawyer, one Scott B. Ennis—a name to remember if you get into trouble in San Mateo—argued in court that what the officers saw as impairment was probably a combination of gout and cultural misunderstanding, though it was not immediately clear exactly whose gout was at issue. At last word, Ennis was carrying on with a $20 million wrongful dismissal suit against Fed Ex.

Kava kava is known for its relaxing qualities, which is part of the problem. The authorities can't abide the relaxants. It's fine for caffeine-crazed javaheads to drive around like maniacs, but relax for a moment and you're headed for the big house. If driving under the influence of herbal tea becomes illegal in California, they won't be able to build new prisons fast enough to hold the perpetrators. Marin County will become a ghost town.

It's that pleasure thing again. What the Republicans really hated about Bill Clinton—apart from his being a Democrat in public office—was not that he received sexual favours from a consenting adult in the Oval Office but that he visibly had fun. A lawyer friend of mine likes to point out that there is no reference to fun in any Act of Parliament, and I suspect the American constitution is just as bad. It permits the pursuit of happiness, as I recall, but it stops short of fun.

When the Republicans succeeded—by hook or by crook, but mostly by crook—in retaking the White House in 2000, we were treated to the spectacle of John Ashcroft becoming Attorney General. Ashcroft was available for the job because the voters of Missouri had tossed him out of office, voting for a dead guy instead and making Ashcroft the first incumbent U.S. senator to lose to a dead person. To be fair to the Missouri electorate, it wasn't easy to tell the difference.

John Ashcroft doesn't hold with dancing. It's not that he doesn't like dancing, or isn't good at dancing, like George W. Bush. He thinks dancing is a sin. He won't dance, don't ask him. Ashcroft is straight out of the world's oldest religious joke: Why do Baptists disapprove of having sex standing up? Because it might lead to dancing.

An Attorney General who thinks dancing is wrong is unlikely to look kindly on America's drinking classes, even though his president is from Texas, the state where drinking while driving is practically an institution. Not that the president does that. Not any more. Indeed, the born-again president quickly barred the White House kitchen from even cooking with alcohol.

But I digress. Like you, I'd welcome safer roads and highways, but the new Puritans will do little to achieve that end. The figures show that the overwhelming majority of accidents are caused by bad drivers, a handful of whom have been drinking as well. Let's get bad drivers off the road, but let's keep the "sinner repent" morality out of it.

# Rex Gladstone,
## or the Meaning of Pub Names

I refer elsewhere in these pages to a Toronto pub called the Rose and Crown. There are many English pubs that bear this name, which commemorates the victory of Henry VII over Richard III in 1485. The rose is that of Lancaster, and the crown is the crown of England, won by Henry. You won't find a lot of Rose and Crowns— or should that be Roses and Crown?—in Yorkshire, which was the losing side.

Pubs called the Royal Oak take their name from the tree in which the future Charles II hid after getting whupped by Oliver Cromwell in 1651. The King's Head can refer to any masculine monarch, but it is most appropriate in the case of the head of Charles I, which became involuntarily separated from the rest of the king one January morning in 1649. Publicans have tradition-ally been more inclined to support the fun-loving Stuarts over the gloomier Roundheads, and there are still pubs called the Blackboys, which is not, in fact, the racial slur it appears but an affectionate reference to Charles I (you had to be there). There are many pubs that pay tribute to royalty with names like the Queen's Arms, the Crown, and the Feathers (a reference to the coat of arms of the Prince of Wales). Older pubs recall the Crusades: the Turk's Head, the Saracen's Head, and the Trip to Jerusalem. And of course there are countless tributes to any number of dukes, earls, and counts. You can learn a lot of English history by hanging out in pubs.

Wouldn't it be nice if we honoured Canadian history in our pub names? If nothing else, it might lend an air of gravitas to our filthy habits if we could say, as we lurch through the front door, "Sorry I'm late—I stopped in for a quick one at the Rowell-Sirois Commission." Or if we could agree to meet later at the Lord Durham's Report. Or at the Avro Arrow Cancellation, or the Discovery of Insulin, or the Anne Murray's First Grammy, or Ye Olde Notwithstanding Clause. I'd even settle for Stephen Harper's Head. And who wouldn't like to call home and report, "I may be a while. I'm in Adrienne Clarkson's Arms"?

There's something powerful about names. You may be familiar with the comic gambit of finding your soap opera name. It's simple: you take your middle name and combine it with the name of the street you grew up on. I know someone whose soap opera name is Kimball Bessborough, which is a really fabulous name. It's hard to do better than that. It's especially difficult for me, as I don't have a middle name. Call me Blank Welbeck. Apparently, there's another version that creates your name as a stripper. It involves the name of your first household pet, and I don't remember the rest of it. It helps if you grew up with a cat called Fluffy. Frisky would be even better.

Any writer of fiction will tell you that finding names for characters is one of the toughest parts of writing. Get the name right, they say, and the character will follow. Call me Ishmael: brilliant. Call me Nigel: not so good. Leopold Bloom, Holden Caulfield, Miss Havisham, Gussie Fink-Nottle, Sir Toby Belch, Heathcliff—the characters are half-written as soon as you read their names.

It struck me one day, many years ago, that one could write a novel—or at least a fairly serious novella—using altogether plausible characters whose names could be drawn from the names of Toronto drinking spots. This had to be many years ago, of course, before we traded in our venerable old watering holes for places with winsome names like the Toad in the Hole or the Friar and Firkin. Even P.G. Wodehouse, who had a gift for hyphenated names, would have drawn the line at someone called Toad-in-the-Hole. "I say, Friar-and-Firkin" just doesn't work.

No, it has to be the old names. A lot of them are gone now: the Morrissey, the Sheldon, the Beverley. Others remain: the Rex, the Selby, the Gladstone. Now, I still haven't actually written that novel, but I've got the characters, so I'm well on the way. I see a man called Rex Gladstone, and maybe you can see him too. He's a good-looking fellow with a powerful jaw, and a biggish chap too. In later years people will see Rex as a bit on the heavy side, but for the moment he cuts quite an impressive figure. He has a pretty serious job, I imagine—something in banking, perhaps—but he's not averse to a bit of fun. He's a loyal friend and an imposing adversary. He looks good in a well-tailored suit, but he can raise a young woman's heartbeat in his tennis whites too.

Rex is engaged to—or has possibly just been romantically linked with—the lovely Selby Linsmore. Of that Fine Old Ontario Family,

the Linsmores. Selby is always immaculately turned out, and needless to say she knows absolutely everyone who needs to be known.
She might be ever so slightly on the cool side, however, and even
the sight of a glistening Rex Gladstone attacking the net at the
tennis club in the mixed doubles semifinal fails to bring a flush to
her exquisite features.

Rex understands that marriage to Selby will be the making of
him, but he's accustomed to a bit more ardour from women. Like
pretty young Beverley Paddock, for instance. Beverley has no family at all to speak of, and in fact she speaks of them as little as possible. She doesn't come from money, like Selby, but there's a certain
spunk to the girl, and she knows how to please a fellow. She's just
not the sort of girl you'd marry. Let alone take to the tennis club.

Enter Clinton Morrissey. Of mixed blood, Clinton came to
Toronto from his native Caribbean, touring as a fast bowler with
a better than average cricket side. He has always preferred tennis,
however, and has just become the assistant teaching pro at the
tennis club to which both Rex and Selby belong. Not surprisingly,
Clinton is a handsome man, and even the ice-cool Selby melts a
little when he makes a curiously effective adjustment to her grip.

Rex—who is, quite honestly, no smarter than he strictly speaking needs to be—sees the change in Selby. He confides his concerns
to his friend Cameron Brunswick. I don't quite have a fully-formed
Cameron Brunswick in my mind just yet, but I certainly like his
name. Cameron suggests that Rex surprise Selby in some way, take
her somewhere she'd never normally go. Like where? asks Rex. How
about the circus, proposes Cameron, who is slowly turning into a
character I like.

The circus—luckily for the plot—just happens to be in town, and Rex books the two best seats in the house, hoping that the danger of aerial daredevils and the sweat of horses will rouse Selby in a way he's never managed. They sit through several acts, including a comic piece involving a troupe of First Nations performers, in which a man called Black Bull quarrels with another man called Red Lion over the affections of a woman they both fancy—pretty little Wheat Sheaf.

And then Rex and Selby are snapped to attention by the loud crack of a whip. A full-grown Siberian tiger snarls and crouches, as if about to attack a woman in an abbreviated leather costume. She cracks the whip again, high in the air above Rex and Selby's heads. Rex is transfixed. The woman is beautiful—dark and lean. Her strong, olive-hued arm ripples as she handles the whip. The tiger, feeling her power, slowly yields to her, finally rolling over and allowing her to rub his furry belly. That done, the woman—now standing feet away from Rex and Selby—acknowledges the wild applause of the audience, bowing deeply, her full breasts threatening to tumble free from her skimpy leather top. (Whew—I'm enjoying this.) The circus announcer cries out over the popular roar, "Ladies and gentlemen—direct from Venezuela, the incomparable Isabella El Mocambo!"

Rex, his lip trembling, cannot take his eyes from this wild creature, so he is unaware that next to him Selby is similarly bewitched. "Brava!" he calls out to the circus performer. Isabella smiles and turns her huge dark eyes to—no, not Rex, but Selby! Then, with one last triumphant crack of the whip, she turns on her stiletto heel and exits, the crowd's cheers still ringing in the air.

A crew of clowns rushes in, but Selby suddenly gets up. "I need some air," she says breathlessly, and she walks out. Rex, uncertain if his legs would even carry his weight, such is his state of excitement, remains in his seat. Should he follow Selby, even if he could? If Cameron Brunswick were there, he'd have advice for Rex, but Cameron—unknown to Rex, whose experience of the world is limited—is, as we speak, in a Church Street leather bar, trussed like a Christmas turkey, while . . . well, I don't know while what. Let's face it, I've never been in a leather bar in my life.

Okay, so I haven't figured out the rest of the story yet, but I really think I'm on to something here. Cameron Brunswick, for starters, certainly came as a surprise to me. I suspect before the story ends someone will need the services of patrician attorney Waverley Drake. The plot is almost certainly going to hinge around something that is said or done by a visiting aristocrat: Sheldon, Duke of Connaught. I think this story has legs. They're not as good as Isabella El Mocambo's legs, but they're legs nonetheless.

# Part II

# Drinking in Particular

# Two Practically Perfect Pubs

**H**aving determined that pub perfection is unattainable, let's cast our little red eyes on a couple of pubs that come pretty darn close. These are both English pubs in slightly out-of-the-way places. They are not tourist meccas, only one of them has a website, and they are generally unknown to people who live more than ten miles away. There are lots of other pubs like them, I'm sure, but these are two that I know.

Lewes is an old town in East Sussex, a few miles northeast of Brighton. It has a ruined castle, a house that once belonged to Anne of Cleves (the locals soft-pedal the regrettable fact that there is no evidence she ever set foot in it), an old priory, several antiquarian bookshops, and an excellent brewery. In the nineteenth century it had seven breweries, but there's no point regretting what we've missed. It has a vibrant high street (despite some major flooding a few years ago), which is not so common in England these days, and a few good pubs. The best of these pubs is the Lewes Arms, an early nineteenth-century inn that has attached itself to the old castle wall like a benign barnacle.

The Lewes Arms has several of my Perfect Pub criteria—no piped-in music, no television, good beer, genial staff, a dog-friendly environment—but it also has those intangible factors that distinguish a great pub from a good one. It isn't a beautiful pub inside, but the moment you step inside you feel you've come to something not unlike home. There is a tiny front room and a slightly larger room on the far side of the bar, plus a third room off the corridor you enter from the front door, with access to the bar via a hatch. There's another room upstairs that is used by the folk music club, among others. The pub also hosts the annual World Pea Throwing Championships, as well as something called "dwyle flunking." If you have to ask what dwyle flunking is, it's probably not for you, though the Friends of the Lewes Arms observe, "The rules of the game are impenetrable and the result is always contested." So there you are.

The pub-minded know a good pub when they see it, and the Lewes Arms is seldom empty. You know you're in the best pub in town when all the interesting people are there, and they're certainly at the Lewes Arms.

Now, I said that it's seldom empty, but that was not the case for 133 days in 2006–2007. The people of Lewes like their Harvey's ale, made in the centre of town in a fine old brewery, and they don't take well to having it plucked from them. In October 2006 the Greene King brewery, which owns the Lewes Arms, decreed that henceforth Harvey's Sussex Best Bitter would no longer be sold in the pub. Only Greene King beers would be available. After all, as a man in a suit pointed out, Harvey's was available in every other pub in Lewes, so why should anyone complain. I don't know if this besuited man flunked his dwyle, but he certainly flunked Public Relations 101.

The Friends of the Lewes Arms formed to protest this decision and announced a boycott of their favourite pub. This was not something you'd do lightly. Think of your favourite pub. Now boycott it for 133 days. This is what the people of Lewes did, until finally the handsomely clad chaps of Greene King came to their senses and reinstated Harvey's delicious ale. Power to the people.

The best pubs have a customer base of all ages. At the Lewes Arms the young mingle with the old, but the young are outnumbered by the old—or at least the middle-aged—so they don't get it all their own way. Any pub that is dominated by the young will almost certainly drive away the older drinker. Some towns are full of young people's pubs. Anne and I spent Christmas in Saffron Walden in Essex some years ago, and all the pubs appeared to be young people's pubs—all loud music and hostile looks when a wrinkly face peered in at the door. We finally found the pub the older people went to, but it was so crowded we couldn't get in.

The landlady of the Lewes Arms, when I was last there, was one Claire Murray, as far as I can tell an altogether sweet-natured woman who wanted the best for her pub and her customers. One night we watched a man who had—apparently uncharacteristically—taken aboard more than the daily maximum recommended by the health authorities. He did a round of maudlin farewells through the place and finally lurched out into the night. Claire watched him go, then put on her coat and followed him to see he came to no harm on his way home. (It turned out that he spotted her when he was most of the way home, then tried to insist on walking her back to the pub.) When I'm in Lewes, you'll find me at the Lewes Arms. It is a true community centre, and I love it.

The town of Dursley in Gloucestershire is celebrated for not much, quite honestly. It is one of the less attractive spots in the Cotswolds, although its setting is wonderful. Dursley is on the route of the Cotswold Way, so hikers pass through town, walking right past—if they're completely daft—a pub called the Old Spot. (Dursley is also the source of the name J.K. Rowling gave to a pack of unsympathetic characters in her Harry Potter books, and the town has mixed feelings about its newfound celebrity. She just liked the name, that's all.)

I have family in the greater Dursley area, so I've spent a bit of time there over the years. My favourite pub for the longest time was the New Inn at Waterley Bottom, just up and over the hill from Dursley. When I first knew the New Inn, it was run by a couple named Ruby and Ric Sainty, and it was heaven on earth. Ric—if the local gossip was to be believed—ran off with a barmaid sometime in the eighties and took over a pub in Bristol, but he came back in 1993 and took over a dowdy Dursley pub called the Fox and Hounds, changing its name to the Old Spot. (Old Spot is a local beer named for a breed of pig raised in the area, so don't complain that you don't learn anything from me.)

Ric now has a different wife—neither the earlier wife nor the barmaid—and together they have transformed the Old Spot into a pub that in 2008 was named the Campaign for Real Ale National Pub of the Year, beating out pubs from across England, Wales, and

Scotland. One of CAMRA's Pub of the Year criteria is "clientele mix," which I can vouch for: everybody's there.

The Old Spot's an attractive pub with an ongoing pig motif, though it's not your classic picture-postcard English pub. It's quiet, even when the local folk music people take over one end and fill it with the unamplified sound of guitars, a fiddle, a dobro, a mandolin, a concertina, a button accordion, a banjo, a double bass, a bodhran, and human voices.

Ric and Ellie have retired, leaving the place in the hands of a genial fellow named Steve Herbert, his wife, Belinda, and their West Highland terrier. Ric has a house up the hill and will doubtless still be seen at the Old Spot on a regular basis, if only to ensure that his glorious vision is not mucked about. If I lived in Dursley, I'd be at the Old Spot every day. It offers excellent beer (including Old Ric, brewed by the local Uley Brewery) and just about everything you want in a pub. On my last visit, the local vicar, the Reverend Janet, was behind the bar, pouring drinks and raising funds for the church roof. And the Old Spot's website has a feature I've never seen before, whereby the regulars can advertise their skills for free. So if you're looking for a plumber, a landscape gardener, or a music teacher, you can find one. And if you don't like the work, you know where to find the person who did it.

Again, it's the intangibles, it's the regulars, it's the dogs . . . it's the practically perfect pub.

# Drinking Globally:
# The Wide World o' Booze

Travel, as we know, can be a broadening experience. I think we all do things on holiday that we don't much do at home. We go to museums, we visit historic sights, and we go on tours. But there's no point being silly about it. For the drinking person, travel offers a rare opportunity to see how people drink in other cultures. Some people actually get grants to do this, and they call it anthropology. You and I do this on our own dime. Mind you, we don't have to write an impenetrable report about it afterwards, so all in all it's worth it. My wife calls it "alcotourism."

I've already written about drinking in England, but they drink in other countries as well. I find the most difficult part of drinking in France is getting anyone to understand me when I try to order a Pelforth. There is a French beer, brewed in Lille, called Pelforth, which is obviously a very un-French name. How to pronounce it? Possibly my favourite sentence by P.G. Wodehouse is the opening line of a novel called *The Luck of the Bodkins:* "Into the face of the young man who sat on the terrace of the Hotel Magnifique at

Cannes there had crept a look of furtive shame, the shifty, hangdog look which announces that an Englishman is about to talk French."

Well, that's how I feel when I try to order a Pelforth. It's not even that Pelforth is the best beer in the world or anything, but I kind of like it. It has more character than most French beers, but how do you say it? Do you Frenchify it and leave off the "th" at the end? Pelforrrr? Do you pronounce the "th" as a Gallic clipped "t"? Pelfort? Or do you recognize that it's one of those odd French things and say it in a vaguely English way, as it's spelled?

Dear reader, I have no idea. I've tried all three approaches on various occasions and have been rebuffed each time. I think we've all suspected from time to time that the French are having us on, that they understand exactly what we're trying to say but they're damned if they're going to give us the satisfaction of thinking that we speak intelligible French. My friend John Jackson and I once went into a patisserie in Paris and ordered, or tried to order, several delicacies. The patronne would not sell us these items until we could pronounce them to her satisfaction. Still, they were very good when we finally left the store a couple of hours later.

Anne and I were in Marseilles once and stopped for lunch at a café. We ordered food for both of us, a glass of wine for Anne, and a Pelforth for me. The waiter looked at me quizzically, but you expect that, don't you? At least he didn't deny that any such thing existed, which is what I usually get. A little while later he reappeared with Anne's wine and a large plate with a sausage-shaped thing on it. "*Et c'est quoi, exactement?*" I said, or something like it. "*Votre franc-fort, monsieur,*" he replied, with the warm glow that comes from having completely foxed a tourist. There is, apparently, an odd quirk of the Marseilles dialect that makes no distinction between a dark beer from northern France and a frankfurter. My French is Wodehousean, but it's not that bad. Pelforth, francfort—even I can tell the difference. It still beats trying to pronounce "33," the name of a very popular French lager. *Trente-trois* is a combination of sounds designed to confound the anglophone palate. Small wonder the locals all drink wine. Maybe they can't say it either.

There's another French beer I like, and I discovered it not all that far from Marseilles. We had rented a car—this was 1986 and I think we're still paying it off—and had stopped for the night in a small town called Brignoles. We found accommodation, settled in, and went out to see the sights. There weren't a lot of them. We visited one café, stayed for a bit, then crossed the street and visited the other café. The second café was more lively than the first, and our hostess, having established that I was in search of interesting beer (or a hot dog), smiled and said, "Adele Scott?"

I smiled back, as you do, but stopped short of answering in the affirmative. The nature of the question was unclear. Should I know Adele Scott? Was I being offered Adele Scott and would it be deemed impolite to turn her down? Driving in the English countryside once, I saw a hand-lettered sign advertising Local Honey for Sale. I didn't stop. I mean, you don't know what she's going to be like, do you? Same thing with this Adele person.

After a bit of this back-and-forth smiling and non-communicating, she held up a beer bottle and said once again, "Adelscott!" I didn't know at the time that Adelscott was a French beer made by the Adelshoffen brewery in a sort of Scottish style using whisky malt. It has a smoky flavour and it's really rather nice. It's also rather strong, which I also didn't know at the time.

There was another woman at the bar, and she might have been there a long time. Certainly hours rather than minutes. Possibly days rather than hours. She might have been a few Adelscotts to the wind, and why not? She wanted to meet these exotic tourists who had breezed into town and wanted—perhaps to keep us from speaking French—to address us in our native tongue. Unfortunately, her knowledge of English made us sound like Charles Aznavour by comparison. She thought a moment, made a facial expression that signified great concentration, and finally uttered a word we slowly recognized as "friend." "Ah," we cried, in international good cheer, *"ami!"*

Another round of drinks seemed called for to help us celebrate this outburst of friendliness. Really, it was all going very well. Emboldened by her success, our new ally recalled that she knew another English expression. Dredging it up was clearly going to take a moment or two, and her brow furrowed at the effort. Finally she had it. She leaned forward toward us, and we leaned forward toward her. The entire bar fell silent. No one wanted to miss this moment. Slowly she formed the words: "You . . . fucking . . . dog."

God knows what she thought she was saying, but she seemed a bit surprised when we broke into laughter. A grim-faced young woman hurried to her side and—clearly bilingual—whispered to our friend what she had said to us. The healthy glow disappeared from her face. She was mortified, both by the international incident she might have triggered and by the knowledge that someone had taught her these words at some point in her life, possibly under false pretences. We tried to assure her that we took no offence and that we still regarded her as our friend, but she was disconsolate. It certainly seemed to sober her up in a hurry.

Now, if we'd been at a museum or some damn thing, we'd have missed all of that. Trust me, if you want to know what's going on in a place, head for the bar.

The Germans get a bit of a bad rap, fun-wise. They are, in fact, capable of feeling and expressing pleasure, and it helps if they've been drinking. They're a bit like Canadians that way. I've enjoyed myself in German watering holes ranging from huge Bavarian beer halls to little hole-in-the-wall sorts of places. As I mention somewhere else in this book, the German language becomes a whole lot easier after a few beers. You start making up nouns the way Germans do, just piling up words on top of one another, and German people seem to understand. The French would give you one of those withering French looks, but the Germans are just as likely to buy you another beer.

One rule of drinking the Germans seem to understand instinctively is that, if you're going to bore the pants off someone in a bar, it's up to you to buy the beer. For the young, impecunious drinker, this is not the worst of all possible arrangements. (This rule is not recognized in many other places. I have met barroom bores who actually expected me to subsidize their drinking. Well, really.) I was in a bar in Bremen one afternoon in the late sixties. I quickly discovered it was obviously close to some sort of military thing, as there were soldiers about. An older man befriended me. I don't know if he hung out in this bar because he liked to be around young soldiers or because it brought back memories of his own military past. I belong to the don't-mention-the-war school when it comes to Germans, so I didn't ask.

He bought me a beer and started talking calmly and in English about, as I recall, Winston Churchill. If he didn't start out on Churchill, he very soon got there. His view of Churchill was not enthusiastic. Well, it was enthusiastic all right, but not pro-Churchill. I recall the expression "the greatest war criminal of all." As he warmed to his subject, he raised the volume a bit and began to lapse back into German. Eventually, he was ranting—there's no other word for it—entirely in German at great volume.

Then he stopped. He bought us both more beer, and began again. Calmly and in English. The same thing happened again. Again he stopped, bought more beer, and resumed as he had before. After about four beers, I decided I had heard enough and made my apologies. It was practically the first time I had got a chance to speak. Don't let them tell you there's nothing funny about the Germans.

Be careful in Switzerland. Don't get me wrong. It's a damned nice country, with mountains and lakes and chocolate and all the things you expect. But twice in Switzerland I got fooled. They have bars in Switzerland that don't sell alcohol. I went into a bar in Neuchâtel that looked like one groovy place. The Rolling Stones were playing through the speakers (this was still the late sixties, so I was happy to hear them), and everyone in the place looked just as they should. Hip, in a Swiss way.

I sat at the bar and ordered a beer. The bartender looked at me a bit funny, but I'm used to that, and he brought me a bottle and a glass. You tend to do a lot of reading in Switzerland, there being several dozen official languages. I once saw *Rebel Without a Cause* in Switzerland, but I could hardly see anything for all the subtitles. I learned a lot of French, German, and Italian that day. Well, it was the same thing with this bottle of beer. I've never had so much to read on a beer label, but I'm enough of a linguist to recognize that I was being warned that there was no alcohol in my beer in several languages.

Only then did I take a proper look at my surroundings. All the hip young folk around me were actually drinking Pepsi or some damn thing. The bottles behind the bar were bottles, all right, but not the sort of bottles you expect behind a bar. The place was a fake bar, and I hadn't spotted it. My non-beer was exactly that: non-beer.

And I'll be damned if the same thing didn't happen several days later, somewhere else in Switzerland. Fool me once, shame on you; fool me twice, shame on me. (Or, as George W. Bush once put it, "There's an old saying in Tennessee—I know it's in Texas, probably in Tennessee—that says, fool me once, shame on—shame on you. Fool me—you can't get fooled again.") I came of drinking age in Toronto, at a time when the authorities did all they could to prevent people from drinking, but even they never tried a stunt like this. Why do the Swiss tolerate this sort of thing? Perhaps it's changed, but I've never gone back to find out.

The Americans would never pull off a trick like that, although Prohibition came pretty close. Actually, Prohibition mostly seems to have meant that Americans got their booze from a different bunch of crooks than they were used to. For that matter, a lot of

Americans continued to get their booze from exactly the same places they always had.

I'm not sure any New York bars ever bothered closing down during that misguided dark age. McSorley's Old Ale House was popular with politicians and never seems to have had any problems with the authorities. I chatted once with the proprietor of the Old Town Bar on East 18th Street, who said that they had removed their sign outside during Prohibition but that otherwise life had gone on as usual.

There's a bar called Chumley's in the Village that still has no sign outside. (At the time of writing, it is identifiable by the construction hoarding outside, after a wall collapsed in April 2007. The owners insist it will reopen, but call first.) It opened in the 1920s, during Prohibition, and has carried on successfully ever since, or at least until the wall collapsed. But you won't stumble upon it, unless you're a charmed stumbler. Even as you stand at the front door, at 86 Bedford Street, you'll have no hint that you're standing outside a bar with many beer taps unless one of the inmates comes lurching out. It's a quiet street, Bedford Street, and you can impress the heck out of people who don't know about Chumley's if you walk along and calmly push open the door and step into a bustling New York bar. Just don't try it until after about four o'clock in the afternoon, or the door will be locked and you won't impress anybody at all.

Chumley's was tarted up slightly in recent years, but the bar area retained its sawdust on the floor and the three large Labs that lie about looking somehow baleful and winsome at the same time. There were two main themes to the decor: dust jackets and photographs of the many authors who have swilled on the premises and photographs of firefighters. Chumley's also had one of the quirkiest jukeboxes I've encountered. I mean, I've seen retro jukeboxes before, but none that offer a full CD of Joni James. You have to be pretty retro yourself to remember Joni James. You can also hear Handel's *Messiah*, if you need a change of pace.

The Chumley's mix of writers and firefighters in more recent years had given way to tourists and non-locals, and who knows what we'll see when and if it resurfaces. I hope the jukebox can be saved.

(It is worth observing that Christine Sismondo, author of *Mondo Cocktail*, a delightful book about the history and lore of cocktails, told me that I was way off base about Chumley's and that I should check out a bar called Marie's Crisis. And I have. I'm not saying it's the best gay show-tune singalong bar in the world, or even in the Village, or even on Grove Street, but it'll do for me. The beer stinks—I'd stick with gin and tonics—but standing in a crowded room belting out *Oklahoma!* is better than it usually gets and is probably worth a month of therapy. I wouldn't want to live upstairs, even if I could afford to. Don't bother arriving before 9:30. The one in the evening, I mean. Thomas Paine died on the site, but you probably won't.)

Until recent years New York was a lousy town for beer drinkers. (Not all that long ago the whole country was lousy for beer drinkers. One of Canada's boasts was that our beer was better than theirs. Ah well.) It used to take me a day to remember that I drank gin in New York. Gin was better value, given the generous servings you tend to get south of the Canadian border. The beer usually went by the name of Bud or his scrawny kid brother, Bud Light, and the purveyors of this stuff charged hefty prices for a thick mug that held paltry amounts. Just as well, really. The only time I was happy to see Bud was July 4, 1983. We were visiting our friend Syd Holden in Brooklyn Heights, and we went up to Yankee Stadium to catch the Yankees against the Red Sox. Syd's from Boston, so we were all cheering for the away team. There's something unhealthy about people who support the Yankees, I've always felt. It's too damn easy. It may have been Red Smith who said that cheering for the Yankees was like cheering for U.S. Steel, but what has U.S. Steel done lately? Beyond taking over Stelco, that is.

It was a very hot day, and we were sitting in the bleachers. I was keeping score on an envelope that I had with me for some reason. Dave Righetti was pitching for the home side, and pitching well. Given that we were all cheering for the Red Sox, I didn't feel it was jinxing anybody to point out after several innings that we were watching a no-hitter. It was still a close score, and Syd was sure that the forces of good could still prevail. With two out in the ninth, Righetti got Wade Boggs swinging on strike three, and we all went crazy. Well, the three of us went less crazy, having hoped to the end that the Red Sox could come back, but it's still the only no-hitter I've ever watched live.

Did I mention that it was hot that day? It was very hot, somewhere in the mid-nineties on the American scale, and we were ready for a cold one. There are a couple of industrial, pour-beer-down-the-throats-of-many-thousands-of-Yankee-fans kind of bars right outside Yankee Stadium, but they were predictably packed and we walked a block or two looking for something more congenial while the area cleared out. We found a backstreet bar not far away, an actual neighbourhood corner bar. We didn't expect anything more exotic than Bud, and we weren't disappointed. Still, it was the Fourth of July, the Yankees had just won a no-hitter, it had maybe cooled down to about ninety degrees, we were in a part of the Bronx we would probably have been warned against, and we pounded back a few ice-cold Buds, the bottles soaked with conden-sation. They were too cold to taste, which is the only way to drink Bud. We were happy, and I haven't had a Bud since.

Even today you can't be sure of getting a decent beer in New York. The Bud brothers are everywhere, unless you know where to look. The lover of good beer (or tequilas mezcals, or single malts, for that matter) heads for a place called d.b.a., down near the foot of 1st Avenue. The frills at d.b.a. are all behind the bar, and I'm not referring to—or at least not just referring to—the bar staff. They don't do food at d.b.a., though they're happy to direct you to local takeout places if you want to eat while you drink. (On a recent visit I saw a couple of guys at a table enjoying a picnic of several cheeses and a fresh baguette; they looked euphoric.) They don't have live bands—though they do make you listen to music—and they don't have banks of television screens. You're there to drink, and to drink well. And the neighbourhood's improved enough in the years since d.b.a. opened (1994) that you're less likely to be murdered when you leave.

There are places in New York with bigger draught beer selec-tions, but d.b.a. always offers an intelligent choice of beers, with at least a couple of real ale opportunities. And it's not every bar that tells you, on a blackboard above the bar, when each of the casks was tapped, so you know how fresh everything is. They love their beer at d.b.a., and they're happy to talk about it, happy to give you a taste of something you're not sure of. Dropping in one night, I found myself in the midst of a celebration of microbreweries from New Jersey. Who knew? The name, by the way, probably stands for Doing Business As, but if you inquire you'll probably be told Don't Bother Asking.

I've spoken to Canadian beer guru Stephen Beaumont about d.b.a., and he reckoned it's either the best bar in America or tied for first with a place called Toronado in San Francisco. If you don't trust me, trust him. Mind you, he might have changed his mind since then.

The venerable McSorley's in the East Village dates back to 1854, and it hasn't changed much since John McSorley first opened the doors, except that there's probably more clutter now. And, as mentioned before, women are now allowed inside.

It's a nice place to be, particularly in the afternoon (or even better in the morning; try to avoid the evening). We were there one fairly busy afternoon, sitting beneath a pay phone, which turns out to be the bar phone. If you call McSorley's, that's the phone that rings. The staff showed no interest in answering the damn thing— hell, the place was already busy enough—so Anne started picking it up. Most of the callers were looking for the address, though some needed directions. She didn't do terribly well with the guy calling from the Lincoln Tunnel, but she was great with the guy who claimed to be on the Upper West Side.

"Can you be more specific?" she asked. "Where exactly are you?"

"I'm near Bloomingdale's," the man replied.

"Bloomingdale's?" my wife from Toronto said. "Then you're not on the West Side, are you?"

I wanted her to add "Welcome to Noo Yawk!" and hang up, but she was too polite.

There's not a lot of choice at McSorley's. There's dark beer and light beer—formerly made locally, but now made by Stroh's—and it comes in little mugs that need constant refilling. They'd need even quicker refilling if it were better beer. And a good mid-afternoon pick-me-up is offered by the cheap cheese plate: soda crackers, cheddar cheese (and not bad cheese either, for the Americans), and raw onions. A bit of strong mustard, and life is close to ideal. It was said soon after the turn of the last century that wives knew when their husbands had been in the safe, floozy-free environment of West 7th Street, because you could always tell a McSorley's onion.

The man who wrote best about McSorley's was Joseph Mitchell, who penned the definitive study of the old saloon for *The New Yorker* in 1940. At that point McSorley's was merely eighty-eight years old and still on only its fourth owner. Mitchell writes of the regular who, on the day of his retirement announced, "If my savings hold out, I'll never draw another sober breath." I'm not sure I haven't seen this regular in there recently. You'll find this piece in Mitchell's book, *Up in the Old Hotel*.

Some years ago I was on a bit of a pub crawl in New York with Syd from a few pages back. We had done Pete's Tavern—an old haunt of O Henry—and one or two other spots I don't now recall, and we were headed across town to the Village when we happened upon the Old Town Bar on a very dark, almost moribund East 18th Street. We never did get to the Village. At that time—this would have been the early eighties—the Old Town was the bar that time had forgotten. It even held to the old (and now virtually extinct) New York tradition that the house bought every third drink. I enjoyed that tradition once at the late and still lamented Lion's Head in the Village, a grand old Manhattan landmark.

East 18th Street is perkier now than it was then, and the Old Town is more popular than it seemed that long ago night. It made it into the opening credits of David Letterman's show, and it even boasts a *Sex and the City* connection, which has drawn the crowds. A hipper clientele has improved the draught beer selection a bit, which it certainly needed. There is Liam Neeson memorabilia on the walls, which probably means that he's moved on by now and drinks somewhere else.

The Blind Tiger used to be an outstanding bar on Hudson Street on the West Side, not far from the famous White Horse Tavern, where Dylan Thomas infamously—and allegedly—drank the many neat whiskies that may have led to his doom. The Blind Tiger met its own doom on December 27, 2005, when its landlord decided that Hudson Street needed a Starbucks more than an outstanding bar, and the latter was out on the street. The owners went looking for a new location, found one (at 281 Bleecker Street), and fixed it up admirably with a lot of wood taken from an old New York State farmhouse, then disappeared into liquor licence hell. The visually impaired Tiger emerged only in March 2007, but I'm happy to report that it's wonderful. The local NIMBYs allowed it only a beer and wine licence, so its famous Bloody Marys are a thing of the past, but the creator of those Marys (a terrific bartender named Louise) is now making a bloody beer. Don't knock it till you've tried it.

Louise is now in charge of food (they never sold food before) and at last word was still doing her Sunday afternoon shift behind the bar. Long may she thrive.

There's a Waterfront Ale House in Brooklyn, but I don't get to Brooklyn much since Syd left town. Fortunately, they opened a branch in Manhattan, on Second Avenue in midtown. Fine beers and good food too. Speaking of Brooklyn, as Manhattan rents have soared, many artists have crossed the bridge to that less glamorous borough, and good beer has followed. There are now just about as many good bars in Brooklyn as in Manhattan. It's worth going just for the Spuyten Duyvil in Williamsburg, which, according to its website, offers "Cheese, Meat, and a wide selection of Beer." Not easy to find, but worth the trek. It couldn't be less like a franchise pub.

Back in Manhattan, when Anne's shopping at Lord & Taylor, I wait for her at the Ginger Man on East 36th Street. With sixty-six taps (and often two hand pumps) on display, there's plenty of beer to choose from, but it's definitely the sort of place where you want to feed the jukebox in the evening rather than listen to the pap you'll have inflicted on you otherwise.

There are now lots of good places to drink beer in Manhattan, and I haven't even mentioned David Copperfield's, the Hop Devil, or the Spring Lounge.

When I'm in Chicago, I try to have lunch at least once at Andy's on East Hubbard. Andy's is a jazz club that used to offer live jazz three times a day: at lunch, after work, and in the evening. The lunchtime session, alas, is gone. But it's still a chance to buy Goose Island Honker's Ale from a woman who typifies a certain kind of big-town barkeep: not as gruff as she seems, but almost certainly tough if she needs to be.

The Goose Island Beer Company has two bars of its own on the way to Wrigley Field, and they give an opportunity to taste the beers on its list other than the fairly ubiquitous Honker's. Not far from Wrigley is a bar called Sheffield's, which has a fine list of beers and a pleasant garden. I like Sheffield's because it was the first place in a quarter-century to ask me for ID. They were checking everybody, including at least one other geezer, but still, it was nice to be asked. The Clark Street Alehouse has a lot of good Midwest microbrewery beer and a sound system to loosen your teeth. Invest heavily in Miles Davis on the jukebox. The room looks beautiful and the people look smarter with "'Round Midnight" playing. A lot of Chicago bars don't open until at least mid-afternoon, so call first. Late in the nineteenth century, Chicago's bars were famous for never closing. Part of the ritual upon opening a new bar called for the proprietor to declare the place open, then take a walk and throw the keys into Lake Michigan or the Chicago River.

A place that opens early is the Map Room in Bucktown. There are other places to drink beer in Chicago, but there's nowhere like the Map Room. I have been insanely happy there. That's all I'll say. Great beer, great bar.

In 2000 the Christian Booksellers Association held its annual conference in New Orleans, which seemed an odd location. A lot of people find themselves harbouring ideas in New Orleans that aren't always in keeping with a strict reading of the New Testament. It seems to me a city that does a better job fulfilling the physical pleasures than the spiritual ones. In a *Publishers Weekly* report of the conference, one Christian bookseller from Texas declared that she had enjoyed herself but added that New Orleans wouldn't have been her first choice. "There's not a lot here for Christian folk to do," she pointed out.

That may be so, but we sinners find plenty to occupy us. Writer Calvin Trillin once asked a local gourmand where he should eat in Louisiana. He was told: anywhere. The same rule pretty much applies to drinking. At first glance, there appear to be no drinking laws at all in New Orleans, but I'm aware of at least two. If you're going to drink on the streets, your beverage must be in a plastic or paper container, not glass or metal. And you can't drink on the streetcar that goes out to the Garden District. That seems to be it, legislation-wise. I'm sure there must be other rules, but those are the only ones that stand out.

I haven't visited New Orleans since Katrina, but the places I mention here are still (or again) doing business, and heaven knows the city needs our help. There are many facets of life in New Orleans that remind you that you're not in Canada any more, but none more than walking around the French Quarter on a hot night with a large plastic cup of beer, listening to live music from the many clubs. Sure, it's become overrun with T-shirt stores—the first evidence of a dying culture—and it's become something of a theme park, but it's a theme park for grown-ups. Leave the kids behind.

Like most hot, sultry places, New Orleans is not a great beer town. The local institution is Dixie, a standard hot-weather lager of no real distinction, though it's useful when you're trying to restore fluids to the system. They also brew a Blackened Voodoo Lager, which got them in bad odour with southern Christian folk, who don't hold with that voodoo stuff. There's some decent beer from the Abita brewery just out of town, and I've enjoyed Rikenjaks when I've been able to find it.

There are as many bars in New Orleans as there are Mormons in Salt Lake City, so you're never far from a drink. If you're restless, there are lots of hole-in-the-wall sorts of places that offer take-away beer as well. The pub-minded tourist simply has to get to a couple of places: the Napoleon (no, he never drank there, but there's a story that they offered to take him in) and the venerable old Lafitte's Blacksmith Shop. The bar I gravitate toward is a place called Coop's, down on Decatur Street. The last time I was there, they were serving a decent Scotch Ale from Rikenjaks, but I guess I went too often because they ran out of it. Along with pretty good beer and an excellent southern bar ambience, Coop's will do you an altogether serviceable meal—the wonderful local food at good prices.

It is worth noting—well, I think it's worth noting; you can decide for yourself—that the fine fellows who own d.b.a. in New York have opened a d.b.a. in New Orleans at 618 Frenchmen Street. It wasn't there last time I was in the Crescent City, but it's there now.

You never know where you're going to find a drink on your travels. The vicissitudes of life have delivered me to Syracuse, New York, only the once, but it was long enough to discover Clark's Ale

House, a bar of great character, multiple fine beers, and only one sandwich. Still, it's a very good sandwich. Just beyond the border of Cambridge, Massachusetts, just as you get into Somerville, you'll find—if you're lucky—Redbones Barbecue, the only place I've ever found Sam Adams Trippelbock on tap, served from a little barrel behind the bar. I don't speak of life-altering experiences lightly, but this was just such an experience.

If good fortune takes you to Denver, especially during the Great American Beer Festival at the beginning of October, you would be ill-advised to miss the Falling Rock Tap House. It's the only place I've ever been where I've heard an announcement over a loudspeaker that a new beer had just been tapped and was now available.

San Francisco has oodles of excellent bars, as you'd expect. Every beer geek is required to get to Toronado. It isn't scenic, but the beer is outstanding. My cousin once took me to a place called the Connecticut Yankee, at the foot of Potrero Hill, and I'm glad he did. Across the bay in Berkeley there are more pleasures to be had, particularly at the sister brewpubs Jupiter and Triple Rock.

Portland, Oregon, has more bars and breweries than I can count, of which probably the granddaddy is the Horse Brass Pub, an English-style pub that was an early adopter of the craft brewing revolution.

A longer-than-expected delay at the Atlanta airport led to the discovery of a bar that sold only Sam Adams beers on tap. I was almost sorry when our flight materialized. It turns out that there's no international law dictating that airports have to sell bad beer. They do it only to make your airport experience even more unpleasant. Maybe someday the touring drinker will even be able to get a decent beer on an airplane, but I'm not holding my breath.

For many Canadian beer tourists, the best trip of all can be a getaway to the nearest town across the American border. Toronto-area members of the beer community are often to be found in Buffalo, New York, picking up some brews at Premier Gourmet or Consumer's Beverage Centers or having a pint at Cole's. Please remember to declare your purchases on the way home.

Our friend Syd moved to Florida a few years ago. When we went to visit him, he took us to the Palace Saloon in Fernandina Beach, which purports to be the oldest saloon in Florida. I'm prepared to believe that claim until I see evidence to the contrary, and I've no doubt there are half a dozen bars in Florida making the same claim. I just haven't been to the others. Syd has lived in a few places in the last twenty years. We used to visit him when he lived in Brooklyn Heights. We visited him when he lived in Cambridge. We visited him in northern Florida. There was a time when he went to work in Riyadh, Saudi Arabia. Riyadh is one of those chop-your-hand-off kind of places when it comes to the pub life. We didn't visit Syd in Riyadh.

# This Sceptr'd Isle:
# Drinking in England

Like everything else, pub life in the United Kingdom is changing, usually for the worse. Pubs are being closed, or they're being gutted and turned into ghastly theme pubs. Where it once cost about the same to drink at home or in a pub, it's now cheaper to drink at home. And many do, especially since central heating became more widely available. Still, I recently saw a figure pointing out that Americans drink only 20 percent of their beer in bars and restaurants, while the English continue to drink 75 percent of their beer in pubs. And rightly so, for the pub is not just a place to drink. It's the village hall. It's where people go to hear the news, find jobs, make friends, meet the people they'll spend the rest of their lives with.

The English pub is something that has evolved over centuries. The earliest pubs existed to serve travellers, usually pilgrims. Chaucer's pilgrims set out from the Tabard, an inn in Southwark. As travel grew more sophisticated, inns proliferated along coaching routes, in much the same way that Canadian towns sprang up along railway lines. Travellers needed a bed for the night and a meal, and while they were there they might as well have a flagon or two of ale as well.

When railways began to supplant the coaches, pubs appeared to cater to the needs of train travellers. Long after the British railway system was gutted in the 1960s, you can still find pubs called the Railway or the Station Inn, far from the nearest train line. It's a little disconcerting the first time you come upon one of these stranded railway pubs.

One of the most impressive pubs in London was built by a man named Frank Crocker, who had been given a hot tip that a major railway station would be built practically across the street. Crocker built the Crown Hotel, an ornate palace of a place, and waited for the fortune that would surely follow. Alas, the train line veered away from Crocker's hotel, and Marylebone Station wound up a mile away. A broke and broken Crocker jumped to his death from an upstairs window. Pub historians are quick to cast doubt on virtually the whole story, but it's a good one nonetheless. If it isn't true, it certainly should be. The pub—now called Crocker's Folly—still stands in a quiet residential street in St. John's Wood, not far from Lord's Cricket Ground. Alas, however, it closed down in 2004 and has sat vacant ever since. English Heritage has added the pub to its register of London buildings at risk; we can only hope for the best.

Call me a rain-soaked anglophile, but there's not much I like better than a good English pub. People talk of a good old typical English pub, but there's really no such thing. Some of them are fancy, with acres of frosted glass, mahogany bars, and great marble urinals a fellow's almost reluctant to pee into. But they're not all like that. In 1967 my cousin took me to a Gloucestershire pub that didn't even have anyone tending the bar. The customers served themselves, then reported what they'd taken to a woman who came around with a change purse. She told you what you owed and you paid her.

That pub doesn't exist any more. Nor does the Berkeley Hunt in Purton, an unadorned pub on a canal that runs parallel to the Severn River. The Berkeley Hunt, when I knew it, was run by a Mrs. Musselwhite, known to all as Ma Musselwhite, rumoured to be if not the oldest licensee in England then certainly damn close to it. The pub didn't have anything as highfalutin as a bar. You came in the front door and found yourself in a narrow corridor with a kind of serving hatch in front of you. There, if you were lucky, stood Ma herself. The beer was behind her in casks, and your beer came straight out of the barrel. By this time the casks were metal rather than wood, but you can't have everything.

Once served, you joined the throng that gathered in the doorway or, in good weather, stood outside in the garden beside the canal, or you moved into either the room on the right or that on the left. There is a general principle in English pubs that if you have two rooms one will be tonier than the other. In the Berkeley Hunt I think it was the room on the left, on the basis that the furniture was a mite softer. But I'm not sure I ever saw anyone drink there. I once spent Christmas Eve in the Berkeley Hunt, and we all gathered in the room on the right, sat in a large circle singing songs and sharing something I've never tried to define. (The Germans have a word for it—*Gemütlichkeit*—which is almost as much fun to say as it is to experience.) Shortly before midnight, Ma Musselwhite herself came around and took orders for a round of drinks on the house.

I once spoke to a younger member of the family who said they were keeping the place open only as long as Ma wanted to run it and was capable of doing so. When I came by one year and saw the place closed up, I knew an era had ended. God bless you, Ma.

You never know when you're going to have a magic pub moment. In May 1980 I found myself alone in London, my wife back in Canada. It was Cup Final day, a big day on the English sporting calendar. I watched the match on television in the afternoon, a surprise win for West Ham over fellow London club Arsenal. That evening I took the tube up to Islington to see a play in a small theatre at the back of a pub called the King's Head. After the play, I decided the King's Head was too crowded, so I headed down the street to find something a little quieter. Islington now is very chic, but it wasn't at the time. It was also the part of town in which Arsenal—that day's losing team—played.

I don't know what the pub was called, but I went in. Similarly, I don't remember what was on tap, but I know that an older fellow played a piano and the whole community was there. Over to one side stood some lads who had been to the match and were looking sombrely at their programs. There were youngsters and there were grannies at this pub, and I may have been the first tourist who ever set foot in the place (statistically unlikely in London, I know). Even though I was actually living in London at the time, it wasn't that part of London and I hadn't been living there for generations; I was a tourist. A Salvation Army couple came in to solicit donations.

They were made welcome, but they weren't allowed out until they sang a song. They did us a rousing hymn, accompanied by the old fellow on the piano, and we all cheered. And I swear that before the evening ended we sang "Maybe It's Because I'm a Londoner," the great anthem of the capital. I was probably the only outsider in the room, but I joined in with gusto, wishing I was a Londoner. For once in my life, I could actually imagine being an Arsenal supporter. The impulse didn't last, but it was powerful at the time.

Not all pubs are friendly, welcoming spots, it must be said. Some years ago Anne and I sought out a Wiltshire pub that was described in the *Good Beer Guide* as "One of a dying breed; as basic as they come." It was what had clearly been a rustic pub, now being encroached upon by creeping suburbia. We drove past it once, because its ancient, weathered pub sign was illegible. When we stepped in, we saw it was indeed basic. The venerable landlady gave us a look that suggested we'd come to the wrong place. In a room to our right sat the regulars. They were men to a man, all in black, with a couple of working dogs. It was hard to say where these rustics lived or worked in this newly genteel area; possibly they were bused in each day.

The regulars fell silent as we came in. Not that we actually entered their room; that would have been an invitation to violence. Feeling a chill in the air, we ordered half-pints as a compromise position. We weren't about to retreat altogether, you understand, but we didn't feel like lingering either. We sat alone in the only slightly more tony room, where we could see into the regulars' room through a doorway, or at least we could until one of the regulars pointedly kicked the door shut. Only then did they resume conversation, which from where we sat sounded rather like, "Orrr, arrr, orrr, errr . . ."

We have not been back to the Bruce Arms, but the pub guides suggest that it is now a friendly, welcoming spot under new management, still retaining its unspoiled charm. Maybe so; I just want a guarantee that the guy who kicked the door shut isn't still there.

There are plain pubs and grand pubs, but the rules are the same. There are generally no waiters in an English pub. You go to the bar and get your drinks. Some of my best friends are waiters, but I have to say that the English setup works wonderfully well, especially if you're just pushy enough to make your way to the bar and get the bar staff's attention. It's an efficient system. One recent New Year's Eve I watched three bar people serving a very busy Sussex pub without making anyone wait for long. Sometimes the landlady pitched in as well, but there was scant space for a fourth person behind that bar. Her presence meant one of the others could take a smoke break and go look for abandoned glasses.

I've worked in a London pub and I know that pub wages aren't bad, or they weren't in 1969, at least compared to other jobs I did in London at that time. I'm not saying anyone's getting rich behind a bar, but they're not dependent on tips. I have seen a London barman get tipped by an American tourist and call the fellow back because he'd left change on the bar. Tipping is not the accepted practice, but if you like the service you're getting from someone behind a bar, you say, as you're ordering your drinks, "And will you have one yourself?" The person will then say, "Thank you, I'll have a half-pint," or whatever, and will charge you accordingly. All is well, and you will be favourably regarded thereafter.

The traditional English practice of buying rounds is slipping away somewhat, for fairly sensible reasons. Traditionally, if two people drank together, one would buy the other a drink, after which the second would reciprocate. If three drinkers gathered, each would play his role, and so on up the scale. Find yourself one of a group of half a dozen, and it becomes clear that you're there for six pints, whether you want them all or not. It was chummy, all right, but not conducive to productivity. And woe be to you if you left before your round came along.

So, what are you drinking? It used to be fairly simple for the beer drinker: a pint of bitter. (Please note "bitter," not "bitters." Bitters is a usually vile herbal drink designed to do battle with a hangover.) This was in the days when pubs were owned by breweries and a pint of bitter was the normal draught ale made by that particular brewery. Nowadays, there is likely to be a choice of bitters, but there are worse things than choice. My advice is to make sure that what you're drinking comes from a hand pump, the tall, slightly phallic device that signals the presence of real ale. English lager exists to separate fools from their money, and the other beers on offer will not be as fresh or as tasty as a real ale. Don't hesitate to ask the bar staff for advice, especially if they're over twenty-five. Mind you, at one time they were likely to be Australian. Nowadays, they're frequently Polish, so be careful seeking advice. You didn't go to London to drink Żywiec, though you might learn how to pronounce it.

You should be aware that if you ask for a martini in an English pub, to this day you will probably be served a glass of vermouth. You may also be asked if you'd like lemonade with that. The standard measures for liquor have grown marginally in the shift from sixths of gills to a metric measure, but they're still smaller than Canadian measures (and a tiny fraction of what you generally get in a good American bar). Feel free to ask for a large one, which will be a double. You're on holiday, for Pete's sake.

English drinking hours continue to bewilder visitors from practically anywhere. Explain to anyone that pubs in London close at 11 p.m. and they'll laugh at you. Hell, you can drink later than that in Kenora. That may be true, but it doesn't alter the fact that at ten minutes to eleven all across London barmen are calling out "Last orders please!" And ten minutes later you'll hear a bell and the cry, "Time, ladies and gentlemen, please, let's have your glasses!"

As noted earlier, English pubs can now stay open beyond 11 p.m., but don't assume that they will. This is part of a very gradual relaxing of pub hours that followed the ending of the afternoon closing laws. They've even made it possible for pubs to stay open all day on Sunday, at least until 10:30 at night. But that's assuming the publican actually wants to open the doors, for he's under no obligation to do so. In smaller, more rustic parts of Britain, most of the pubs are run by a family who live on the premises. They open at lunchtime, close for a few restful hours, and reopen for the evening. As far as they're concerned, they're working plenty of hours, thank you very much, and I suppose they have a point. If they stayed open longer, they'd either have to work longer hours themselves or pay someone to work those extra hours when they wouldn't have enough customers to justify it.

When I worked at the Argyll Arms, just off Oxford Circus in London, I turned up at 9:30 a.m. to get the place ready to open at 11. We were busy at lunchtime, but I got a short lunch break myself. We then closed at 3 p.m. for the afternoon. All being well, I got away at 3:20. We reopened at 5:30 p.m., which meant I had to be back ten minutes earlier, and we then worked through till 10:30, with a dinner break in there somewhere. We were quiet during the evening, which was a blessing, so we closed half an hour earlier than the other local pubs, which meant I could get away for a couple of quick pints elsewhere after we closed. Still, it was a long day with a virtually useless two-hour break in the middle of the day. If you went home in the afternoon, there wasn't enough time to do anything, and it wasn't as if you could go to a pub, because they were all shut. As I recall, I was taking home £16 a week, with Wednesday evenings and Sundays off. Still, I've been less happy in jobs.

Then there's food. There are few English pubs today that don't offer some sort of lunch. The ploughman's lunch, which is not a traditional meal but something that was created in the sixties as a cheese marketing initiative, is served in many pubs. Much of southeastern England boasts a baked potato—called a jacket potato there—served with cheese, chili, tuna, or baked beans, depending on your needs. Farther north, you might get Yorkshire pudding served with a choice of fillings.

Dinner, in some parts of England, is still an adventure. The Cotswolds are chock-a-block with pubs serving dinner, while other parts of the country are still incredulous that people might want a meal after dark. Once it was even worse. Anne and I almost reached the point of consulting legal persons in the late seventies and early eighties whenever we visited the British Isles. A cheese sandwich in Mansfield once saved our marriage, as did a couple of leftover ham rolls in Gretna, up in Scotland. Travel writer Bill Bryson has written of the stunning ability of the English to take pleasure in the smallest things. The cheese sandwich in Mansfield was as glorious an experience as I can recall in England, with the possible exception of the 1983 FA Cup semifinal (Sheffield Wednesday 1, Brighton and Hove Albion 2). Fainting with hunger, we asked the landlord if there was any food at all of any sort to be had. He thought for a moment, it being later than 2 p.m., and admitted that, if pressed, he could invent a cheese sandwich or possibly two. There was never a better cheese sandwich than that cheese sandwich, and I raise a glass to the unknown publican of Mansfield. I hope that success and happiness have dogged his every step since that evening.

You should know that even the pubs that stay open all afternoon seldom serve food after about 2 p.m. This falls under the "There's no call for it, guv" rule that says the publican is the sole judge of what his customers want, not that he'd ever actually ask. There's a pub in Lewes that serves food from noon until 7 p.m., so you can get a nice meal at four in the afternoon but will probably be too late if you get peckish at, say, your normal dinnertime.

But enough carping. The English pub continues to evolve, sometimes for the better, sometimes not. Many pubs, for any number of reasons—tough drinking and driving legislation, the increasing likelihood of people staying in to watch *East Enders* instead of going to the pub, or the growing tendency to drink at home, throwing back smuggled French lager which bears a much lower tax rate than English beer—are closing their doors forever. London has lost countless pubs in recent years, simply because there's more money to be made from turning them into housing. Chelsea is now almost pub-free. This loss is incalculable. As pub-lover Hilaire Belloc said, "When you have lost your inns, drown your empty selves, for you will have lost the last of England." Amen.

# Patrick Kennedy's Subway Game, Eastbound

There are lots of games involving drinking, most of which take place inside pubs and usually require a display of physical dexterity or the total recall of arcane trivia. A hospitality industry professional friend of mine has invented a drinking game of an altogether different sort.

If you've ever visited a Toronto pub called Paupers, you have probably encountered Patrick Kennedy. Patrick's a bit of a local star. To his embarrassment (he's not an attention seeker), he finished runner-up in the 2000 *Now* magazine Best of Toronto readers' poll in the Best Restaurant Server category, but then this is the same poll that named Red Lobster the Best Seafood Restaurant in town, which gives you some idea what sort of people are voting. Democracy's a slippery notion. When not waiting on tables, Patrick is frequently to be found somewhere near the bar, chatting with his regulars long after his shift has ended. Many people assume Patrick to be the owner, such is the proprietary attitude Patrick takes toward the place. This misapprehension is helped along by his authoritative manner and aldermanic bearing, although he sports a rather un-aldermanic ponytail. Well, let's just say that I've never seen an alderman with a ponytail.

Patrick's Subway Game requires the use of a subway, so this is a game that can be played only in select cities, and then only in areas of those cities that are served by a subway. A bus or a taxi simply won't do. It is important that you can't see what you're getting into, so it's essential to arrive at your destination from beneath the ground.

The idea is this: you take a subway map and find a station you've never been to before, in a part of town you don't know. Then you board the subway and travel to the station you've selected. Emerging from the tunnel of transit, you proceed to find some kind of licensed premises. Then you have a beer. And, well, that's about it really. It's not about winners and losers and scoring points. It's about finding hidden treasures, and it's the playing that counts. Canadian radio personality Stuart McLean once spoke about Patrick's Subway Game on his show, but chose to leave out the subway part of it (there aren't a lot of subways in Canada) and the beer part (it's a family show), which quite honestly doesn't leave a lot.

In some cities, of course, the Subway Game could keep one occupied for years. The relative ubiquity of the English pub would make the London version rewarding, if possibly a trifle too easy. Though who knows what you might find near the South Ruislip station, or Theydon Bois or even Gants Hill. What pleasure to go a-searching, though. New York, as well, offers a wide variety of subway, stations but I don't know what joy you might find in, say, mid-Queens. (And I still don't, as you'll discover in a later chapter.)

I decided to put the Toronto version of Patrick's game into action. The Toronto subway, alas, is limited, and there are too many stations I can already identify with a pub of some sort. The east end, however, is a bit of a cipher to me, so on my first outing I settled on the Coxwell station, out on the Danforth. I may have seen the corner of Coxwell and Danforth at some time in my life, but I certainly don't remember it.

You can possibly imagine my excitement as the subway rolled to a stop and I left the train. You might then imagine my frustration as I realized I had got off a stop early, having miscalculated the number of stops after Pape. The doors closed behind me, and the train sped off to wherever it goes after Donlands, where I now found myself. Well, actually, I know where it goes: it goes to Coxwell, and that's where I eventually wound up as soon as another train came along. Tip number one: in almost all cases, subway stations have their names emblazoned on the walls so you know where to get off. Sometimes the driver or conductor will also announce the names of approaching stations. When you hear the words, "Next stop XVBERRRGGSVMP," you'll know enough to read the signs on the station walls.

When you leave the Coxwell subway station, you come out on a quiet residential street. Well, first you have to negotiate a brace of piranha-like Girl Guides selling their celebrated cookies inside the station, *then* you come out on a quiet residential street. Cost so far: subway token, purchased in moderate bulk, $2.25; box of Girl Guide cookies, $3.00. Well, you never know—there might be nothing to eat at Coxwell and Danforth. And you didn't meet these Girl Guides. It would have taken a braver man than I to say no to them.

And, for that matter, I wouldn't be surprised if they were actually Brownies, though I'm no authority on the subject.

The only sign of urban life on Strathmore Boulevard is a cheerful, if aggressively Protestant, church called Church of Christ, but soon you're out on Coxwell Avenue. To your left you see the law office of one T. Edgar Reilly, working out of an old house across the street from Rocco the Cobbler. A moment later you're on the Danforth, standing in front of a bar called TKO's: The Sports Pub. I had expected the Subway Game to be more difficult than this.

Uncharacteristically reluctant to seize the first pint offered to me, I walked along a few blocks eastward. After all, there seemed little purpose in travelling all this way only to have a quick pint then head back to the subway, never knowing what pleasures have been laid on for the proud denizens of the Coxwell-Danforth area. Surely people don't live there just because the houses are cheap or because they like to live as close as possible to Rocco the Cobbler, as fine as I'm sure his work is. Though I didn't see his name in the *Now* magazine readers' poll.

As I passed a storefront operation called Open Heaven Ministries Inc., I began to wonder if this was perhaps not a big drinking part of town. My limited experience with enthusiastic Protestantism tells me that the people who frequent places with names like Open Heaven Ministries Inc. do not pop into TKO's for a bracing snifter afterwards. Yet I pushed on. I was excited to find a place called the Prince of Wales, which proved to be a supermarket. I passed on Europe Planet Bar-Grill-Pub, although I liked the name, and I may regret my decision for many years to come.

On the south side of the street I saw a place called Cheers

Tavern, with a sign outside that was about the same size as the set of the television sitcom. Since that successful show, there can be hardly a city, town, or village on the planet that does not have a bar called Cheers. I tend to stay out of these places, because of the perhaps irrational fear that everybody will know my name. Can you imagine anything worse? Also, the beer they served on *Cheers* looked pretty insipid. Did you ever notice that nobody ever seemed to get drunk at Mayday Malone's?

Turning back, I passed a place I had missed going eastbound— The Bus Terminal Family Restaurant, which was a building that had very clearly once been part of a bus terminal. Had I been in the mood for a milkshake or a slice of cherry pie, I'd have been in there like my late cat Nosey on a bowl of kibble. I had my Girl Guide cookies with me, however, so I wasn't hungry. A neon sign in the window promised Molson Export on tap. I took this as divine warning and headed back to TKO's.

Sports bars always have lots of TV screens in operation, and TKO's was no exception. It also had some decent beer on tap, which is not always the case. So I sat at the bar with a pint of Conner's Dark Ale and watched a bit of US college football. This is something I do every couple of years or so, and it always strikes me that football is a game played with a ball that the majority of play ers never touch. Am I alone in finding this odd? Imagine a baseball player who never made contact with the ball. Okay, we could name a few of those, but at least they're trying. Another thing about American football is that there are guys whose job it is to catch footballs that have been kicked toward them, who then as often as not very pointedly don't catch it. I mean, they deliberately don't catch it. They just stand there and let the ball bounce around until someone on the other team grabs it. Having then grabbed the ball, does the other team get to keep it? Of course not. And sometimes the team that's supposed to catch the ball catches it in the end zone and the guy then genuflects and everything stops, and it doesn't cost them a single point. I'll never understand the Americans.

Another thing I think about sometimes when I find myself gawking at a pub TV screen is sports uniforms. For the most part, you can figure out how modern uniforms have evolved, although figure skating costumes seem to adhere to a set of rules that haven't been explained to the rest of us. Can you imagine leaving your house in figure skaters' clothes? Maybe it's something to do with ice, because I've never been able to understand hockey uniforms. These guys are wearing shorts. Shorts and tights. Ugly padded shorts and frequently striped tights. What sort of fashion statement is that?

The other thing about sports bars is that most of the time there's nothing of much importance going on. Sure, any night of the week you'll see live hockey or baseball games, and Saturday and Sunday afternoons there's usually at least a golf tournament or something. But the rest of the time can be pretty bleak for the stations that usually carry sports events. Maybe if I were a fisherman I'd take more pleasure in watching guys in a boat fondling the fish they've just caught, but I doubt it. And in recent years, there's been an explosion of poker shows. What's next? Scrabble?

The absolute worst thing—and I've seen this only once—is turkey hunting. I once went into a Wal-Mart in rustic Pennsylvania during what I assume was wild turkey season, and there, by the gun section, was any amount of expensive stuff for turkey hunters, including every sort of camouflage and turkey caller you can imagine, and maybe a few things that you can't. All this to outsmart a turkey. I've always held that you can learn a lot from platitudes, and I've never heard anybody use an expression like "wily as a turkey" or "smart like a turkey." So to look up from a bar and see four TVs showing a couple of guys in full camouflage creeping through a field hoping to fool a turkey is not a life-affirming experience, especially when the other three sets are showing Golf Channel infomercials.

TKO's is a bar for Toronto Maple Leaf fans. This is made very clear. A sign behind the bar reads PLEASE BE ADVISED THIS BAR SUPPORTS THE TORONTO MAPLE LEAFS LEAF FANS RECEIVE PRIORITY SERVICE. Fair enough, you know where they stand. If you're hellbent on the Anaheim Ducks, I'd advise you to try the Europe Planet Bar-Grill-Pub. Still, even though I was wearing no Leaf-abilia I was served hastily and pleasantly, and the Conner's wasn't too shabby.

(I've been back to TKO's more recently and liked it very much. Conner's Dark being a thing of the past, I had a pint of Mill Street Tankhouse Ale, served by a fine barmaid who combined efficiency with warm friendliness. She knew everyone's name but mine. We all watched the last seventeen entries on something called approximately The 50 Most Damn Inspiring Sports Moments Ever to Happen to Americans. Foreigners, when they appeared at all, existed only to be defeated by Americans. Number 16, as I recall, involved Whitney Houston singing the American national anthem. At the bar of TKO's, we found that amusing.)

Rather than get back on the subway and find another unknown destination, I started walking westbound, back toward what I tend to think of as civilization. Though I kind of liked the Coxwell-

Danforth area. There were a couple of big chain things a little east of Coxwell, but it was mostly small local businesses of a frequently offbeat nature. I like that. There are no major universities in that part of town, but the Danforth Dance Studio is not far from the Danforth Karate Academy, so there is no shortage of opportunities for self-improvement.

I continued to walk westward because I had remembered an old watering hole on the way to Greenwood Avenue, a traditional old taproom called the Linsmore Tavern. Surely it could not have survived the last quarter-century of gentrification unscathed, but suddenly there it was, untouched. Ever wonder what happened to those old six-ounce draught beer glasses? They're at the Linsmore, and for a mere dollar or so the kind of waiter I hadn't seen since the Morrissey Tavern locked its doors will bring you one filled with Labatt's 50 on tap. I haven't seen Labatt's 50 on tap since Christ left Cobourg. Labatt's 50 might have been what drove him out of Cobourg in the first place. He could turn water into wine, but there isn't much you can do with Labatt's 50.

I sat a spell in the Linsmore, watching a golf tournament on one of those early prototypes of large screen TVs, the kind that gives you a dim picture that disappears altogether if you're not directly face-on. The Linsmore still has old snowshoes nailed to the ceiling, and I was glad to see them. And I still had a few Girl Guide cookies left, so I wasn't tempted by the pickled eggs on offer.

Just west of Greenwood, I found the apartment building I've long thought of as the ideal Toronto address for the stay-at-home drinker. Sure, Rosedale has its charms, and I know people who swear by Forest Hill, and the Annex has plenty of admirers, God knows. But the Adella Apartments at 1169 Danforth have a beer store immediately to their east and a liquor store immediately to their west. Only in the worst imaginable weather would you need anything more hardy than slippers. I must have walked past the Adella Apartments a hundred times in my life, but I've never seen an APARTMENT FOR RENT sign outside.

The drinking person is always on the lookout for a new little spot, some undiscovered gem your sophisticated friends don't know about, and I found just such a place west of Donlands on the north side of the Danforth. I had never even heard of The Only Café, and frankly I'm reluctant to tell you about it now. It's not a big place, longish and narrow, as city bars tend to be. The sign outside boasted 101 bottles and thirteen taps and I still had the taste of Labatt's 50 in my mouth, so I did what any right-minded drinking person would do: I walked in.

It's an odd kind of place, The Only Café, clearly not designed by some concept guy in an office several miles away. The concept guy would have demanded a more mainstream selection of beer, for starters. I mean, why scare the Coors Light drinkers away? And then there's the music. First we heard a bunch of songs by Woody Guthrie, and I don't recall ever hearing Woody Guthrie in a bar before. When that was over we got Frank Sinatra, in particularly good form. The old couple sitting near me at a table seemed to enjoy that especially, but the young tattooed guy next to me at the bar didn't seem to mind it either. The father-son duo at another table were too engrossed in their game of chess to notice.

I sat at the bar, supping my Kawartha Lakes Brewery Raspberry Wheat beer—at the time an excellent lightish beer, though it has since been taken over and is not quite what it was—and thinking warm thoughts about a bar that serves good beer and plays music for grown-ups. I was by now probably close to a mile away from Coxwell and Danforth, but Patrick Kennedy's Subway Game had brought me to a great discovery. I would—I resolved then and there—return to The Only Café.

As I left, I was still thinking about the Adella Apartments. Until his death in 2006, Canada's richest man, Kenneth Thomson ("Lord" to his friends), lived in Toronto's deluxe Rosedale area. The publishing mogul was worth an estimated $24 billion, yet he lived an unhealthy mile-and-a-quarter from the nearest beer store. Frankly, the weight of a two-four could kill a man of his age over that sort of haul, and I wouldn't be surprised if that was a factor in his demise.

The official residence of the president of the University of Toronto is only slightly closer to a beer store, and there's a difficult crossing of Mount Pleasant to negotiate. It would be treacherous with a case of beer under your arm. Fortunately, the president is a younger man than Ken Thomson and, in any case, he's got vice-provosts and people of that ilk to fetch his beer.

Residents of the Adella Apartments on the Danforth may lack the niceties of life—like vice-provosts—but they don't need them. Door to door, they are a mere thirty-three paces to the beer store and only nineteen to the liquor store. What price happiness?

# While You're Up: What's My Poison?

I'm a fairly flexible drinker, but my specialty is beer. I liked beer back in the dark times of the sixties and seventies, when consumer choice, particularly in North America, was declining dramatically. I like the taste of it—when it's good—and I like the strength of beer. You can feel drunkenness coming on when you're drinking beer, and you can decide how quickly you want to proceed toward that end. You can pace yourself with beer, unless you're a college student.

I made a decision at some point in my life to try to stop drinking bad beer. I've heard a Canadian beer expert say in public that there's no such thing as bad beer, but I'm not convinced. If I'm at a party where there's no good beer on offer, I drink wine. I have a better tolerance for uninteresting wine than dodgy beer.

As noted earlier, my last Budweiser happened on July 4, 1983, and I think it likely I'll get to my grave without another one. Thank you, but no Bud, no Bud Light, no Coors, no Coors Light. In fact, I don't really want anything that's marketed as "Light" or even "Lite."

The English brew beers of varying strengths, beginning at about 3 percent alcohol by volume. The lighter beers are often called "session" beers because you can drink them over several hours without falling down. The notion of light beer confuses the English, and early in 2001 Anheuser-Busch announced that it was pulling Bud Light out of the UK because of poor sales.

The excellent Fuller's brewery in London makes three standard draught beers: Chiswick Bitter (3.5%), London Pride (4.1%), and ESB—or Extra Special Bitter—(5.5%). These could be characterized as ordinary bitter, best bitter, and strong ale, respectively. If you're going to be at it all day, you might at least start with Chiswick Bitter. If you were having a few, you'd be grateful for London Pride. And if you have only a short time before last orders, bring on the ESB. These are all wonderful beers, but I would never denigrate the Chiswick Bitter or the London Pride by calling them "light" beers. All three of these beers have been named Champion Beer of Britain at least once, and they deserve to be drunk on their own merits, not because you're trying to beat the Breathalyzer or save a few calories.

One of the wackier features of America is that you're actively discouraged from knowing how strong your beer is. A few American bars post the strengths of their beers, but you seldom see it on a bottle or can. Why is this? Presumably because they're stupid. This is a country so full of lawyers that a bottle of tranquilizers will come with a warning: "Caution. May cause drowsiness." Well, I should bloody hope so.

It was a decree of the Bureau of Alcohol, Tobacco and Firearms that made it illegal to advertise or even mention the strength of beer in America. This measure was presumably undertaken to keep breweries from plugging their extra-strength beers around the time they started making malt liquors like Colt 45 in the 1960s. Ironically, not long thereafter, health-conscious beer drinkers began to look for lighter beers but were barred by federal law from finding out which beers contained less alcohol and exactly how much (great taste, less filling). In 1995 the Supreme Court struck down the law, but at last count the lawyers were still bickering. Meanwhile, American drinkers are still in the dark.

How many Americans are charged with drunk driving every year? Oodles, that's how many. And has not one lawyer been able to defend a client with the argument that the poor sod had no idea how strong his beer was? Not one? I'm no lawyer (he said boastfully) but this defence seems a walk in the park. I have beside me a bottle of Old Crustacean barley wine from the Rogue brewery in Oregon. I know it's strong because it's a barley wine and because it comes in a small bottle. There are some odd numbers on the label, like 120 IBU, which I know stands for International Bitterness Units (120 is extremely high). It also claims 38° L and 73.1 M, and I'm out of my depth there. It does, however, cite a figure of 26° Plato, and I know that Plato is an obscure European measurement of beer strength. Doing my calculations, I reckon this beer is in the rough ballpark of 10 percent to 11 percent alcohol by volume.

So I know roughly how strong this beer is (very!) because I'm at home with my reference materials, and I'm also reasonably sober. Now, take some American guy who stops in at a bar and decides he wants a change from the usual swill he drinks (but almost certainly doesn't know the strength of). Gimme something out of the ordinary, he tells the barkeep, who sees this as an opportunity to offload some of the Old Crustacean he brought in on a whim. Our guy takes a drink, recoils a bit, and asks the bartender how strong this stuff is. Beats me, says the barkeep, checking the label. It's either 26° Plato or 120 IBU, he reports. That's probably about normal, he says, unwilling to admit that he has no idea.

After a few Old Crustaceans, our guy says Nood Gight to the bartender, walks outside, gets into his car, and kills a family of eight on its way to Bible class. Just before our new friend is put away for years, his lawyer (maybe Kevin Reddington, from five or so chapters ago) points out that no one in America—including the judge, the jury, the DA, and the court reporter—knows how strong Old Crustacean is, least of all his client, and that he cannot possibly be held responsible. Acquitted of all charges, our man sues the bar, the bartender, the Rogue brewery, and the United States government, which has to sell off a couple of tanks to pay for the damages. It might have been such a case that led the Supreme Court to rule against the Alcohol, Tobacco and Firearms law.

There's no such thing as Old Crustacean Light, nor should there be. A beer, whatever its strength, should have its own integrity. The Canadian government, uncharacteristically wisely, requires that brewers print the strength of their bottled beers on the label, so I know that my Arkell Best Bitter from Wellington in Guelph weighs in at a cautious—but tasty—4 percent, while my Trois Pistoles from Unibroue comes at me aggressively with the gusto of 9 percent. I'm grateful for this information, so it seems churlish to ask if we could make them list their ingredients on the label as well. If you're putting it in your mouth, you ought to know what's in it, no? Oddly enough, our brewing friends resist this sensible suggestion, presumably because they'd rather not tell us how much corn syrup and other beer cheapeners they're using, not to mention assorted foam-enhancing agents and the like. Canada's Food and Drug Act permits more than a hundred ingredients and chemicals and stabilizing agents and things in general in our beer, so we might start seeing much larger beer labels if they had to include all this information. Perhaps some of our brewers are afraid that consumers might be put off beer altogether if they saw what was in it. Remember that all you really need to make beer is grain, hops, yeast, and water.

So what's on tap in our pubs? For the most part, the choice is dismal, even in the places with eighteen beer taps. One might almost say *especially* in the places with eighteen beer taps. You'll see the standard imports: Guinness (served too cold), Kilkenny, Boddington's, Smithwick's, and Stella Artois (the beer cleverly designed to fool the unwitting into thinking Belgium makes dull beer so the Belgians get to keep the good stuff for themselves). Then there are the standard domestic brands: Blue, Blue Light, Carlsberg, Carlsberg Light, Foster's (it's Australian for beer, but it's made by Molson), Keith's, Moosehead, Rickard's Red. Then, for the discerning drinker, what we call the premium beers: Creemore Springs Premium Lager, Amsterdam Nut Brown, Amsterdam Natural Blonde, Upper Canada Lager, and Sleeman Cream Ale. You'll see slight variations from mainstream pub to mainstream pub, but those are your most likely choices.

There was a time not terribly long ago when we would have killed for this sort of beer selection, but we get jaded so quickly.

The international picks are not inspiring. It isn't the publicans who insist on serving the Guinness so cold; it's Guinness. Nowadays they even offer an Extra-Cold Guinness to cater to people who want to be seen drinking Guinness but really don't want any taste at all. The domestic choices range from dull to execrable, and the premium brands run the gamut from overrated to good but unsurprising.

There are no microbrewery beers on this list. (Please note that Rickard's Red is not a microbeer made by some reclusive artisan named Rickard. It's a Molson beer brewed in the same factories that produce the other stuff and marketed to seem to be a beer made by a reclusive artisan. There used to be rumours that it was Molson Export with food colouring, but I couldn't comment on anything as libellous as that.) Sleeman, which also owns and brews Upper Canada, is now a national player owned by the Japanese. Creemore is now owned by Molson. Amsterdam is a fair-sized regional brewer and has left the micro world far behind it. Amsterdam is okay, but not exciting, so over the years I've downed a lot of Creemore as my default beer. It's good beer, all right (Michael Jackson, the beer demigod, once called Creemore the best North American lager), but I wouldn't mind a bit of variety sometimes. A bartender recently said to me that it's good when the staff know your name, but it's better when they know your brand. I agreed quietly, but in fact I don't like to be that predictable. I'd like to go into an eighteen-tap bar and have to think about what I'm going to drink. Or what I'm going to drink first. That's when you know you've got a real choice: I'll start with one of those, move to one of those, and graduate to one of those.

Having done most of my drinking in Canada and England, I

lean toward ale over lager. Canadian lager has, in my lifetime, been mostly insipid and characterless. The best you can say for it is that it's cold. If it isn't cold, you're in trouble. Not that the ale has always been much better. When the Big Three—now the Big Two—did all the brewing, one sought out the oddities in their lists: Molson Stock Ale ("The Original Blue"), Toby, Labatt's IPA. The IPA was so good they had to stop making it altogether to avoid embarrassing the other brands.

In 1993, worried about losing a tiny bit of market share to the burgeoning microbreweries, Molson launched its Signature series. These were beers that were brewed by craftsmen in traditional ways, or so we were told in a series of commercials that showed real craftsmen doing authentic artisanal things, then switching to the genial, down-home Molson brewmaster making fine ale and lager. Molson was walking a very thin line in this campaign, trying to boast of making beer the proper way without coming right out and saying that everything else they made was crap.

Interestingly, the Signature beers—an ale and a lager—were fairly decent, but the people who had switched to microbrewery beers didn't switch back, and the drinkers of Golden and Canadian were unwilling to pay the slightly higher price for better beer. Before long, the commercials stopped appearing, and finally, without any fanfare, the Signature brands disappeared forever. Molson's experiment in brewing good beer had come to an end. In fact, of course, they probably sold more of the stuff than most microbreweries were selling, but that's not enough for a company as big as Molson.

The mass brewing scene in Canada is a minefield. The big brands are consumed largely by young folks, who are as fickle as all get-out.

A new advertising campaign comes along, and they're off in hot pursuit. It's all about risk. There are fortunes to be made and lost. But you take a beer like Molson Stock Ale and you're dealing with easily predictable numbers. Molson knows, almost to the bottle, how many cases of Stock Ale it's going to sell every month. The only variable is if some old fellow dies carrying his case home. They brew in smaller batches, which is less cost-efficient, and they use better ingredients, which costs a bit more. On the other hand, they never have to advertise it and there's virtually no waste. Ergo, profit.

What would I like to see in a pub? Something surprising. Lately I've seen the occasional Continental beer on tap, a Hacker-Pschorr or a Pilsner Urquell, and I'm encouraged by that. But I see none of the great English beers on draught. The handful of English beers you see here are beers I would never drink in England. And on the rare occasions the good beers turn up, they're never in their real ale form. Sometimes I see them in New York, but never here. The names of Harvey, Adnam, Taylor, and Bateman are unknown in this barren land. Recently, the good people of Fuller's have been known to ship over the occasional cask of one or more of their award-winning beers, and Ralph Morana of Caffe Volo has served it in its natural, cask-conditioned manner.

I met an American guy one evening at the Victory Café in Toronto, a fellow called Matt who has been living in Toronto a handful of years. We were drinking Cameron's Auburn Ale, a pleasant enough beer from the Toronto area. Cameron's advertising material makes the point that their president is also their brewmaster, which is certainly not the case at most breweries you could name. Matt told me he had looked forward to coming to Canada and tasting the great microbeers of our land, but that he had been disappointed. He felt that Canada's mass-market breweries were better than Anheuser-Busch, Coors, and Miller, but that our microbreweries were left in the shade by their American counterparts.

I wanted to disagree with him, but I wasn't sure I had any grounds. Most of our microbreweries are a mite timid, in that characteristic Canadian way. Nobody wants to give offence. The problem is that the market is already packed with beers that don't offend, beers that are bereft of personality. What's the point of going head-to-head with that market? And why would you go into brewing if you're just going to make another predictable beer?

If Quebec ever separates, many of Canada's most interesting beers will become imports. The brewers of Quebec put the rest of Canada to shame. The McAuslan Brewery of Montreal, founded in 1989, creates beers of an English nature, including the celebrated St-Ambroise Oatmeal Stout, perennially rated one of the country's finest beers. St-Ambroise is named for the Sulpician monk who was said to be the first brewer in New France. If his beer was as good as this, McAuslan was justified in elevating Frère Ambroise to sainthood.

The other superstar of Quebec brewing is a company called Unibroue, located in Chambly. Unibroue's inspiration is Belgian beer, and head brewer Gino Vantieghem produces a number of beers that could hold their heads up proudly in Brussels. Like their Belgian counterparts, Unibroue's beers start at 5 percent alcohol by volume and climb sharply from there. All the bottled beers are bottle-conditioned—that is, they undergo a second fermentation in the bottle—so you'll find sediment in your beer. You have the choice of pouring carefully and getting a clear glass or getting the full bottle with some cloudiness and a slightly yeastier flavour. They're all pretty heady beers, so you'll want to pour carefully in any case. And if you're having a few, don't make any serious travel plans. Unibroue was swallowed up by Sleeman in 2004, which of course has since been swallowed up by Sapporo. This has had beer lovers worried about the fate of some excellent beer, but so far our fears have not been realized, though, oddly, being taken over by an Ontario brewery has not led to greater distribution in this province.

Back in the early eighties a man named Ed McNally decided that Alberta was ready for some decent beer. Unfortunately, the Albertan authorities were not ready, and McNally had to jump through hoops to get a licence for his Big Rock Brewery. This is a story that is repeated practically everywhere beer is made: a pioneer has to go in and get laws changed to allow someone whose name isn't Molson or Labatt to set up a brewery. These days we can get Big Rock Traditional Ale in a few places in Ontario, but I'd like to see more of McNally's Extra Ale, a strong ale more easily found in the western states than in Canada. Pity.

Actually, drinking beer in Canada is
a bit like drinking beer in England
thirty years ago, in that, apart from
the brewing behemoths, most of the
interesting beer is very regional by
nature. Even within, say, Ontario,
there's a limit to how far beer can
profitably be delivered by a small brewer.

But even more significant is the
absence of free trade within Canada. I can go
to a beer store in Buffalo, New York (and all the
best beer stores in the Toronto area are in Buffalo),
and I'll find American beers from across the country,
from Vermont to California. Yet if I go to a beer or liquor store
in Toronto, it's as if Canada doesn't exist. The only beer I'll find
from the Atlantic provinces is Keith's or Moosehead, but, until
very recently, nothing from Garrison or Propeller. I'll see some
McAuslan and Unibroue beers from Quebec and some Big Rock
from Alberta, but that's it. British Columbia? Dream on. If I'm curious about what's new from the Crannog, Phillips, or Tree breweries,
I have a very long drive ahead of me.

The microbrewery movement in Canada began in British
Columbia. They had the first brewpub and the first microbrewery,
and the rest of us must bow to them for that. And they're still
brewing good beer, much of it of the west coast hoppy variety. Not
that we hear much about it in other parts of the country, for the
reasons lamented above. I just wish there were more good places to
drink it once you've made the trek to Vancouver. Maybe it's that

Vancouverites have fallen under the sway of other drugs. When I first visited Vancouver, I don't recall seeing coffee shops on every corner. Nor, by all accounts, had the cultivation of hydroponic marijuana reached the advanced state I gather it has now attained. British Columbians are either in a state of frenetic caffeine-ridden activity or blissful cannabis-generated catatonia. Given these extremes, a pint of decent craft-brewed beer hardly stands a chance, I guess.

The last time I got to Nova Scotia I was very impressed with a tiny brewery called Shippey's, which operated in the Historic Properties. It was a pleasure to sit with a glass of fine beer and look out on Halifax Harbour. My Maritime informant, Craig Pinhey, advises me that Shippey's is no more (bad news), but that its brewer, Greg Nash, moved to Garrison Brewing Company (good news) and made it a better brewery. Indeed, Garrison won four medals at the 2007 Canadian Brewing Awards, including the Beer of the Year award for its Imperial Pale Ale. Since then, I'm sad to say, Mr. Nash has left Garrison, and I have no idea what the future holds for either party. Both Garrison and Propeller have improved their facilities and are making more aventurous brews, and Kevin Keefe of the Granite Brewery is expanding as well. Craig also tells me that Tom's Little Havana has become the best pub in Halifax: "Just your style, I think." Rogue's Roost was an excellent brewpub, and apparently still is.

I live in Ontario. (Cue the abuse from all other parts of the country; when you've got that out of your system, I'll continue. There we are, thank you. Oh, sorry—you need more time? Look, go for a walk or something; I'll be here when you get back.)

There, better now? Not only do I live in Ontario, but I'm even in midtown Toronto, which makes it worse. And I'm sorry for that, but it can't be helped. If you drink beer in Toronto, or even if you're thinking of visiting us and drinking beer, you are required to pay attention to BarTowel.com, a lively website for local beer geeks established by one Cass Enright. Apart from the latest news about beer events and new, usually temporary, acquisitions at the government-operated liquor store, Bar Towel hosts an active discussion forum, which allows members of the beer-consuming community an opportunity to carp, complain, and criticize practically everybody and everything, especially one another.

We're a bit of an ungrateful lot, we suppers of ale. We want more choice, we want the world to change more quickly, we want everybody to abandon the megabreweries and embrace craft beer. And people are coming around to it, as they're coming around to real cheese, real bread, and slow food. But slowly. And until there's a critical mass of people desperate for beer that tastes good, our brewers will be nervous about turning out unusual beers and our publicans will be timid about serving them. And if a biggish city like Toronto can support only so much quality stuff, what does a smaller place do? A fairly extreme brewer in the States like, say, Dogfish Head, has a domestic market of 300 million potential drinkers. It's going to get only a very small share of that, but it's still a bunch of people. A similar brewery in Southern Ontario might have a possible market of 5 million or so. Do, as they say, the math.

But, as I keep telling the hotheads, look how far we've come. Some of the beers we once embraced seem kind of dull now and have been replaced in our affections by much tastier brews. The Granite Brewery's two cask-conditioned ales are terrific. Denison's Weissbier is stunningly good. Beers from Black Oak, Grand River, Durham, Church Key, and others are stellar.

And take a look at cask-conditioned beers, unknown in these parts a scant few years ago. The Wellington Brewery in Guelph began making British-style beers in 1985, offering them to publicans in the authentic format, but not many publicans were up to the job of handling cask-conditioned ales.

Here's the problem. It takes three kinds of people to make something like this work: brewers who are willing to make something risky; publicans who are willing to give bar space to something risky; and punters who are prepared to seek out and pay for something risky. Any two of those groups are not enough. It takes all three.

And in recent years we've seen the growth of just that sort of synergy, as the business geeks say. There still aren't many pubs selling cask ales (even some of the specialist beer joints don't), but the exposure is growing. I keep hearing customers at the Victory Café asking what that unusual hand pump is all about.

The King of Cask in Toronto is Ralph Morana, proprietor of Caffe Volo on Yonge Street. A few years ago, Bar Towel posters started reporting that an Italian restaurant was serving good beer. Ralph had discovered good beer and was going at it with the enthusiasm of a zealot. I ran into him and his wife, Aina, at the Great British Beer Festival, which he was attending to drink beer but also to pick up the equipment to operate his own beer engine for cask ale.

In 2005 Ralph held his first Cask Days, for which he challenged his brewers to produce a variety of cask-conditioned beers. His motto began as "13 brewers, 15 beers, 2 days," but as his brewers warmed to the prospect it became "15 brewers, 23 beers, 2 days." Finally, he was turning brewers down because he was out of space. By 2007, demand for this annual event was so high that all tickets for four separate sessions sold out in little more than an hour and Ralph had something like thirty-four cask ales from twenty-three breweries, including two casks flown in from Fuller's in London. There was also an excellent cheese table (Aina has become a cheese authority). Mere sainthood would seem an inadequate reward for Ralph.

Ralph Morana is a publican who challenged Ontario brewers to lift their game and challenged Toronto beer lovers to come and get it. They did and we did. Most of the brewers were there, as were a number of other publicans and a packed house full of happy punters. I get a warm feeling all over just thinking about it.

We have a lot more choice than we used to (trust me: I was there), even in Ontario, a province not celebrated for fun, or even the pursuit of fun. Older readers may recall the song we heard far too often in 1967: "A place to stand, a place to grow (Ontari-ari-ari-o!)," with a tune by Dolores Claman, who also wrote the *Hockey Night in Canada* theme. This might make her even more annoying in your eyes. The lyrics by Richard Morris had a lot about trees and snow and lakes and free winds, but nothing about decent pubs and good, honest beer. At the time, you weren't allowed to stand in an Ontario beverage room; I've long thought that "Give us a place to stand" was a cry for the liberalization of Ontario's drinking laws, but I'm guessing I'm mistaken again.

But there is now an association called Ontario Craft Brewers, which exists to promote beer from, well, as you'd expect, twenty-nine craft brewers in Ontario. I know some of these guys (and the ones I know, I'm afraid, are all guys), and they're all guys you'd be happy to have a beer with. Some of these guys make the beer, answer the phone, deliver the beer, and restrain themselves from violence when a beer geek complains that it's not hoppy enough. Many of them are making all the beer they have capacity for and sell pretty much all the beer they make. All they need now is to figure out how to make a living doing it.

But is my American friend Matt right? Do Canada's microbrews lack the excitement of their American counterparts? If you take Quebec out of the equation, then I have to concede, albeit grudgingly. We certainly lack the variety. I can't remember who brewed the hazelnut-flavoured beer I drank in Chicago in the late nineties, but I do recall going back for more. Imagine if I actually liked hazelnuts. That said, Ralph's 2007 Cask Days included a herbal mild, an oak chip–steeped Irish stout, an English dark ale with vanilla beans, two pumpkin ales, and a peppermint stout.

The character of the western hops used by most American breweries lends a flowery note to a lot of American beers, which some people like and others don't. The Americans have clearly been more adventurous than we have, experimenting with fruits and spices and a wider range of styles than we see in this country. They have some advantages, of course, with lower alcohol taxes, cheaper gas, and a lot more thirsty people. They also—although this varies from state to state, county to county—tend to have more relaxed legislation governing the making and selling of beer. Canada still hasn't overcome laws that prevented beer from being sold in a province in which the brewery did not operate. Moosehead Lager was a famous Canadian beer in the United States long before Canadians outside New Brunswick ever got to taste it. My first Moosehead was in Detroit. (And my last, I hope I'm right in saying.)

Compared to Anheuser-Busch, practically everything's a microbrewery, but many of the American beers we may think of as micros are rather bigger than that: Anchor, the San Francisco brewery rescued by Fritz Maytag of the appliance family; the Boston Beer Company, creator of the Sam Adams line of beers; Sierra Nevada of Chico, California, among others

All right, I'll take questions. Yes, you in the back? What's in my barf ridge? I don't . . . Oh, my beer fridge. Let's have a gander. (Man walks downstairs, says "Hmmm" a couple of times, returns to his desk.) Three bottles of Mill Street Tankhouse Ale, a Black Oak Pale Ale, a Wellington Imperial Russian Stout, and one of Perry Mason's (yes, it is his name) 2005 Tsarina Katarina Imperial Stout, all from Ontario. From the United States: a Stone Ruination IPA, a Southern Tier IPA, a 2007 Anchor Merry Christmas Ale, a Victory Old Horizontal barley wine, a Great Divide Titan IPA, Sierra Nevada's Harvest Ale and Anniversary Ale, and a Dogfish Head grand slam of Chicory Stout, Raison D'Etre, 90 Minute Imperial IPA, and Midas Touch (an attempt to replicate the traces of beer found in King Midas's tomb). From Britain: a Belhaven Twisted Thistle IPA and a Fuller's 1845. And from Belgium: a Mort Subite Framboise, Cantillon's Kriek and Organic Gueuze, a Hanssens Oude Gueuze, a Rochefort 8, a Rodenbach Grand Cru, a Saison Dupont, and from Liefmans a Goudenband and a Framboise. I'd forgotten I had a couple of those; they might not see out the night. (Most of those beers on my list were purchased in Buffalo, needless to say.)

Okay, I hear you ask, but what's my favourite beer? It's the sort of question a beer enthusiast does all he or she can to avoid. One day it's going to be a nutty stout, next day it might be a tart cherry-flavoured lambic, and the day after that it'll be a big, strong ale. But if the beer Nazis made me pick one beer to drink day in and day out for the rest of my life (and promised to make unlimited supplies available, fresh and impeccably maintained), I'd probably hem and haw a bit.

As noted above, there are more fine beers produced locally, and only a fool would say that imports are necessarily better than the domestic product, whatever country he lives in (though there are some exceptional countries that make almost nothing of note). And the Belgians and Americans make some truly magnificent beers. But, for everyday drinking pleasure, I'd probably wind up narrowing down my selection to English draught beers, and then to Fuller's London Pride and Timothy Taylor Landlord. They're both delicious ales, both have been Champion Beer of England (Landlord has won a record four times), and any serious—or even frivolous—drinker would smile with unrestrained pleasure to be handed a pint of either. I've certainly had a good deal more Fuller's, only because the Timothy Taylor is hard to find.

Once, on holiday in Dorset a few years back, we found our-selves in a very good pub with a fine selection of beers. I came back from the bar and handed Anne a pint of ale. She sipped it casually and said something not dissimilar to, "Wow, what is this?" It was Timothy Taylor Landlord, and a week or so later it was named Beer of the Year at the Great British Beer Festival. Wow, indeed. So, with respect to Fuller's—not to mention Adnam, Harvey's, Uley, Young, Black Sheep, Bateman, Hop Back, and all my other English favourites—make mine a pint of Landlord.

# If You Ever Go
# Across the Sea to Ireland

There is an Irish pub in Chicago . . . No, let's start again. There's a place in Chicago called Fado—although the Irish probably pronounce it in some way the rest of us will never be able to replicate—that purports to be an Irish pub. Actually, it purports to be six Irish pubs in one. In which case, it is probably the first Irish pub—or the first six Irish pubs—to offer valet parking. I have been to this alleged pub, because nothing is too good for you, dear reader, and I encourage you to think of a multi-storey quaint Irish pub filled with possibly authentic bric-a-brac and a soundtrack of deafening American pop music. Jaysus, the missus and me exclaimed, let's get the Fado out of here. And so we did.

The Irish have become very sexy in recent years—well, perhaps not the actual Irish themselves, but the larger concept of Irishness—and there has been a lot of money to be made from the notion of Celtic wonderfulness. And rightly so, up to a point. Ireland truly is a grand place. I once spent a week in the West Cork town of Baltimore without ever finding out when closing time was, which was possibly due to the story we heard that the local Garda—the one local policeman—was retiring and perhaps didn't want any outstanding charges hanging over him.

I like Ireland, and nowadays so does everybody. Across England, perfectly decent pubs have been transformed into mock Irish pubs for the duration of the Celtic craze, presumably to be changed into German bierstuben or Greek tavernas or whatever becomes sexy once we all tire of celebrating the craic in fake Irish pubs. New York, of course, has long had Irish bars, frequently staffed by young Irish bartenders who have usually arrived that morning from Limerick. What New York Irish bars are going to do for staff now that young Irish people are all far too busy toiling in Silicon Bog and becoming dot-com millionaires I cannot imagine.

The irony of fake Irish pubs is that the true Irish pub is even less easy to typecast than the English pub. Many of them double as grocery shops, newsagents, or undertakers. Outside Dublin, many Irish pubs look like someone's living room, and they sometimes are. In Limerick, with my friend Kieran Simpson—a native of that city—we were sat in a pub in his old neighbourhood when he exclaimed that we were sitting in what had once been the bedroom of an old boyhood friend.

Irish pubs are now global, to the point that some clever economist developed what came to be called the Irish Pub Index of Economic Development, which is now apparently used by hedge fund johnnies. The gist of this idea is that the number of Irish pubs in a (presumably non-Irish) city reflects the wealth of that city. Apparently, it's a more reliable economic indicator than anything the World Bank or any of those experts has to offer. Luxembourg, it is said, has the most Irish pubs per capita of any European city, and is also the wealthiest city on the continent. You might be able to win bets with this.

And so to Fionn MacCool's, a large Irish pub on Toronto's Esplanade. Once an ignored, almost shunned, part of town, the area behind the Sony Centre (as we must now call what used to be the O'Keefe Centre, then the Hummingbird Centre) has a number of old warehouses that now accommodate entertainment concepts. It began, I suppose, with the Old Spaghetti Factory, a lively barn of a place that brought "fun" to Italian food. Like spaghetti had always been deadly serious before.

Fionn MacCool was, by all accounts, a legendary Irish hero and father of Ossian, but I suspect that the pub's name was chosen because it sounded, like, MacCool, you know? I am told that on St. Patrick's Day the young people start lining up in early afternoon for the evening's festivities, and good luck to them.

On one of the other 364 days of the drinking year, Fionn MacCool's was a little quieter, with only the insistent, if discreet, boompety-boom of the pop music without which no one would know if they were having fun. Otherwise, it was just the craic, or what other people call conversation. The drinkers closest to me were talking about golf. Does that constitute craic, I wonder? I noticed that when the Celtic rage began (and before he got sent up for eight years for doing in Jez Quigley), *Coronation Street's* Jim McDonald started talking about the craic a lot more than he formerly had, as in "What's the craic, boys?" Also, before Celtomania, we used to spell it crack, but that might have confused the users of the cocaine by-product. If Washington mayor Marion Barry had been smarter, he would have claimed that it wasn't the crack cocaine he was after but a bit of the old traditional Irish craic. He might have got away with it too. Like O.J. Simpson, he could have vowed to spend the rest of his natural days seeking out the perpetrators of craic.

I wasn't hungry, but I did take a gander at Fionn MacCool's menu, because I know my readers care about these things. It boasted Celtic Fare like Bunratty Castle Caesar and Roast Beef Panini, presumably just like Granny used to make, saints preserve her. Sometimes it's a blessing not to be hungry. I did notice that the female servers were wearing those pert little tartan skirts, which I'm guessing are meant to suggest step dancing rather than private-school girls. No doubt once the live music gets going in the evening the servers break into a sort of Riverdance routine. Unfortunately, I couldn't stick around for that.

There's no shortage of Irish-style pubs for the Toronto drinker, though most of them—it must be said—are not so much Irish as "Irishish." The James Joyce on Bloor Street West used to be a hamburger joint, but now it bears the proud Irish name of the writer who left Ireland as soon as possible and never went back. The sign outside carries the promise TRADITIONAL IRISH PUB—but I tried in vain to buy a pound of potatoes and the *Cork Examiner*. The only concession to Irish decor comes from a number of promotional items for assorted Irish beers, but there's a kind of Irish honesty to that as well. Real Irish pubs are very much as you find them, and if they have illustrations of Killarney on the walls, you can bet they're pitching themselves at the tourist market.

Scruffy Murphy's, up on Eglinton Avenue East, seemed a nice enough place, with a lively bartender and a number of contented regulars, but the design spoke to me of the faux-genteel English suburban pub of the sixties, not of anything you'd see in Ireland. And I wonder how Irish people feel about this perpetual scruffy thing. In his fine book *McCarthy's Bar*, Pete McCarthy writes of seeing in Killarney a hotel bar called Scruffies, which employed a couple of large men to guarantee that no one scruffy got in.

This whole Irish pub business is presumably based on the notion that no one drinks like the Irish. What's interesting about the Irish and drinking is that they settled pretty quickly on what they liked. There's whiskey or three kinds of beer: stout (usually Guinness), ale (inevitably Smithwicks), or lager (which was traditionally Harp). If you were close enough to Cork, you might get Murphy's or Beamish's Stout, by way of variety. Harp—the national lager—has given way to the global Carlsberg, and indeed if you find a drop of Harp in Ireland today it'll probably have been brewed in Canada. That's how mad the world is. Long the only ale choice in Ireland, Smithwicks has in recent years been joined by the likes of Kilkenny and Caffrey's, fine traditional ales of the 1990s, shot through and through with traditional Irish nitrogen to make it sm-o-o-o-o-o-th. There was, for a time, even a Canadian guy brewing new and interesting beers in Dublin, practically in the shadow of Guinness's St. James's Gate Brewery, and living to tell the tale. (He was last seen in Newfoundland.)

Bordering dangerously on being an Irish Concept pub is Dora Keogh, on the Danforth. Opened in 1997, Dora Keogh is a handsome room with that vaguely Georgian look of the Dublin pub, all high ceilings and right angles, but with the hard, unupholstered furnishings of the country pub. What it also had for me was a surprise.

I didn't expect to meet Fionn MacCool at his eponymous pub, or James Joyce at his, and I'm not sure I'd have wanted to encounter Scruffy Murphy. But there really is a Dora Keogh. She's an attractive redhead. I met her just standing there at the bar, so she was. She told me her mother was very proud of her, having her name on a pub and all, and quite rightly too. I'm sure the Duke of York's mother is similarly proud of her son whenever she comes to town.

Not being an investigative journalist, I never quite established Ms. Keogh's role in the operation, but I had a nice chat with John Maxwell, who actually owns the place. Maxwell—who also owns Allen's, next door—is a slight former New Yorker who has been in the hospitality lark since 1964 and clearly knows what he's about. Running places like Dora Keogh, he says, is about "passion," and he wants his bars to be not only places where someone like me might be comfortable, but also places his deceased father and elderly mother could be proud of. It was getting a bit late when he mentioned that he hoped he died before I did, because he didn't want to be in this business when the likes of me were no longer around, which was rather sweet. Maxwell does not cater particularly to young people, which is a blessed change in this youth-crazed marketplace. Looking worriedly around, he confides that he doesn't even particularly like young people, referring darkly to "feral youth," an expression I liked so much I made a point of writing it down on a paper napkin.

One of the key things in today's hospitality biz is catering to groups, and Maxwell has thought of this in his design for Dora Keogh. The pub has a self-contained snug with its own access to the bar, which is a nice touch, and a kitchen in the back that can be booked for a group of eight to fourteen for a private dinner. And private it is, with your own Irish server and plates stacked high with roast lamb (it's usually been the lamb when I've been there, though there are other choices) and vegetables and two kinds of potatoes. It's like having a big family dinner without actually having any of your family there. You can decide for yourself whether that's a good thing.

If it's authenticity you're looking for, the toilets at Dora Keogh are labelled *Fir* and *Mna*, a couple of Gaelic words not in common use in these parts. My wife got caught by this confusing dilemma in Limerick once, so we've learned the hard way which is which. You might think that F and M might correspond to Female and Male, and *Mna* is clearly an anagram of Man, but you'd be barking up the wrong tree in this case. I wonder how often in an average evening the staff are called upon to usher non-Irish drinkers to the correct loo.

John Maxwell opened another Irish pub downtown some years ago, but it is now owned by Pat and Anne Quinn, who are as Irish as can be. P.J. O'Brien's is a handsome room, the bartender wears a long white coat, and the food is good. Typically of an Irish pub, the beer selection isn't packed with surprises.

Probably the most Irish pub in Toronto is McVeigh's, at Church and Richmond. It's been there forever, or at least since 1961—which, in the drinking life of this town, is pretty close to forever. It's a dark room, with the odd Irish mural you can't see terribly well in the gloom. I was served one day by Mr. McVeigh himself, a gentleman of a certain age. I felt sheepish asking for a receipt—listen, when you write this sort of book, you keep receipts—and I got the feeling I was the first customer who had asked for a receipt in his forty years on the premises. I got the receipt, but he didn't talk to me again.

Luckily for me, other people did. Fair enough, they weren't Irish, but we can't all be. They were at least Scottish, which is not far off. Patrick was over from Motherwell to visit family, particularly his uncle Jimmy, who hadn't been well. Jimmy looked pretty good that afternoon, with teeth that occurred enthusiastically if sporadically. Patrick is a train engineer back in Scotland. Although he acknowledges that driving a train is a lifetime dream for some people, it's just a job for him. What he likes is something going wrong, something he can fix. That's the job satisfaction for him. I wasn't sure if I'd want to be on Patrick's train, knowing that the guy up front was aching for some misadventure.

When I arrived, the conversation—craic, if you like—was about Billy Connolly, the Scottish comedian who apparently drops into McVeigh's whenever he's in town. Mr. McVeigh was hearing no ill of Billy Connolly, whom he described as a "humble man" who could, after all, drink anywhere at all. Jimmy and Patrick acknowledged that he could indeed drink anywhere at all, but felt nonetheless that he had forgotten his roots. As Patrick said, "His personal remarks about Scotland do not sit well with me, Mr. McVeigh." There was unlikely to be a lasting consensus about Billy Connolly, and Mr. McVeigh went off to serve other customers.

We were joined by Ian, another expatriate Scot, who likes darts and jokes. Patrick told a variation on a Superman joke of which I am very fond, and Ian followed with the story of a long-married couple, the wife of which finds her husband drinking intoxicating beverages early one morning, clearly in an upset state. When asked what the matter was, he reminded her of the time she was sixteen and pregnant and her father had told him that if he didn't marry her, he (the father) would have him (the husband) charged with rape and that he'd serve twenty years for it. "You're not still bothered about that," the wife says. He shakes his head sadly. "I'd have been a free man today," he says.

We had a good laugh over that, and Jimmy's teeth—well, you couldn't take your eyes off them—were much in evidence. Ian followed with the other Superman joke I know, also well received, and Jimmy joined in with a Newfie joke. Patrick made it clear that he didn't appreciate racist humour, but Jimmy would not be gainsaid.

Patrick told me that, as a Celt, he cared most about family—he was not in Canada to see the sights—and having a sociable time in a pub. The English, he said, looking at me a bit accusingly, I thought, were more concerned with their houses. I'd have stayed longer, but I had to go and see a guy about getting a conservatory added on to the library in the west wing.

I forgot to go to the gents' and check the place for condom machines. In Ireland in the summer of 1993, I recall seeing such a public convenience in a public convenience and thinking what a revolutionary sight this was in a country that not long before had banned any sort of birth control, even for respectable married couples. There was no mistaking this machine for anything else. It used strong words like "ribbed" that had not been seen in Ireland since St. Patrick drove the snakes out. No doubt some people were made uneasy by this blatant display of the prophylactic arts, and a few days later in a different pub I saw a plain white metal box attached to the wall of a corridor leading to the facilities. It gave no hint of its contents, but a small sign beside a coin-collecting device asked the passerby to insert two one-punt coins. Perhaps it dispensed condoms, perhaps small tokens of absolution. There was no evidence that the machine issued receipts, so I didn't take the chance. And now I'll never know.

If you ever go across the sea to Ireland—and if you haven't, you should—it's important to keep your wits about you. Certainly it seemed to be the case that the barmen of West Cork greeted their customers with the words "Y'all right?" Which, to a polite Canadian, deserved the response, "Yes, we're fine, thank you very much." Whereupon the barman turned away with a quizzical look and went back to preparing the perfect pint of stout for the fellow down the bar. What we slowly discovered was that "Y'all right?" was a short form for "Do you need a beverage of some sort, given that you've come all this way, so?" It still seemed presumptuous to respond straightaway with a drink order, so we settled upon a Canadian compromise: "Yes, thank you, we're fine altogether except for the lack of a drink, so perhaps we could trouble you for a couple of pints of Smithwicks, thank you very much."

# I Am Canadian
# (But I Also Like the Taste of Beer)

The people of Canada have a pretty mixed bag of drinking choices. A lot of it is luck. Denizens of the Atlantic provinces are rightly praised for their lively drinking scenes, with the possible exception of Prince Edward Island, which was technically dry for practically half of the twentieth century. (Fortunately, they grow a lot of potatoes, which can be turned into a robust intoxicating beverage.) And nowadays, especially in Nova Scotia, they even have some very decent beers to drink.

And then there's Ottawa. I've never had much luck in Ottawa, though the last time I was there I found a pub called the Manx, which seemed a great improvement. In early 1990 I was in Ottawa for a spot of business, and late in the day I found myself downtown, thirsty and with an hour or so to kill before I headed for the airport. I was aware of the reputation Canada's capital city had enjoyed vis-à-vis fun back in the past, but I was confident that things had changed. I walked into one bar, and about five minutes later I walked into a second bar. Friends, I heard the words "last call" spoken in earnest twice before seven o'clock. I was never so glad to get on a plane bound for Toronto, which suddenly took on the aura of at least Gomorrah, if not Sodom itself.

People who know Ottawa tell me I was just in the wrong place. (It was worse than that: I was in two wrong places.) I am assured that there are pubs in Ottawa that stay open as late as eight or nine, and if I'd had a couple more hours before my flight I might have found them.

Here I am perpetuating the notion that Ottawa is a dull place. When my friend John Jackson was an undergraduate at Carleton in the mid-sixties, I went to visit him. This was, of course, still the era when you were required to be significantly older than we were to drink in Ontario, so we—like practically everyone else in Ottawa— drove to Hull to raise a little heck. In Hull—it being Quebec and all—all that was required was that you had the cash to pay for your beer. That was exactly the kind of ID I was carrying, and I had a wonderful time, though my recollections are admittedly fuzzy. I vaguely remember singing along with the Beatles' "Act Naturally," a popular hit of the time.

Those were my first several beers in Quebec, but not my last. The Québécois, of course, laughed at us Ontario types and our absurd drinking laws. Our bars closed at midnight, if they opened at all. We were repressed; they had joie de vivre. In Ontario, joie de vivre was an indecency. Practising joie de vivre in the presence of minors constituted a major violation of the Criminal Code. When I got to Montreal, I was, like, wow, as the young people say. They had joie de vivre and style as well, which put them two up on us. It was at Expo 67 that I first got drunk twice in one day. It was my overenthusiastic attempt at joie de vivre, if not necessarily style. Mind you, it's easier when you're young, isn't it? You recover from lunchtime and off you go again. Those were the days.

For all their superiority, it must be said that there were a couple of questionable traits to Québécois drinking life. I mean, what was with these tavernes, for Pete's sake? They seemed to close at midnight, just like our bars, and they didn't allow women. I think drinking with women is fun. In the early eighties I tried to take my wife to Toe Blake's celebrated bar in Montreal. Nothing doing. That chromosomal thing was a problem. Did she just sit back and take it? Of course she didn't. She went shopping, leaving me to drink at Toe Blake's. What a woman.

Although it was the extremes of the country—Vancouver (Horseshoe Bay and Granville Island Brewing) and Halifax (the Granite Brewery)—that got good beer going in Canada, it was Quebec that took it to new heights. Unibroue even makes a 6.5 percent beer for the St. Hubert chicken restaurant chain in Quebec; there's nothing like that at Swiss Chalet.

As you cross this great country, you encounter all sorts of interesting local customs. In the summer of 1972 ("Didn't it rain, children? Lord, didn't it rain!") I was hitchhiking in an easterly direction across the Prairies, whenever the rain let up enough. The rains of 1972 verged on the biblical. This particular day was a cool one, with a sinister wind at my back. I was on the outskirts of a town called Lloydminster that straddles the Alberta-Saskatchewan border. I might have been there a day or two at this point. Every hour or two a car passed me by, pointedly speeding up as it approached.

Suddenly a Volkswagen van stopped. The pulse rates of hitchhikers of that era were known to accelerate at the sight of Volkswagen vans, such was the hitchhiker-pickup quotient of their drivers. Unfortunately, this particular Volkswagen van was on the other side of the Trans-Canada Highway and pointed in a westerly direction, but it was nice to see that vehicles in the Prairies actually did have brakes. I hadn't seen much evidence of any slowing-down mechanism so far. Anyway, what the hell, maybe I'd go back westward. Eastward was no great shakes.

You know what they say about Canada, that it's a very small population strung out (and I do mean strung out) across a huge land mass. So we should not be surprised to run into our friends in a place like Lloydminster. I'd never been to Lloydminster before, so I was surprised. I wouldn't be now. Yes, the Volkswagen van carried three old pals from Toronto who were driving west to Victoria.

We decided to call it a day, travel-wise, and we booked into a campsite somewhere in the greater Lloydminster area. Settled in, someone proposed a beer. By a narrow four-nil vote, the measure was passed, so we made our way downtown and found a bar. I don't remember what it was called—possibly the Palace or the Paramount or something like that—but we walked toward it with resolution. These were four young fellows who liked a drink. As we arrived, we saw a sign on the front door, a sign that stopped us big-city guys in our tracks. The sign read: PLEASE USE DOOR. Our bravado left us. What kind of place was this that drinkers had to be informed to use the door? How did they usually get in? Would we look like a pack of wussy eastern bastards if we didn't come bursting through the wall like everybody else? At the risk of standing out, we used the door. And we were just fine. Funny what you remember about a place.

I stand by my theory that you can learn a lot by hanging out in bars. I got drunk in Dawson City one evening with a guy who was AWOL from the Dempster Highway building project. It took them twenty years to build a 450-mile road through country that didn't take to road building, and every now and then one of the guys would get a little stir-crazy and hitch a ride into town for the purpose of sitting in a bar and getting shit-faced. I, for one, would not blame such a man.

This particular man was well into the process by the time we fell into conversation, and it became clear to me that this was a man with a dream. The dream in question was to build and operate a sort of lodge somewhere on the Dempster Highway, catering to the many travellers who would surely make their way up that gravel road once it finally got done. What he needed—and this was where I came in—was a partner. Was I such a person? Frankly, I didn't think so. My lack of capital was matched by the absence of any relevant lodge-building skills, and an aversion to remoteness and an antipathy to blackflies and mosquitoes wouldn't have helped much either.

I hope his dream came true, and that enough people drive up the Dempster Highway to make such a dream viable. If you haven't been up there, I can tell you—having done it all via the hitch-hiker's thumb—that it's a hell of a long way from practically any-where. To get to the Alaska Highway, you need to get to the top of British Columbia. Then you drive a very long way north-by-northwest into the Yukon. When you get to Whitehorse, you leave the Alaska Highway and head farther north again. Quite some time later, when you've gone farther north than most North Americans of European origins ever go, you're at the very beginning of the Dempster Highway. No wonder people get thirsty.

As a resident of Toronto, I am a bit reluctant to write about Vancouver. Torontonians and Vancouverites don't get along very well, even though it is only the regular infusion of Torontonians that keeps Vancouver from losing its status as a city. Scratch a Vancouverite—not that it's a practice I advocate—and chances are you'll find an expatriate Hogtowner. Like religious converts, these newfound westerners are the most wild-eyed believers in the mythology, the most likely to promulgate the idea that Vancouverites routinely go skiing in the morning and sailing in the afternoon. There is no recorded instance of anyone actually skiing and sailing in the same day, but the belief that it can be done holds a lot of people in thrall. In fact, Vancouver's traffic nowadays makes such a practice unlikely, and in any case Vancouverites don't have the time for it, having to work like Torontonians to make the payments on their leaky condos.

What the residents of these two cities have in common is an irrational smugness, an utterly unfounded belief that they are living in the best city in the world. We grasp desperately at warm comments from visitors, keen to be noticed by outsiders. The best of all is when we get acknowledged by international studies that rank the cities of the world. These surveys invariably come up with widely divergent results, and sometimes Toronto does well and other times it's Vancouver.

Early in 2001 we learned—and don't think there wasn't a bit of teeth-gnashing in Toronto—that Vancouver had been named the best city in the world for "quality of life," and for the second year running. (We'd have been more upset in Toronto by this news had we not been preoccupied by the impending arrival of the International Olympic Committee, coming to judge our Olympic bid. We were desperate to host the 2008 Games, if only to annoy the hell out of Vancouver. The joke was on us, of course. We got nothing, and Vancouver got the 2010 Winter Games, though they had something of an advantage, what with actual mountains and all.)

The point, of course, is who's conducting these studies. If the Campaign for Real Ale names Vancouver the best city in the world, I'll be on the next plane. If Mick Jagger or John Updike or Jan Morris tells me Vancouver's the best city in the world, I'll at least pay attention. You should know that Vancouver was actually tied for first with that most exciting of cities, Zurich, justifiably famous for its discreet banks and not a lot else.

Who decreed that Vancouver is the best city in the world? Does the name William M. Mercer mean anything to you? William M. Mercer, it turns out, is not so much a guy as a bunch of guys. A bunch of accountants and actuaries, if you must know. (No wonder they also liked Zurich.) Frankly, being named the best city in the world by a firm of accountants and actuaries is not the highest possible recommendation. I doubt they're losing sleep in Paris and New York. (And if you like, you can label this sour grapes from a resident of Toronto—tied for nineteenth with Montreal.)

And it's happened again. I have at hand a printout from the BBC website with the news that, once again, Vancouver is the best place on the planet to live, with Toronto back in ninth spot. And who determined this? The Economist Intelligence Unit, those arbiters of fun and a diverse drinking life.

What I remember about drinking in Vancouver the first time I got there, back in 1971, was the funny licensing hours. Someone explained to me that bars could be open for any consecutive twelve hours. The obvious twelve hours were noon to midnight, but I remember a Granville Street bar that opened at 9 a.m. It had to close early, sure enough, but it got a bustling breakfast crowd. And I mean bustling.

British Columbia was the vanguard of interesting drinking in Canada. It had the first microbrewery and the first brewpub. By all that's right and decent, it should be far and away the pub capital of the country. So where did it all go wrong?

I went to a booksellers' conference in Vancouver in the latter half of the nineties. I looked forward to it, I really did. It had been a decade since I had been out to lotus land, and I eagerly anticipated supping some of these celebrated BC microbeers in the new pubs that had surely popped up all over town. I got into Vancouver in mid-afternoon, made my way to my hotel, and at about five o'clock strolled out for a refreshing pint. I was centrally located, so I foresaw no difficulties. At 7:30 I sat down and celebrated the first of the day. I seemed to have covered miles. I had a couple of pints, listened to an alarmingly redneck conversation going on at the next two barstools, and got a definite whiff from the barkeep that the place was about to close. When I say whiff, I mean he said it was going to close, which might have been his way of getting me out of there before the guys next to me noticed I had a beard. It was still light. I went to a nearby liquor store, bought a six-pack of decent beer, and headed back to my hotel room.

While I was in Vancouver, I tried to find out where I had gone wrong. I kept meeting local residents and I made a point of asking them where they drank. Many of them weren't sure, which I took as a bad sign. A number of them had to think about it for a long time, which wasn't encouraging either. The handful who were able to come up with a name all came up with the same name. Where else would that happen? Ask twenty New Yorkers where they drink and you'll get at least eighteen different answers. Ask twenty Torontonians and you'll get at least ten. The only bar Vancouverites could think of was the Yaletown Brewing Company, and that was probably because many of the people I talked to were in the book trade and the conference had held its opening night party there.

(All right, to be fair to British Columbia—and it goes against the grain, I have to say—I observe that Stephen Beaumont, in his most recent edition of *The Great Canadian Beer Guide*, awarded three or more stars to seventy-five beers across Canada. Of these, twenty-four were BC beers, compared to twenty-one Quebec beers and a mere twenty Ontario brews—the Prairies muster six and the Atlantic provinces four, by the way—so I'll shut up now. Well, actually, I probably won't. If BC has all those fine beers, it's all the more criminal that you can't find anywhere to drink them.)

Coffee you can get in Vancouver. This was just before designer java hit Toronto in a huge way, and it was a novelty to see coffee shops on every corner. But novelty takes you only so far. My theory is that Vancouverites are so laid-back that only caffeine keeps them from sinking into total torpor. As a hypertense central Canadian, I need the calming effect of the depressants to simmer me down a bit. You can keep your stimulants, thanks very much; the last thing I want is to stay awake through all of this.

It turns out, of course, that there were at least two decent places to drink in Vancouver. A friend at the same conference went to a ballgame at the old Nat Bailey Stadium and reported a fine environment and a choice of decent beers, which is more than can be said for attending a game in Toronto. Mind you, Vancouver's baseball team has since left town (and gone to Zurich, for all I know), so I can't vouch for anything of the sort now.

My beer discovery was even less predictable. By a quirk of scheduling for which I can't take the credit, I had a free day before the conference began. This was a booksellers' conference, so I had some bookstores I needed to see, one of which was the University of British Columbia Bookstore, a considerable bus ride from downtown. I had a good look around and contemplated my next move. It was the sort of day the rest of Canada assumes never happens in Vancouver. We hope it doesn't, anyway, unless we're actually there. It was warm and sunny and perfect in every way. An afternoon at the beach seemed called for. Sadly, I hadn't thought to bring swimwear; happily, I happened to know that the beach nearest to the UBC Bookstore had no dress code. More of an undress code, if the truth be told.

I had been to Wreck Beach—Canada's most celebrated (and possibly first) nude beach—half a lifetime before, on just such a day, and I made the long trek down the hill in a fury of nostalgia. I hadn't kept my boyish figure, but I thought it unlikely I'd run into anyone I knew, and I didn't. Though heaven knows the place was busy. Wreck Beach had retained its raffish, sixties feel, but it had changed a bit. For all I know, the people were the same people I had seen a quarter-century before, or possibly their sons and daughters, but there were no easy government grants or anything of the sort any more to sustain today's residents.

The people of Wreck Beach had to support themselves now, and they seemed to be doing so excellently. There was hardly anything you couldn't get or have done at Wreck Beach. You could rent a hammock or an umbrella, have your hair braided (not likely in my case—see author photo), get a henna tattoo, or buy freshly baked goods. A young man in a fez and a change belt flogged Turkish coffee, an admirable young woman sold shot glasses of Southern Comfort, and several vendors did the rounds with coolers full of beer. It wasn't clear to me how all this commercial activity was being carried out. I assume some Mr. Big was bringing the beer in by boat, but it was always cold and there were some palatable microbrewery beers available.

For all my obnoxious Toronto-centric prejudices, I had to admit that, with a snow-capped peak off in the distance across the water, I couldn't think of any watering hole back home that offered such a view or such a relaxed dress code. (I've often wondered, for instance, if you'd be served at a Shoeless Joe's franchise if you turned up barefoot.) Where Vancouverites drink in bad weather I still don't know, and it was another five years before I got to the Yaletown Brewing Company.

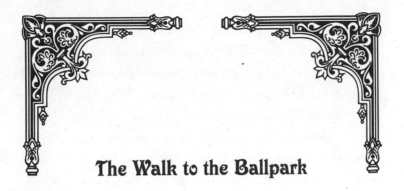

# The Walk to the Ballpark

**I** hate to go on about how primitive drinking conditions in Toronto used to be, but it is a recorded fact that in 1977 there was one major-league ballpark on the planet that catered expressly to abstainers, and it existed in Toronto. Not that it was much of a ballpark. Tacked onto one corner of a concrete football stadium, the baseball part of Exhibition Stadium was a cold, windy spot where most of the seats faced somewhere other than the makeshift baseball diamond. Frankly, sitting on a cold metal seat, absorbing a cold wind off Lake Ontario, did not always make one cry out for an equally cold beer.

Still, it was the principle of the thing. There is something in human nature that hates to be told we're not allowed to do something. Our political leaders in this part of the world have never liked to trust us—the drinking public—to do the right thing. Older readers may recall a series of television ads in the eighties that were designed to encourage us to behave sensibly. "You are your own liquor control board," we were told. Hallelujah, we Ontario drinkers cried. Power to the people! Alas, we learned the next day that the Liquor Control Board of Ontario had not been disbanded. The government had not, in fact, relinquished control over us and our nasty habits. It wanted merely to get us to do its work for it. We were our own liquor control boards but, just in case we didn't manage it properly, we could be overruled by the government.

It was that kind of thinking that determined that beer in the ballpark was a bad idea. People might actually drink it, and then where would we be? (Not long afterwards the province of Ontario permitted bars to sell drinks cheap at certain times of day. Happy hour proved to be wildly popular, so it was quickly banned. It would have been fine had people not spoiled everything by taking advantage of it.) Eventually, of course, the forces of progress took over and beer drinking was allowed at Exhibition Stadium. It turned out to be all right, needless to say, because the beer was so bad and so expensive that only a fool or a lawyer would want or could afford to abuse it.

The idea, then as now, is to have a drink before you get there. That was definitely the case in 1977. Watching the early Blue Jays sober was a mug's game. One July day I decided to go see the locals in action. I knew that a little advance drinking was needed, so I started at noon. I would have started earlier, but noon was when the bars opened in 1977. I like to walk, so I went to a second bar, then a third. I know for a fact that the Blue Jays were playing the Minnesota Twins, but don't ask me who won.

Thus the Walk to the Ballpark was born. Drinking alone from noon until game time could be interpreted as evidence of a drinking problem. Or possibly a social problem. In any case, the Walk to the Ballpark needed more people. Terry Shoffner, a genial graphic artist from Arkansas, was persuaded that this combination of walking and drinking was a good thing, and he and I constituted the second Walk, with sporadic help from friends along the way. I don't even remember who was playing.

With the passing years the Walk to the Ballpark grew in popularity. Otherwise responsible people—some of them with mortgages, then cellphones and eventually BlackBerries—took the day off work to tour the bars and pubs of Toronto in congenial company. And, at least in the early years, we actually went to the baseball game. We went to baseball games even though the Blue Jays were becoming more competitive and more of a draw. We sat way out beyond the right field fence one year and couldn't see the ball, sitting in seats that faced practically nothing but an empty football field. I vaguely recall being cranky that year. I recall it because people regularly remind me of it. I believe it was the last time the Walk to the Ballpark went to the ballpark.

The following year—this might have been about 1982—Walk day was cold and raw. We sat in the old Palace Hotel at King and Strachan, the last bar before the ballpark, and the younger, keener participants were beginning to whine about it being close to game time. I wouldn't have sent a dog out on an evening like that, let alone fifteen or twenty people who had been drinking for more than seven hours, but tradition seemed to call for some sort of action.

Just then a vision appeared in the form of a man called Bill Martin, who does something in advertising. I believe it's something creative, if that's possible. Bill had missed the Walk so far, but suddenly here he was, standing in the doorway with our waiter, a man in the mandatory white shirt and black pants of the day and holding a tray filled with glasses of beer. As the proprietor of the Walk to the Ballpark, I had to make a snap decision. We stayed exactly where we were. Hypothermia, after all, is a dreadful thing, and I didn't like to think of the legal repercussions of sending people off to a freezing cold ballpark. In any case, since then the ballpark has been more a metaphor than a destination.

The year of 1982 might also have been the one that featured The Only Punch Ever Thrown (to Date) on the Walk to the Ballpark. We discuss it to this day. Was Russ Hughes justified in introducing his fist to the general region of Jon Comerford's nose? History has yet to pass its definitive judgement. What we know is this: Russ Hughes was sitting in a chair, while Jon Comerford stood behind him, behaving in what Russ saw as an annoying manner. I believe I'm right in reporting that the words "Cut it out" had escaped Russ's lips at least once, which is possibly fair warning. (Pashley's Seventh Rule of Drinking: if a big fellow known to have played a lot of hockey tells you to cut it out, consider revising your behaviour.) Did young Comerford cut it out? He did not. Finally—and I have run this episode through on my internal VCR a hundred times—Russ, without leaving his seat, turned around and delivered a blow to the Comerford beak. This caught us all by surprise, but especially Jon Comerford. The power with which Russ connected from a seated position, his back to the punchee, was impressive.

Apart from the Hughes-Comerford dust-up, the Walk has been violence-free, if you discount the occasional food fight. Well, okay, there was the time that one Michael Lee was removed from the Wheat Sheaf for defending the honour of his sister-in-law, but no punches were thrown. What is far more likely is the spectacle of people falling in love, or something that might pass for it. Sometimes this attraction is ill-fated, if not altogether inappropriate, but it is not completely unknown for people to get lucky on the Walk. (See the chapter on Drinking and Sex, with particular reference to the possible debilitating effects of large quantities of beer.)

It seems extraordinary now, but in our early days we used to get to some thirteen bars and still get to the ball game by 7:30. Nowadays, we get to eight bars over about thirteen hours, which is thoroughly manageable. (Mind you, we're drinking out of much larger glasses today.) It's all about pacing, eating whenever possible, and taking on water as if one were running a marathon. Even so, we still see the occasional sprinter on the Walk, and the consequences are usually dire. In the early eighties a young man called Ray—I won't embarrass him by mentioning his last name (Chong)—was regularly the first drinker with an empty glass at each stop, egging the rest of us on to drink up and keep moving. At the El Mocambo he stood up, informed us that we were crazy, and vanished. Two years later he attempted to do the Walk on a diet of nothing but Black Russians. This was a spectacularly bad idea, though he did get two bars farther this time, not crashing out until the Rex Hotel. I wonder what Ray's up to these days.

It's a mixed group of people who make up the Walk to the Ballpark. We usually have at least two lawyers (when what we really need is doctors), some riff-raff from the book trade, a philosopher, an importer of hi-fi equipment (or whatever we call it these days), the odd teacher, an actor, an accountant, a comedian, a landscape architect, a historian, one or two guys who seem to do things with computers, several people who work in offices, and a growing number of people who may or may not have jobs of any sort. The beauty of the Walk is that the constant change of venue encourages one to consort with different people along the way. If you stay long enough, you'll talk to everybody.

The Walk has traditionally taken in a variety of watering holes, from really quite nice places to joints you'd go to only if you'd been drinking for several hours and had parted with your critical faculties. It helped, of course, to be in a group of people.

Some of the old places have shut down, which helped us make the decision to move to an all-good-beer Walk. Most of this is spent on the world's longest street, Yonge Street. Well, it certainly seems like Canada's longest street while you're doing it, especially when you get a long haul between micturition facilities. The good news is that, apart from part of the stretch between the Bow and Arrow and the Rebel House, it's pretty much downhill. You can't put a price on that.

If you're in Toronto and you'd like to put yourself to the test, here's what usually passes for a route these days (times are massively approximate):

11 a.m.: Duke of Kent, 2315 Yonge St., north of Eglinton.

Noon: Granite Brewery, Mount Pleasant and Eglinton. Have lunch.

2:07 p.m.: The Bow and Arrow, 1594 Yonge, north of Davisville.

3:14 p.m.: The Rebel House, 1068 Yonge, near Rosedale Subway.

4:16 p.m.: Caffe Volo, 587 Yonge, at Dundonald. Getting serious now.

6:17 p.m.: beerbistro, 18 King Street East. Eat again.

8:38 p.m.: C'est What, 67 Front Street, near Church.

By this time there's really nowhere nearby to walk to, so we usually hop in cabs and go to Kilgour's Bar Meets Grill (509 Bloor Street West) around 11 p.m. Well, when I say we hop in cabs, I don't mean Walk stalwart Igor Martin. Igor walks everywhere. He walks from his home in central Etobicoke to the Walk. He walks from C'est What to Kilgour's. Sometimes he walks home afterwards. One year he even walked the route ahead of time so he'd know how much time we needed. I like that dedication.

Anyway, Kilgour's is the sort of place that tends not to look down on people who have been drinking for twelve hours. That's important.

Somewhere after midnight, when people are beginning to look just a bit ropey, I set the remaining drunkards on their way, send them home to their beds (or the beds of others, where appropriate—or inappropriate). It's over.

So if you're on Yonge Street some year in June (or occasionally September) and you see a pub crawl lurching by, it might be us. Introduce yourself.

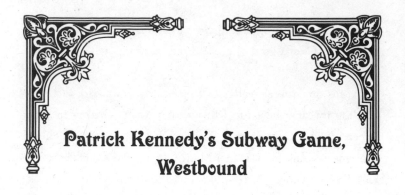

# Patrick Kennedy's Subway Game, Westbound

Having given Patrick's Subway Game a try, I went back to the source to try to fine-tune the rules. It turned out there weren't many rules, which is jake with me. Patrick insists on the sacredness of using the subway to get to your destination, and that's as it should be, though he has no objection to using any means at your disposal to get away from it. In some suburban locations you might find yourself far from the subway by the time you find your beer.

Upon reflection, Patrick did manage to come up with another rule: the Subway Game must be played solo. And I think he's right. The point of the game, after all, is to discover new parts of town and take a look at what goes on there. If you're with friends or loved ones, you're just going to talk about whatever you usually talk about and forget about where you are. It's human nature. I'm sorry, but these are the rules. I didn't make them up. If you've got a problem with the rules, talk to Patrick.

As an avid supporter of Brighton and Hove Albion Football Club, I'm used to games having a competitive thrust. (All right, not all that competitive a thrust, and I'm used to losing more than winning.) I began thinking of ways to make the Subway Game conform to traditional gamesmanship. Player A, say, could send Player B off to one subway station, while Player A would go to a destination of Player B's choosing, points awarded on the basis of how quickly beer is found, possibly with points added or subtracted according to the quality of the beer found. Or the whole city could be handicapped by a knowledgeable drinker and transit user, with points awarded on the basis of difficulty. So finding a beer at Yonge and Eglinton would be worth maybe half a point—anyone who can't find a beer at Yonge and Eglinton shouldn't be playing this game—while High Park station might be worth ten points.

Patrick listened to this sort of talk with the patience of a man who has worked a long time in the hospitality industry, a man who has heard everything at least once. He's not a big sports guy, Patrick, and I could see he didn't think much of my idle speculation. The Subway Game would remain as it was. I don't see it becoming an Olympic sport any time soon.

Having sampled the east end, I turned my attention to the west. Unlike most people, I actually know of about three pubs in Etobicoke, so there were a couple of subway stops at the western end of the line that were disqualified on the basis of prior knowledge. There was no question that I could find drinking spots as far west as Dufferin, and I didn't feel up to trying Lansdowne. When he first told me about the Subway Game, Patrick mentioned getting off at Lansdowne once and finding a place that seemed to be filled with drug dealers who didn't much like the cut of Patrick's jib. I've always found Patrick's jib to be well tailored, and I thought that if these guys didn't like his jib they probably wouldn't like mine either, so I decided to save Lansdowne for another day. (It turns out that there actually is a very good bar right there, but that's another story.)

I could vaguely picture the area of the Jane Street subway station but couldn't imagine any drinking spots around it. I didn't know of anything between Bert and Ernie's at Runnymede and the Whatsit and Firkin just short of Islington. Right, then, Jane Street it would be, knowing I could always walk east to Runnymede in a pinch.

Jane Street, I guess, marks the western limits of Bloor West Village, a cheery, upmarket stretch of boutiques and specialty food stores. I know that part of town only because I've had to visit a funeral home along there a couple of times. What the living did in Bloor West Village was anybody's guess. I do know that, heading home from one of these funerals, my wife and I had the devil of a time finding a drink. So Jane Street seemed as if it might represent the sort of challenge the Subway Game thrives on.

I don't care where you're coming from, it's a long ride to Jane Street, and I emerged from the subway with the sort of thirst you associate with the genre of cartoon that usually features two guys crawling through a desert looking for an oasis. It takes a minute or so to hit Bloor Street from the station, but as soon as you get there the first thing you see across the street is a place called Bryden's, very obviously a licensed establishment. I was beginning to wonder if there was any challenge to the Subway Game at all.

Once again, I strolled about the neighbourhood to see if there were any alternatives to Bryden's. What I found was Billy Bob's Bistro and Saloon. Now, I like the ring of "saloon." This town can boast of lots of neo-quasi-English pubs and more sports bars than I care to think about, but saloons are thin on the ground. P.J. Clarke's on Third Avenue in New York is a saloon. Billy Bob's, from where I stood, did not look like a saloon. So I went back to Bryden's.

Bryden's was a bit upmarket, with couches and armchairs for those who like to lounge while they drink. I headed for the bar toward the back of the place and cast my jaundiced eye along the row of beer taps. The choice was noticeably lager-heavy, I couldn't help noticing, the only ales being imports of the "smooth" variety. Here I go again about smooth. This smooth business is a mite tiresome, I have to say. You take what might once have been a decent enough beer, then you shoot it full of nitrogen. This gives it that "smooth" quality and simultaneously removes any discernable flavour. It is important to remember that, although lots of people drink beer, not many people actually like the taste of beer, so brewers are constantly finding new ways to take the taste out. Remember when "dry" beers became all the rage? Remember the proud "no aftertaste" boast? Why would you . . . oh, don't get me started.

I had a pint of Tetley's bitter, ruined by the patented Smooth-Flow process, and studied the menu. With delight I spotted the entry for Caeser Salad. Very few menus spell "Caesar" right, but this was a new twist. Usually it's the first syllable they get wrong. It quite perked me up, it did. Peter Kilgour, co-proprietor of Kilgour's Bar Meets Grill, historically spells it "Ceaser," which I enjoy more than I can say. There's a theory that places that misspell it usually actually make it better, but I don't know if that's true.

The music that day was a bit more eclectic than most piped-in pub music. It featured some jazz with even some recognizable people such as Ella Fitzgerald, not the annoying generic lite jazz you get sometimes. Still, Bryden's was not going to hold me for long. I headed east, keen to see if the trendy Village had gained a drinking spot. And it had. A Dark Horse—not, please note, *The* Dark Horse—was a new pub from the Empire Freehouse chain. It was bright and modern and offered Muskoka Cream Ale on tap, which you don't see every day. With a pint of Muskoka in front of me, I was well placed to listen to the piped-in music, which was Adult Contemporary Crap Pop. (On a recent revisit I drank Tankhouse Ale and chatted with an off-duty beerslinger named Simon, brother of a late barkeep called Claire I mention elsewhere. The bartender on this occasion was a woman who addressed me as "Honey," which I admit to liking. I'm not sure what George Orwell would think.)

Soon I was off again. Across from Bert and Ernie's (now the Swan and Firkin) at Runnymede was a new spot called the Yellow Griffin, which seemed to serve only imports on tap for some reason. The people of Bloor West Village have my sympathy. The area used to be dry by law, but the publicans of this town have not come storming in.

Walking along, I came to the High Park subway station. Here is a challenge for the Subway Game. Not much in the way of intoxicating beverages around here. The resourceful might step into the park and walk briskly for ten minutes due south, knowing the Grenadier Restaurant was there. Let me advise you to preserve your strength. If you want to drink in High Park, you'd better bring something with you. (My revisit to these parts revealed a new place called MacKenzies. I can't vouch for it, but the Subway Game just got a lot easier.)

East of the Keele Street station there was finally something to celebrate. Whelan's Gate was a splendid pub, sporting plaques by the bar commending both the bar's record of selling Guinness and keeping it in good condition. The Gate is a small pub with an upstairs bar that opens in the evening. The piped-in music is of the Irish variety, ranging from the "Whack Fol the Daddy-Oh" variety to U2. I know it was U2 because I looked at the CD case.

Whelan's Gate filled me with that warm sense of contentment that a good pub can generate, and the locals who cheerfully filled the room seemed happy as clams. Once again, Patrick Kennedy's Subway Game had delivered me indirectly to a fine local watering hole.

And, as one of those only-in-Canada moments, if you continue walking eastward from Whelan's, you'll see, across the street, a store called Goalie Heaven. Yes, it appears to be a store that sells stuff of use to hockey goalies, and not much else. Where else could you make a living doing that?

# The Belgians, Beer, and God

One morning in the late sixties, I found myself strolling through the streets of Antwerp. That's what the late sixties were like: somebody handed you a dodgy-looking cigarette, and the next thing you knew you were in Antwerp.

As I strolled, I came upon a young man attempting to push his car along a major Antwerp street, holding up a fair chunk of Antwerp traffic in the process. Having been raised to help out in times of need, and estimating that the car in question couldn't weigh much more than a standard toaster with tires, I pitched in. In no time we had this fellow's car safely stowed on a side street and out of harm's way.

Astonished, the young man asked where I was from, quickly adding that no Belgian would have helped him out. Obviously, no Belgian had helped him out, so he was right on that score. Keep that in mind next time your car breaks down in Antwerp. Look for a Canadian.

Clearly the young man was eternally in my debt. I can't stress

enough how effusive he was about this. Belgians must really be a
mingy bunch of bastards if one small act of consideration can turn
into a deed of Mother Teresa-esque proportions. Would I accept a
beer or two as an expression of Belgian gratitude? Well, of course I
would. Belgium might be one of those countries in which rejection
of hospitality is a hanging offence. You can't be too careful.

By a stroke of luck, we were perilously close to a watering hole
dear to the heart of my new friend and his fellow students, and in
we went. I was introduced around the table as the sort of saint that
was seldom seen these days on the streets of Antwerp, and beer
was quickly ordered. There I remained for some hours, as I vaguely
recall.

All these years later, I wish I could tell you that we opened with
a couple of interesting lambics—possibly a gueuze and a kriek—
and followed with a characteristic spicy white beer, from which we
moved on to some of Belgium's great red and brown beers, making
our way through one or two strong ales before settling in with a
choice of the great Trappist beers. But I cannot. I was young and
stupid, and beer was beer. I have no idea what I was drinking, just
as I had no idea at the time that I was in the most interesting brewing country in the world.

Belgium is, in some ways, the Canada of Europe: an uneasily
bilingual country widely regarded as intensely, almost aggressively,
boring. This is partly because the French have routinely stolen all
the best Belgian stuff and claimed it as their own. Jacques Brel, for
instance. What we call french fries are actually Belgian, and are
served with mayonnaise or other tasty toppings in the streets of any
Belgian town. But the French have yet to produce many beers that

could crack the Belgian top twenty. (Admittedly the French have made the odd decent wine, which confirms my theory that countries can produce good beer or good wine, but seldom both. There are, sadly, countries that do neither.)

Most people, if pressed to name a Belgian beer, would eventually come up with Stella Artois, just about the only boring beer in the country. This is not surprising: the most famous beers of most countries tend to be the dullest. Think of Budweiser or Heineken, for starters. For years, the most famous beer of England was Watney's Red Barrel, which says it all. But get beyond Stella Artois, and you're into a stunning range of beers of all sorts and colours.

Belgium hasn't yet become as sexy as Ireland, but one can drink Belgian beer in many jurisdictions these days without having to push anybody's car. The trend may have begun in London with a chain of restaurants called Belgo that must account for hundreds of thousands of mussels a week. But I'm not aware that there's any sort of Belgian Pub Index of Economic Development.

There used to be a very nice place called Café Brussel in Toronto, but it's gone now. It was, strictly speaking, a restaurant, and didn't hold much with people coming in just for a drink. They let me in for that purpose once. Perhaps they recognized me from Antwerp. (There may be something to this karma thing, after all.)

There's no trouble getting a drink at the Esplanade Bier Markt, down on Concept Bar Parkway. Owned by Prime Pubs Inc., proprietors of Fionn MacCool's next door, the Bier Markt is a big, labyrinthine place where mussels go to die. I'm more impressed by the Bier Markt than by its mock-Irish neighbour. The design actually turns a barn-like room into manageable, almost intimate, areas, and there's a nice long bar for someone who wants to have a beer or two without murdering any molluscs.

Most of the Belgian beer you'll find in Ontario, particularly on tap, comes from one brewery: InBev, formerly Interbrew. Here in Canada, only a few beer people had even heard of this Belgian brewery, makers of the unnecessary Stella Artois, until they snaffled up Labatt in 1995. Just gobbled them down like a dish of mussels, they did. Labatt was just one of their many acquisitions on the way to becoming the biggest brewing megacorporation on planet Earth. (As I write, there is recurring speculation that InBev will merge with Anheuser-Busch, the number two brewer in the world, to create the biggest thing in the history of human development, which will make me nostalgic for the old lumpy beer of ancient Mesopotamia.)

In buying Labatt, of course, InBev unwittingly became the principal owners of the Toronto Blue Jays. Now, I'm keen on Belgium, but no one suggests that they know beans about baseball, and the InBev years will not be remembered warmly by many people. Remember that Flemish third baseman they had for a spell? Rubbish. And that relief pitcher? A complete Walloon. More important, did the InBev years mean an improvement in the quality of beer served down at the Big White Thing? They did not. Could you get proper Belgian frites served with a big dollop of garlic-flavoured mayonnaise? You could not. (Nowadays, of course, the Blue Jays are owned by Ted Rogers, whose company sporadically provides me with cable service. I doubt the beer's any better.)

InBev owns more breweries than you could wave a glass at. Stella, Beck's, Labatt, Brahma, Staropramen, and Boddington, not to mention a few brews even the keener elements of the beer community might scratch their heads about: Klinskoye, Chernigivske, Ožujsko, and Antarctica. I'm guessing that last one is designed to be drunk very cold.

This huge corporate thing started with a stable of Belgian beers: Stella, Hoegaarden, Leffe, and Belle-Vue. Stella is a celebrated global lager, advertising for which succeeds in suggesting that it dates from 1366, when in fact it first appeared in 1926. It has been promoted as "reassuringly expensive" and a cut above the rest, though the *Brighton and Hove Argus* in November 2007 reported that pubs across the southern English county of Sussex were removing Stella because of acts of violence perpetrated by its consumers. Said one publican, "My customers are loopy enough without any help." The beer is also known in some quarters by the attractive nickname "wife-beater," though I'm sure there's absolutely no cause for that. I am also reliably informed that the best-known drag queen in Blackpool operates under the name Stella Artois.

Anyway, if you go to Belgium, and you should, you'll find plenty to drink besides Stella. The Belgians treat beer with reverence, pouring it expertly into glasses designed for each brewery. The really good beer bars of the country stock an amazing array of glassware, ready for any request. Part of the pleasure of Belgian beer drinking is visual.

Then there's the beer itself. Nowhere else in Europe, or possibly anywhere, offers the variety of beer you'll find in Belgium. Sure, they have a few wimpy Euro-lagers, but you're under no obligation to sample them. Pretty much everything else is worthy of your attention. They tend to begin at about 5 percent alcohol by volume and head north from there. If you think the end of the world has arrived, it might be simply the impact of the Belgian beer. Cease intake at once, seek out a couple of Aspirin, and lie down for a good long spell.

If you'd like to see brewing at its weirdest—and why wouldn't you?—you need to get to Brussels and visit the Cantillon brewery. They do tours. But get there before some EU functionary decides that this is no sane way of brewing and shuts the brewery down for being nuts or unsanitary.

I don't know about unsanitary, but it's certainly nuts. Cantillon makes beers called lambic, a style that goes back to the early days of beer. They boil up their mixture of barley and wheat, using very old hops because they want the preservative effect of hops without the hop bitterness, and leave it to sit in a shallow vat upstairs in a room with open windows and louvred vents. And there it sits while any number of different wild yeasts in the air drift by and start fermenting the beer. Madness! Can you imagine Molson's brewmasters doing anything as crazy as that? For most brewers, the idea of corrupting your yeast source would keep them awake at night. It is reckoned that as many as eighty-six different strains of yeast might come into play.

If you've ever visited a brewery, you will probably have been impressed with the cleanliness of the place. You don't want anything infecting your beer. Dark and dusty Cantillon bars its employees from disturbing spiderwebs, as they might harbour useful microflora that give the beer its character. Spiders also kill flies, and you don't want flies.

Once it has begun to ferment, the beer is placed in wooden barrels and left there for, oh, maybe a year. A year?! Are these people loopy? The resulting beer is flat and sour and can be seen being merrily consumed in any number of Breugel paintings. Most lambic today is used to make either gueuze or a fruit-flavoured beer, usually with cherries or raspberries but also with apricots and other fruit. Gueuze is the result of blending at least two, and often three or more, lambics: a young one and older ones, say, a one-year-old and a three-year-old. Gueuze is a wonderful beer that, for many people, just doesn't taste like beer. Except, of course, that it does; it just doesn't taste like most beer. Now it is no longer flat, but very bubbly. There is still some sourness, but it's dry like a dry champagne. It's the beer that most closely resembles champagne. It's tart and refreshing, but keep an open mind. Be warned: the last time my wife tasted a gueuze, she looked at me and said, "You *like* that??"

Incidentally, if you're from Ontario, don't mention it at the Cantillon brewery. Any beer sold in Ontario has to be approved by the Liquor Control Board of Ontario labs. It's good for us, all right? In 2004 an attempt was made to get several of Cantillon's excellent beers into Ontario, but their kriek was rejected. Kriek is made, in the best of all worlds, and certainly at Cantillon, by dumping whole cherries into a bunch of lambic and leaving them to engage. Eventually, all that is left of the cherries is their pits, which are removed.

The problem, according to the LCBO, is that the cherry pits were ever there at all, because, as you're probably aware, cherry pits contain a trace element of cyanide. And our saviours at the LCBO are not about to approve for public consumption anything with a known poison. At last word, whole cherries are still available at most grocery stores in this province, but for God's sake don't swallow the pits. Many Belgians succeed in living to a decent age despite being poisoned by their brewers, but we Ontarians aren't nearly as tough.

Now Cantillon has sworn off Ontario forever, and if you say the name of that province at the brewery you will be a figure of contempt. Just a warning. And if you want the beer in Ontario, cross a border.

So go to Brussels, but go other places as well. Belgium is a small country with good train service. Bruges, Ghent, and Antwerp (say hello for me) are easily within reach. Hell, go anywhere. You can't miss. The people are friendly, the food is terrific, and the Dutch-speaking Belgians tend to speak excellent English. (And they're much happier to speak English than French, Belgium being not entirely cheerfully bilingual. It was effectively without a functioning government for more than six months in 2007 because the Flemings and the Walloons were at constitutional loggerheads. I'd stick to discussing beer if I were you.)

Perhaps the saddest fact of modern Belgian life is that fewer monks are active in brewing strong Belgian beer than at any time within the last eight or nine centuries. There's something very appealing about the thought of monks doing God's work, whether it's brewing beer or making odd liqueurs. Saint Bridget (born AD 439) is reported to have transformed water into beer for the benefit of the unhappy lepers she was administering to. We should all get such nursing care. And sixth-century Irish-born Saint Columbanus exercised the power of prayer to double his supply of bread and beer while toiling among the heathens of Germania. Neither of these saints became the patron saint of brewers and brewing, an honour that fell to one Gambrinus, about whom we know unfortunately little.

It's very Catholic, this pro-alcohol line. Having said that, of course, I recall the accounts of Pope John Paul II's first triumphant visit home to his native Poland. Addressing a crowd of a million souls, he berated his fellow Poles for their excessive drinking. According to the newspaper reports, his audience responded spontaneously by crying out at once, "We swear we will be teetotallers!" I've always been suspicious of this story. Any time you read about a crowd crying out as one, it's always people speaking a foreign language (unless it's a stadium full of English football supporters). And it's usually reported by an English-speaking journalist. I don't know how you say "We swear we will be teetotallers!" in Polish. Perhaps it's a well-known catchphrase that comes naturally to Poles, though I doubt it. In any case, I doubt that the annual intake of alcohol has seriously diminished since that moment of delirium. Poland, after all, is the only country I know of that has a Beer Lovers' Party represented in its government.

Although the Anglicans are generally pretty good on the subject of the demon drink, you don't hear about Anglican monks operating breweries and making perilously strong ales. Mind you, for many years my parents' Anglican church in Etobicoke, of all places, held an annual pub night in the church basement, though the beer fell short of

Trappist standards. (Most beers do.) And there's a Cornish pub called the Seven Stars in Falmouth, England, whose licensee is the Rev. Barrington-Bennett, with whom I once had a pleasant chat about Bill Bryson. I've never talked religion with Bill, but I suspect he'd like the Seven Stars. The Rev. Barrington-Bennett certainly liked Bill Bryson.

No, it's the Protestants—and when it comes to drinking, the Anglicans are definitely not Protestant—who rail against drinking. And it all seems so arbitrary. As Housman writes, "And malt does more than Milton can / To justify God's ways to man." Some years ago, Anne and I attended a Presbyterian wedding. It was not Presbyterian simply in the sense that the bride and groom were both Presbyterians, which they were, or even in the sense that the bride and groom were both Presbyterian clergypersons, which they were. No, practically everybody in the room was a Presbyterian clergyperson, or was married to one.

We had been warned ahead of time that drink would not be forthcoming at this wedding, and we were grateful for the tipoff. Fair enough, we're open-minded people who can adjust to different cultures. Our friends—the aforementioned b. and g.—were not teetotallers themselves, and have, in fact, attended the Walk to the Ballpark, which comes up somewhere else in this book. What rankled, however, were the repeated references throughout the service—and there had to have been at least three or four such references—to the wedding feast at Cana. You'll recall the story, in which the founder of Christianity saved a wedding party at which the wine had run out by transforming a vat of water into wine. And not just any wine, either, but clearly a grand cru from a fine château.

Don't wedding-feast-at-Cana me, I thought to myself. "Any chance of lightning striking twice?" I asked my wife. "Don't torture yourself," she replied. The bartender at the Duke of Gloucester very likely never saw two such thirsty faces as he did later that afternoon.

The anti-booze activists of the church tend to waffle a bit when you bring up the wedding feast at Cana. It's a metaphor for something else, they might say, or they come up with biblical quotes to justify their stance, most of which come from that Saint Paul chap, as far as I can figure out. Look, I'm sure Saint Paul was a decent fellow and good to his mother, but he was not a barrel of fun. Old Miseryguts—as I'm sure his former friends called him after his conversion—was against practically everything that makes this vale of tears at all palatable. You will look in vain for a joke of any sort in either of the Epistles to the Corinthians, and the Thessalonians don't get off much lighter.

I picture a couple of Thessalonians running into each other in town. What's happening? says Thessalonian One. Just had a letter, says Thessalonian Two. Oh, says Thessalonian One, who from? Paul, says Thessalonian Two, and it's addressed to all of us. The fellow who used to be Saul? inquires Thessalonian One. That's the fellow, says Thessalonian Two. What's he on about? asks Thessalonian One. This and that, replies Thessalonian Two. Oh, and you'd better put that beer down. Especially if it's ever been in contact with cherry pits.

(Oddly enough, particularly given the important role beer has played in human history, there is no reference to beer in the Bible. Not in the King James version, at any rate. The New International version, on the other hand, offers no fewer than nine beer entries, all in the Old Testament and all appearing in verses where the King James version uses the words "strong drink." Take Proverbs 20. In it King James says, "Wine is a mocker, strong drink is raging," while the NIV prefers "Wine is a mocker and beer a brawler." Or Proverbs 31: "Give strong drink unto him that is ready to perish, and wine unto those that be of heavy hearts" (KJV); "Give beer to those who are perishing, wine to those who are in anguish" (NIV).

Interesting, that. Most of us don't think of beer as "strong drink." I'm told there's a John Ford movie in which a character is told he can't have a beer because there's no drinking allowed on election day. The man moans to the bartender, "Hell, just give me a beer. Beer ain't drinkin'!" But, when you think of it, what other strong drink did our biblical friends have? I don't think the Israelites had the benefits of distillation, so most of what we would consider strong drink today would not have been available to them. I just thought I'd bring it up.

For that matter, while I'm still in parentheses here, there is another theory that all those Old Testament references to wine are the product of inadequate translation, that in fact they were far more likely to have been drinking beer. Now I really must get out of these brackets and into something more comfortable.)

And it's not just the Judeo-Christians. A few years ago I was in an Afghani restaurant and found myself having a look at the bottled beer selection behind the bar. There was a label I didn't recognize. "Is that an Afghani beer?" I naively asked the barkeep. "No sir," he replied, "if you make beer in Afghanistan they kill you."

I used to work with an Iranian who came into my office one day looking for advice. Quite honestly, more people offer me unsolicited advice than seek it from me, so I put on my best Ann Landers face and vowed to do my best for the poor wretch who had been reduced to seeking me out. He had, he said, a problem with kidney stones. Ah yes, I said, nodding sympathetically but not sure how I could help. His doctor, it seemed, had called for plenty of fluids, but especially beer. Nothing would help like beer. A good Muslim, Ala had never bought beer before; what should he buy? I was happy to help, but I couldn't help thinking that if he'd been brought up Catholic, he probably would never have suffered from kidney stones in the first place. Not that I'd say that in public, of course.

The last word on divinity and alcohol belongs to Benjamin Franklin, though I'd not be surprised if he'd been drinking when he said it: "Beer is living proof that God loves us and wants us to be happy."

# Mind the Gap:
# The Subway Game in London

It stands to reason that a city with a bigger subway system offers more scope for players of Patrick Kennedy's Subway Game, and they don't come a lot bigger than the London Underground. That said, it should be noted that much of the Underground—once you leave central London—is in fact Overground, so not strictly speaking in keeping with the spirit of the game. (The same applies to the New York subway, which is elevated over much of Queens and Brooklyn.)

The real difficulty in playing the Subway Game in London is, in fact, the London Underground itself. There's a lot to be said for the Tube: those dizzyingly long escalator rides, the racy lingerie ads, the cute rounded trains built to fit the cute rounded tunnels, the recorded exhortations to Mind the Gap, that distinctive London Underground smell. I love it all. Unfortunately, no money—public or private—has been spent on the system since about the time of the Crimean War, so it's inclined to be falling apart.

On one of my visits to London, I resolved to see if Patrick's game travelled well, and I picked up my London Transport one-day Travelcard for zones 1 and 2, determined to find out. And, of course, I have to admit to lying to you in the last paragraph. Money has been spent on the Tube, most of it by the long-suffering user of the system. But in recent years an extension to the Jubilee Line was built to take workers to the newly developed Docklands area and tourists to the Millennium Dome in Greenwich. Apparently, some of the new stations on this line are quite impressive. Unfortunately, I have to take their word for it.

I had decided to have a look at the Canada Water tube station in Rotherhithe, which had a nice ring to it. Would I find an ancient dock workers' pub or something modern for whoever now works in Rotherhithe? I took the Northern Line down to Waterloo and followed the signs to the Jubilee Line, stopping only when I heard the announcement that it was shut down until further notice. I read the next day that Prime Minister Tony Blair had also been inconvenienced that day while attempting a morale-boosting visit to the wildly unsuccessful Dome. Part of the boost to morale—though possibly not for him—was to be a Tube ride. Presumably, the sight of the prime minister waving cheerfully as he entered the Underground station would lift the hearts of the working masses. Sadly, the Jubilee Line—in its democratic way—was working for neither the prime minister nor me that day.

Thinking quickly, I changed my plans. Checking the map, I determined that the farthest I could go on my Zone 1–2 ticket was North Acton, so I took the Northern Line back to Tottenham Court Road, then transferred to the Central Line westbound. It worked.

Well, it worked inasmuch as I got to North Acton. Somewhere around White City the Central Line emerges into the daylight, and you get a very good view of Wormwood Scrubs, the venerable prison with the excellent name. This is the highlight of the trip. At North Acton the train is in daylight but sunk in a sort of trench. Unable to see anything, I decided that the fundamental rules of the Subway Game had not been violated.

The North Acton station is not the most prepossessing of sights. There are ramps leading left and right, the only directional indications being signs for buses that promise to take you away from North Acton. I picked right—as opposed to left, not wrong—and came out on what was a very good impression of a superhighway. North Acton appeared to be something that got in the way of motorists and caused them to slow down, though not much. Most of the traffic took the form of very large trucks, or lorries, as they say there.

I may have been the first tourist North Acton has ever seen, or at least the first tourist who wasn't utterly lost, who had gone there on purpose. There's a BBC building in North Acton and an Elizabeth Arden building. There is something called the Victoria Industrial Estate, which has probably won some sort of award from the British Tourist Authority for being the part of England least like a quaint Cotswold village. There's a sandwich bar and a caff, and most important there is the Castle. This is not a castle in the sense of Edinburgh Castle or Leeds Castle or any castle you may have heard of. It is a pub, and a fairly big pub too, with a kind of fifties design to it.

What made my heart soar was the discovery that the Castle was owned by Fuller, Smith and Turner, the great brewery of west

London. In the first twenty-three years of the Campaign for Real Ale's Champion Beer of Britain competition, Fuller's beers won five times. I am more than partial to Fuller's beers. I love Fuller's beers. There, I've said it. After my adventure south of the Thames, it was 11:30 a.m. when I arrived at the Castle, apparently the first customer of the day. I took my pint of London Pride to a table and listened to the Christmas fare on the sound system, to a backbeat of massive great lorries thundering by outside. If you've ever been to England at Christmas, you will be familiar with the roughly four popular Christmas songs that get played over and over in pubs and shops. There's that Band-Aid song of some years ago, there's one by Paul the Beatle, one by John the Beatle, and one by a band called Slade, apparently called "Merry Christmas Everybody." It was the last that was playing as I sat down. I knew the others would not be far behind.

Another customer came in shortly thereafter, only he turned out to be someone looking for work. The next real customers appeared at 12:15, around the time I was leaving. They may have been there for the Food of the World menu, which ambitiously features the cuisine of England, Scotland, the USA, Mexico, Thailand, and

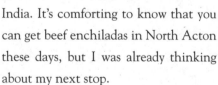

India. It's comforting to know that you can get beef enchiladas in North Acton these days, but I was already thinking about my next stop.

If you're ever in London and want to cheat at the Subway Game, take the District Line to Parsons Green. Turn right from the station and walk about half a block until you see the White Horse. Parsons Green used to be west of Chelsea, but Chelsea continues to expand westward as property values rise, and Parsons Green is very much part of Chelsea now. Every time I go to the White Horse, its clientele gets posher and the lunch gets fancier. The beer, however, persists in being wonderful. The 1994 Champion Beer of Britain was a hard-to-find Suffolk ale called Adnam's Extra, which very quickly ran out on the first day of the Great British Beer Festival. That afternoon, I took a bus down to the White Horse, where they offered Adnam's Extra on tap as a matter of course. At that point, the pub accounted for some 60 percent of the output of that fine beer (it has since been discontinued by the brewery). That's the sort of pub the White Horse is. There's no music in the White Horse, unless you count the snippets of popular classics that announce incoming cellphone calls.

From there I decided to try the east end and settled on Bethnal Green as a destination. Once again, the challenge lay in actually getting there. The sign in the Tube station suggested one destination, the train that eventually appeared suggested somewhere else, and they were both wrong. After what seemed a lifetime, I got to Mile End station. I was close to Bethnal Green—only one stop away on a different line—but I was by now desperate to get off the system altogether, so I changed my plan. Mile End was my new destination.

The area around Mile End station featured another very busy road, but—unlike North Acton—there were actually people around on foot. I was a long way from Chelsea, I quickly discovered. The locals were not as successful as the denizens of the White Horse, and they—or probably their parents, for their accents were mostly London—were once from somewhere else. Again, you don't get a big tourist trade around Mile End.

Getting off the Underground, you have no sense of direction, and the dim light of London in December gives you little hint of where the sun might be setting. In one direction seemed to lie acres of housing estates. There was something that looked like a prison, with loads of barbed wire keeping people either out or in, and I encountered two pubs that offered no real ale at all that I could see. I'm pickier than Patrick Kennedy about what I drink, so I held on for a pub called the Matter of Time—formerly the Flautist and Firkin—and a pint of Greene King IPA. Novelist Graham Greene was a member of the Greene brewing family, and indeed the brewery issued a celebratory bottled beer to mark the writer's eightieth birthday.

The Matter of Time was an okay pub, and I was happy to have found it (not that it was difficult; it was right there on the very busy road), but it was starting to get dark. Actually, it had been starting to get dark since about noon, which was roughly when it had stopped getting light. The days are short in England in December, especially when it's overcast, which is most of the time. The sun— if "sun" isn't too strong a word for it—rises in the south and then, not long afterwards, sets in the south. But I knew that Anne's day of shopping would be drawing to a close and that I needed to get home to be husbandly. So I caught the Tube—reasonably uneventfully this time—and went to Euston station for a quick Christmas ale at the excellent Head of Steam, a railway-themed pub. An interesting day, all in all, and good value for my Travelcard (£3.90 at the time; more now, I'll bet).

# How Your Granddad Drank:
# Canadian Drinking as It Was

**W**hen I arrived in Canada, back in my boyhood, Toronto was still being labelled the Belfast of North America. This, I think, was not intended as a compliment. It spoke of a grey dourness, of uneasy relationships between Protestants and Catholics. It was the tail end of an era in which membership in the Orange Order was a prerequisite for becoming mayor or, for that matter, anything at all of any importance.

At least Belfast had pubs, which set it apart from Toronto. Even after warring factions started blowing up Belfast pubs from the late sixties on, it still had more than we did. The paucity of drinking establishments in Toronto was actually a fairly recent development. In 1837 there were fifty taverns in the tiny quadrant bordered by King and Front streets and Yonge and Church, according to *Tavern in the Town*, the definitive study of early pub life in Ontario by Margaret McBurney and Mary Byers. Alcohol was cheap and plentiful, and there was no shortage of places selling it. Booze is an integral part of the development of Toronto. Bloor Street is named for brewer Joseph Bloor, and Finch, Steeles, and Sheppard avenues are all named for innkeepers who kept premises at the intersections of those streets and Yonge Street.

As in England, Canadian inns sprang up along coaching routes. Horses and passengers needed rest and refreshment, and before long there was no shortage of places offering such services. By the time the traveller up Yonge Street got to Holland Landing, he could be in quite a state. Given that tavern-keepers usually treated coach drivers to free drinks in return for bringing passengers their way, the driver might be in even worse shape.

Nor was the early Canadian drinker certain of what was in his drink. McBurney and Byers offer a few recipes of the day. Wisely they note: "These old recipes are presented for interest only; they should not be used." I'll say. Their recipe for port calls for twenty-eight gallons of cider, nine gallons of whiskey, fifteen pounds of white sugar, as well as cinnamon, cloves, orange peel, ground cochineal, carbonate of potash, and—if necessary—two ounces of ground alum. I don't think that's the way they make it in Portugal. There are no grapes, for starters. I'm trying to imagine how I'd feel the next day. Now I'm trying to *stop* imagining how I'd feel the next day.

Inns were, in many instances, the only buildings around big enough to hold large groups of people, so they became town halls, Sunday schools, courtrooms, and concert halls. Jordan's Hotel on King Street hosted a session of the legislature of Upper Canada in 1814, after American forces had torched the original building. The Wheat Sheaf at King and Bathurst and the Black Bull on Queen Street continue to serve intoxicating beverages more than a century and a half after they first opened their doors. The Jolly Miller on Yonge Street south of York Mills was built in the late 1850s and survived in greatly altered form until quite recently. It has since resurfaced as the Miller Tavern, obviously less jolly but also less disreputable than before.

We complain of life in Canada today (well, I do), but mid-nineteenth-century Canada must have been a daily series of adventures. No wonder they drank. When I say they drank, I guess I mean that the men drank, and they drank like bejeepers, to use a technical term. Men, after all, are weak creatures and need the aid of intoxicants to get through a day. It was only a matter of time before somebody started a temperance movement, and in the nineteenth century somebody did. The first temperance society in Upper Canada was established in 1828 in the appropriately named Bastard Township. Temperance, to begin with, is not necessarily the same thing as abstinence. The initial idea was to encourage more temperate rates of drinking, but as always the hotheads of the movement gained the upper hand and soon the drive was for zero tolerance. Some witty Upper Canadian publicans favoured abstinence for their customers, but only in the sense of abstaining from unpaid tabs.

I blush to admit it, but I have sung in a temperance choir. Strictly for historical reasons, you understand. I have stood before paying audiences—fair enough, they weren't paying much—and sung songs with such titles as "I'll Drink No More Rum Punch" and "The Teetotallers Are Coming (With the Cold Water Pledge)." My fingers were crossed behind my back all the while. We frequently retired to a pub after our gigs. We were being ironic. Our audiences didn't always pick up on the irony, however, particularly an audience we wowed in Kitchener, Ontario, which missed all our postmodern signals and invited us afterwards to perform at the annual general meeting of the Woman's Christian Temperance Union. Personally, I'd have done it, but our leader begged off on grounds of insincerity. He may also have worried about beer on the breath of the bass section.

The best of the temperance songs invariably involve drunken fathers who persist in not coming home from the tavern, even though either a wife or a child is quite obviously dying at home. In "Come Home, Father," a child turns up at the tavern at one, then two, and finally three, pleading with her father to return home before poor little Benny succumbs to Fatal Absent Father Syndrome. "Has Father Been Here?" has yet another wretched child seeking a father from Mr. Barkeeper, Mr. Policeman, and Mr. Jailer, trying to free his old dad with the words: "Oh 'twas not my father who did the bad deed, / 'Twas drinking that maddened his brain." In "Father's a Drunkard and Mother Is Dead," a barefoot and tired child observes that "We were so happy till Father drank rum! / Then all our sorrow and trouble begun." The song ends, "God pity Bessie, the Drunkard's lone child." Not a dry seat in the house, as my late mother-in-law was fond of saying.

With songs this powerful, the temperance movement was bound to make a dent, and it did that and more. As always, it's the people who have time to hold meetings who change the world, and the non-drinkers tend to have plenty of time. If you're ever in Westerville, Ohio, you can visit the Anti-Saloon League Museum, Monday to Friday, 10 a.m. to 6 p.m. Well, what else is there to do in Westerville? I imagine they do good business while people are waiting for the town bar to open.

By the turn of the century, the temperance movement was hitting its peak. In 1901 the government of Prince Edward Island banned the sale of alcohol. The First World War—a time of madness on a global scale—seemed an opportunity to criminalize alcohol as a patriotic measure, and one by one the provinces climbed on board. Quebec, not surprisingly, resisted the longest, and eventually barred the sale of distilled alcohol briefly in 1919. Soldiers returning from the trenches presumably found it difficult to believe what had been going on in their absence, and the Canadian experiment with Prohibition gradually ended. (Very gradually: PEI finally broke down in 1948, long after the rest of Canada. Ontario went wet, in a limited way, in 1927.) The Americans, of course, clung to Prohibition until the end of 1933, a position that made happy millionaires out of Canadian distillers and smugglers.

The end of Canadian Prohibition didn't mean a return to the days of anarchy and cheap booze, however. As provinces repealed their bans on booze, they placed strict government controls on its manufacture and sale, putting in place the systems that survive across much of the country to this day. There was also the local option legislation (the Canada Temperance Act of 1878) that gave local jurisdictions the power to ban the sale of alcohol in their areas. Even today, the unlucky drinker is apt to find himself in such a spot. The last dry part of Toronto disappeared only in 2000, which is a good stick with which to beat obnoxious Torontonians who see themselves as the zenith of sophistication.

In 1947 the cocktail lounge was decriminalized in Toronto, and the Silver Rail became the ne plus ultra of cosmopolitanism. It remained a decent place to drink until 1998, when the by now venerable old bar was evicted. The space was required for an upmarket outdoorsy store, which lasted for about a year and a half, by which time it was too late to give us back the Silver Rail.

In the early sixties, an American actor named William Redfield came to Toronto to play Guildenstern in the celebrated Richard Burton/John Gielgud production of *Hamlet*. In his account of the experience, a fine book called *Letters from an Actor*, he writes of trying to make himself at home in a strange town during the rehearsal period. Lacking the necessities of life, he went out in search of a corkscrew and a cocktail shaker. He went to Eaton's, he went to Simpson's, all in vain. Finally, in Aikenhead's hardware store, he found the goods he needed. As a bonus, he was given a special reduced price, given that the items in question had been sitting in the store, unsold, for so very long.

The Toronto of my young adulthood was a city of taprooms, places of bad beer served up in small glasses by hefty beerslingers who expected the worst of their clientele and were seldom disappointed. Their customers sat at small Formica-topped tables and drank beer, usually on draught. Bottled beer was available but more expensive. Men without women sat in a men-only room that was usually undecorated to the point that it could be hosed down after an evening's drinking. Fights were not uncommon. The idea of these places was to get drunk, and few failed to meet this target. The streets after closing time were thick with drunkards. For all I know they still are, but closing time is much later now and I seldom see it any more.

By 1976 we began to develop more sophisticated drinking spots, places in which one could, if one chose, drink standing up. This had formerly been a crime. The Duke of York on Prince Arthur was the first of what would become a good many mock-English pubs. Eventually, we started to grow American-style sports bars as well. Almost overnight, our public drinking life began to change. Entrepreneurs could suddenly get liquor licences without having to be a close friend of a cabinet minister. The days of the Ontario taproom were numbered.

Most of the old beverage rooms of one's youth are gone: the Morrissey, the Embassy, the Babloor, the Place Pigalle. A handful linger on. The Linsmore, as we go to press, remains, still selling lousy beer in six-ounce glasses. On my last visit, they no longer seemed to be selling pickled eggs; the ones I had seen previously may have been the same ones I first saw decades ago. I even overheard some talk about painting the walls, which might be the kiss of death.

In my university days, I was not an habitué of the Brunswick House, the fabled student hangout of Bloor Street. In those days, if you succeeded in persuading one bar's set of waiters that you were of legal age (and hardly anyone was in those days), you were reluctant to break in another team. Still, alone of the University of Toronto bars of my day, the Brunswick survives. The resident dwarf of the sixties and seventies, mind you, is long gone. Or short gone, if you're a stickler for accuracy.

A few years ago, the Brunswick was the site of a minor kerfuffle during Orientation week, when a troupe of Victoria College freshpersons were brought to this bustling bar on what turned out to be Show Us Your Tattoo Night. Unfortunately—but possibly not coincidentally—this coincided with Smirnoff vodka night. I gather people today have tattoos in fairly remarkable places, and some of the more delicate freshpersons complained that their education was not scheduled to begin until the following week. A spokesperson for the Brunswick noted afterwards that no genital regions had been exposed during this event, because, after all, the place had a reputation to uphold. It was widely agreed that the Brunswick's reputation had been upheld admirably.

There are old Toronto taprooms that have adjusted slightly to the modern era, offering marginally better beer in pint glasses while continuing to maintain the grim, authoritarian feeling of the sixties. Others have adapted very well to a new age. The Rex Hotel on Queen Street used to be a standard Toronto taproom, manned by the standard waiters in white shirts and black pants, their change holders suspended before them like Ontario sporrans. Somehow, the Rex has transformed itself without sacrificing its blue-collar appeal. One of the city's prime live jazz venues by night, the Rex continues by day to be a thoroughly decent Toronto beverage room, its beverages a lot better than they used to be. They might even take credit cards now, but don't count on it.

And then there's the Paddock, at Queen and Bathurst. The Paddock was never, in my experience, much of a bar. It wasn't the sort of place you'd take your mother to, unless your mother was a tough old bird who liked to drink draught beer out of little glasses. Well, the Paddock has changed. It's smaller now, with a handsome retro-cocktail-lounge look to it, though probably a bit ironically retro. It's hard to know, because I was the least hip person in the place. That's all right. These things are relative. I was the hippest person at the Linsmore. Practically anybody I know would be the hippest person at the Linsmore.

I was probably also the oldest person at the Paddock, but the staff didn't seem to mind. On one of my visits, a pretty bartender moved a candle closer to me so I could read my book more comfortably, and I don't know many bars where that would happen. (I can think of bars where they'd move the candle closer in the hopes of setting you on fire.) She stopped short of calling me Gramps, bless her. The Paddock also offers a decent choice of beers, although the kids seem mostly to be drinking martinis of various flavours. (I'm old enough to remember when martinis had one flavour, maybe two if you were liberal about these things.) On my first visit I even quite liked the music; even if it was retro, I listened to it non-ironically.

The trick about the Paddock is that it doesn't open until late in the afternoon, so the really ideal hours for enjoying the place are not available. It would be perfect about 3 p.m., the place mostly empty, a bit of Old Blue Eyes in the air. By prime time in the evening, the place is often uncomfortably busy and noisy, but that late afternoon/early evening lacuna is pretty good. I'm a bit dubious about turning old drinking establishments into trendy nightspots, but even I have to admit they've done a pretty good job at the Paddock.

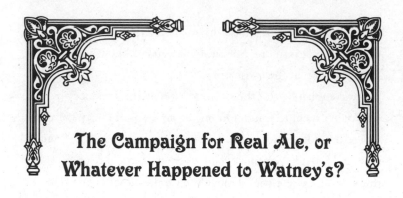

# The Campaign for Real Ale, or Whatever Happened to Watney's?

**W**hen I worked at the Argyll Arms in London in the late sixties, we offered several draught beer choices to our many customers. Having come of beer-drinking age in Canada, however, the subtleties were lost on me, I blush to admit. One day while it was quiet, an older gent seated at the bar took it upon himself to point out to me that only one of our selections was worth allowing down one's gullet. That beer was Bass. It was served from a hand pump, and I was informed that this was proper English beer, served in the way it should be served. Right, Gramps, I thought to myself, but his words stuck in my mind. He didn't call it real ale, as the expression hadn't been invented, but real ale was what he was talking about. It's funny how some things stick with you.

At the time, traditional English ale was an endangered species, being rapidly supplanted by mass-produced beer made in gigantic beer factories and shipped the length and breadth of the country. The new beer—pasteurized keg ales and lagers—had an indefinite shelf life and promised greater profits for the new megabrewers that were busily taking over smaller regional breweries. It wasn't as good as the old beer, but advertising made it highly attractive to a new generation that didn't want to drink the tired old beer of its father's day.

You can't stand in the way of progress, we are often told, but a small group of English beer lovers on holiday in the west of Ireland in 1971 thought otherwise. They might have been drinking at the time. They created something they called the Campaign for the Revitalization of Ale, which by 1973 had become the Campaign for Real Ale. Real ale, as these visionaries saw it, was unpasteurized ale allowed a secondary fermentation in either cask or bottle and served without artificial carbonation. In other words, traditional English ale as it had been served for centuries. It wasn't broke, it didn't need fixing.

The campaign received a boost in the early seventies when the annual report of Young's, a family-owned brewery in southwest London, revealed that the company was making a better profit per pint of beer than the big guys while offering its ales to the consumer at a lower price. (It didn't need to be pointed out that the beer was better too.) The trumpeted efficiency of mass brewing was obviously a lie. Bigger was not necessarily better, or even more profitable. The big brewers were not helped by the energy crisis that arose at the same time. If you've ever rented a car in Britain, you will have gasped at the price of gas, or petrol, as they like to call it. Suddenly, the efficiency of hauling kegs of beer from Reading to Hartlepool made less sense.

Still, the real ale guys were swimming against the tide, but if progress always had its way we'd all be eating our cheese out of plastic tubes by now. Sorry, perhaps you do. The founders of CAMRA struck a nerve with a public that slowly began to realize that it was being gulled by brewers who cared for neither the beer they made nor the punters who were expected to drink it. Wisely, CAMRA picked out a villain, someone we could all isolate as the guys in the black hats: Watney's.

In the late sixties Watney's owned an alarming number of pubs, having taken over and closed down countless breweries in order to pillage their pub holdings. England was being overrun by pubs painted red and black, with little red barrels hanging over their doorways. The barrels referred to Watney's Red Barrel, the new-style beer on which Watney's had staked its future. "What we want is Watney's," cried the advertising material, but CAMRA's campaign led the public to think twice about what they really wanted. As the campaign advanced, Watney's (or Grotney's, as CAMRA preferred to call it) became something of a laughingstock among astute consumers. Being seen going into a Watney's pub was a risk to one's social standing.

CAMRA's first *Good Beer Guide*, in 1974, rashly used the words "avoid like the plague" in connection with Watney's beer. The printer, fearing legal action, forced a change to "avoid at all costs," but the direction was clear. Watney's responded to the increasingly successful campaign by painting its pubs green, then by taking its name off its pubs altogether. It even tried painting some of its pubs the same colours as its more successful and more honourable local competitors, but people continued to stay away. In the eighties it started labelling its pubs with the posher name of Watney Combe Reid, presumably hoping to sound like a law firm. The egregious

Red Barrel was by now long gone, utterly unsellable in the UK. By 1990 Watney's had stopped brewing beer entirely, though some might argue that they'd stopped brewing beer long before.

The Campaign for Real Ale marches on all these years later, publishing its annual *Good Beer Guide*, organizing the Great British Beer Festival every August, and lobbying to improve the drinking lives of decent people everywhere. It lobbies against brewery closings, for more civilized licensing hours, for lower taxes on beer, for full measures, and for practically everything that is good. Watney's is gone, but new enemies crop up all the time. They win some, they lose some, but CAMRA's still at it. As a regular visitor to the UK, I keep my membership up to date. They're working for me, too.

# If You Can Make It Here:
# The Subway Game in Gotham

I'll make it clear from the start: I heart-symbol New York. I've heart-symbolled New York since the first time I saw it early one morning in 1967 as I tumbled off an all-night Greyhound bus. Even then, the Bronx was up and the Battery was down. And in 2001, in a Broadway theatre, I sat two rows behind Betty Comden and Adolph Green, the lyricists who wrote those words in 1944. That's the kind of place New York is, and it's why I heart-symbol it.

It wasn't always a good beer-drinking town. Well into the 1980s, America's biggest city was awash in Budweiser, and even today it's easy to wind up in a place that hasn't heard of anything more enterprising. There have always been good bars in New York, but until recently you had to drink hard liquor if you took drinking at all seriously. It's a competitive town, of course, and rents are crazy, so even a semi-regular tourist sees good bars come and go.

There used to be an Irish bar called O'Lunney's on West 44th Street, attached to a fleapit hotel called the Mansfield. In the early nineties the Mansfield reinvented itself as a hip and expensive (and presumably fumigated) hostelry, and O'Lunney's was evicted, too dowdy and old-fashioned for the hotel's new demographic. Some time later, Mr. O'Lunney resurfaced on the south side of West 43rd Street, hopeful of a long tenure just off Times Square. But the Disneyfication of 42nd Street was under way, and the pub sat in a space that was needed for Garth Drabinsky's new theatre. O'Lunney's closed its doors again, and the pub-minded mourned again. Still, he's nothing if not determined, is Mr. O'Lunney, and in March 2000 he opened yet another eponymous establishment on West 46th Street, a few steps east of 7th Avenue, and he got it open two days before St. Patrick's Day. But don't get used to 46th Street either; he's now on West 45th. Bless Mr. O'Lunney from County Cavan and his intrepid family, and I hope they get to stay where they are for a while. The beer choice could be better, but the O'Lunneys run a nice bar.

If you're apt to go to the theatre, as Anne and I do, you get to know the places to drink near Times Square: O'Lunney's, Virgil's BBQ, the St. Andrew, and Langan's. (The best ones, of course, are gone; I think of McHale's and the Collins Bar, both recent victims of the destruction of 8th Avenue. Hell's Kitchen is turning into Hell's Toilet.) They have all saved our lives a time or two.

And I like the Waterfront Ale House on the East Side. I was there late on Oscar Night 2001, drinking Stoudts Mai Bock when the Best Actress category approached. Our bartender was a woman of strong views, and she had it on good authority that Julia Roberts was not only not the nicest person on the planet but that she hardly scraped into the top ten. For her money, it was anybody but Julia Roberts for the little gold statue. I don't go to a lot of movies (they cut into pub time something fierce), but I learned long ago not to argue with a good bartender. As the moment drew closer, the bar-keep issued beermats to those of us at the bar (Brooklyn Brewery beermats, as I recall), with instructions to whip them at the screen if Ms. Roberts came up trumps, as of course she did. The TV screen suddenly filled with several dozen unnaturally shiny teeth, and we barflies let rip. For a moment or two the teeth vanished behind a sea of beermats. Yeah, I kind of like the Waterfront Ale House.

That said, I wasn't about to take the subway to 2nd Avenue at 30th Street to play the Subway Game, New York version. For start-ers, the subway doesn't go there, and anyway there wouldn't be any surprise. Playing the Subway Game in New York offers an embar-rassment of choices. There must be hundreds of stations, from Van Cortlandt Park in the Bronx to Mott Avenue in Far Rockaway. All within reach for two bucks (early 2008 prices). There's a Prospect Avenue station in the Bronx and another Prospect Avenue station in Brooklyn. There's a 71st Street in Brooklyn, a 72nd Street in Manhattan, a 74th Street in Queens, and a 75th Street in Jamaica. From Mosholu Parkway to Sheepshead Bay, there's almost nowhere you can't get to on the New York subway. Except the Waterfront Ale House.

I settled on Coney Island. Born in an English seaside town, I have a grim affection for out-of-season resort spots. In England, of course, out-of-season can be any time of year. This was late March, on a day that smacked more of late or even mid-February, and I felt that Coney Island would represent that sort of mortification of the flesh we all need from time to time. Or, at least, writers of this sort of book do. You know you wouldn't be happy if I'd taken the subway to Columbus Circle and stepped straight into some swank bar. Nothing's too good for you.

I caught the N train at 49th Street, along with a number of other people. The N train was popular, at least in midtown Manhattan. By the time we travelled under the East River, however, we had lost most of our pilgrims. Clearly not many other people were playing the Subway Game that morning, or if they were they were taking easier options. It took me an hour and five minutes to reach the end of the line, by which time I was the only passenger on my car. This answered my question as to whether Coney Island had an off-season clientele.

Not that it's any of your business, but I actually lived in Brooklyn for a spell in the early seventies. Even so, I'm not sure I ever got to Coney Island. None of it looked familiar to me. The station gives the impression of having seen no fiscal investment since the Second World War, but maybe it looks more cheerful on a sunny day when it's filled with festive New Yorkers. The exit to Surf Avenue looks pretty permanently sealed off, so you come out of the station on Stillwell Avenue, which is not a particularly prepossessing street, it must be said. As you look left, however, you see the bright lights of Nathan's, Coney Island's original fast food extravaganza. Off-season, even Nathan's looks kind of frumpy, and smaller than one expects.

What I don't see right away are any bars, but an area that caters to millions of heat-escaping Gothamites on a summer day must have all the mod cons, right? The forecast is for rain, but it hasn't quite started yet, so I head for the beach. I walk past a number of boarded-up fast-food places, all presumably waiting for warmer weather, and

Brrr

the Coney Island Batting Cage, which is open. There's even a young guy in there taking his cuts. The boardwalk is quiet but not entirely deserted. One of the fast-food spots is even open, and I buy a potato knish. When I lived in Brooklyn, I was no stranger to the knish, but either I've moved on or they're not making knishes the way they used to.

I could have had a cold beer to take away with the knish, but at this point I still have my heart set on a beer indoors, somewhere out of the wind. I go out on the sand and look around; I go back to the boardwalk and look around. There's a fun fair and a big old wooden roller coaster, all sitting abandoned but for a handful of workers who seem to be making a less than fully committed effort to get it all in working order. They seem no more convinced than I that summer is a realistic prospect.

I move back inland, where it's less breezy, and I walk along the apparently bar-free Surf Avenue. I turn right on the bar-free Stillwell Avenue, then left on what proves to be a pretty bar-free Mermaid Avenue. Don't get any naive aesthetic notions about Mermaid Avenue; it's not as nice as it sounds. The ubiquitous security measures suggest a level of insecurity among the locals. Clearly, the gentry have not swarmed to this seaside paradise, elevating property values. I see a couple of restaurants along the way, established presumably in the hope that tourists will tire of the beach and will make their way a block inland in search of fine dining. On a cold March day, this seems a trifle optimistic.

Still no bars. What I do see are corner variety stores, most of them billing themselves—a little grandly, I think—as delis. Deli is a fairly elastic term. These places sell food, all right? Eventually,

Mermaid Avenue loses its charm and I turn left again, back toward Surf Avenue. I am slowly and reluctantly concluding that there are no bars in the greater Coney Island area, so I let myself be seduced by the Express Deli Supermarket, which looks slightly bigger than the other delis I've seen. Not that bigger is necessarily better, you understand, but I'm hoping that bigger might possibly mean a bigger beer cooler and possibly more choice.

I realize that I haven't fully absorbed the rules of the Subway Game. Get on a subway—check. Go somewhere you don't know—check. Have a beer. Does that mean a sit-down beer in a bona fide bar? I'm a long way from Patrick at this point, and I have to make a decision. The only sit-down beer I've seen has been Nathan's. I could sit down at Nathan's with a cold mug of Bud, surrounded by the other pathetic people who find themselves at Coney Island in March, all needing somewhere warm to go. No, Nathan's is too depressing.

The beer cooler at the Express Deli Supermarket has the stuff you'd expect—Miller, Bud, and all of that—but it actually holds a few surprises. I'm all set to pick up a chilled Sam Adams Cherry Wheat when I notice a bottle I've never seen before. A moment or two later I've put back the Sam Adams and I'm headed for the cash with a bottle of Riga Strong Beer, a product of Rigas Alus, Latvia. Contrary to the dictates of the Bureau of Alcohol, Firearms and Tobacco, the label on this bottle actually tells me that Riga Strong Beer packs a wallop of 7 percent alcohol by volume, which is the kind of oomph I need on a day like this. For a mere $1.25 I leave the Express Deli Supermarket with my booty cleverly concealed in one of those distinctly American paper bags that cover the entire

275

Brrraaa

bottle except for the mouth. The young man behind the counter kindly removes the bottle top, and I'm free to go.

I return to the boardwalk, marvelling that I've just bought the first Latvian beer of my life from a Puerto Rican deli on Coney Island. The wind is up and the rain is starting, but I'm packing a strong beer from Riga and I feel all right. They know a bit about bad weather in Riga, I reckon, and they make a beer that's designed to help Rigans (Rigaites?) deal with it. And it's not bad either, though I'm drinking it in less than optimum tasting conditions. I walk by a ballpark under construction—home of the brand-new Brooklyn Cyclones, bringing baseball back to that much-maligned borough—and I think that maybe summer will come again. Soon I've done a big figure eight of downtown Coney Island and I'm feeling the warmth of my Riga Strong Beer. I get back on the subway and head for the bright lights and high prices of Manhattan. I don't know if swigging a beer from a paper bag meets the letter of the Subway Game's laws, but it certainly captures the spirit.

# That's Where You'll Find Me:
# Some Not Bad Places to
# Drink in Toronto

As one of those glass-half-empty people, I thought this was going to be the toughest section of the book to fill. Could I manage a top ten list of Toronto watering holes? I asked myself. Indeed I could, and a few more besides, and I'd still be leaving out places I think highly of. That said, assembling a guide of this sort is an exercise for dopes. I can be sure that by the time you read this, if you do, at least one of these places will have been evicted by a landlord living with GBS (Greedy Bugger Syndrome), and another will have turned against good beer, or have become too noisy, or perhaps simply have barred me.

What are my criteria? Crikey, if you've got this far in the book without knowing what I like in a pub, you've got a short attention span. Anyway, I want decent beer to drink and an interesting environment in which to drink it. I don't think that's asking a lot. To state the bleeding obvious, these experiences are subjective, and one can be lucky or unlucky with one's encounters with bar

Brrraaaaaa

staff, ambient noise, other customers, and other such variable factors. You may be drawn to big, noisy places whose purpose is to get young people drunk and horny. I'm not, and even if I were, I'm sure I wouldn't get past the guy at the door. I try to avoid places where people kill each other, though one of my top five lost one of its patrons when he encountered a hit man downstairs in the parking garage after lunch.

For all I know, all of these places are utterly uninhabitable late at night. I'm usually safe at home by that time. I don't often eat in pubs, so this list should not be seen as an endorsement of the food served, though if I have any information of that sort I may just pass it on. And it's entirely possible that I've missed some wonderful place the regulars have succeeded in keeping to themselves. It's the risk you take.

## The top five

In approximate order of longevity, these are five local establishments that should be considered compulsory for anyone who likes the taste of beer and happens to be in Toronto, if only briefly. I once spoke to the former owner of a pub in Florida who refused to serve Budweiser at all and kept a few bottles of Coors Light on the premises in case of fire. These places are a bit like that. They're also damn pleasant places to drink.

**C'est What**, 67 Front Street East, opened its doors in 1988, declaring itself a place that sold only local microbrewed beers. That doesn't sound so bold now, but nobody was doing that in 1988. It's a big place with two rooms, one of which hosts musical events by evening. There are people, it has to be said, who complain of the service and the general attitude of the place, but I've managed to avoid any such trouble. Get along with anybody, I do.

In the late nineties (*the* late nineties, not *his* late nineties), my dentist moved into the Gooderham Building, also known as the Flatiron Building. He's at the sharp end, not the blunt end, right at the top. Apart from enjoying a bit of local heritage (where else do you find not only an antique elevator but an actual—albeit not antique—elevator operator?) whenever I go for a bout of bloodletting, I have the pleasure of taking aboard a bit of general anaesthetic afterwards practically across the street at C'est What.

It's the sort of place that makes me almost look forward to a dental encounter. It's even better if you go there when you're not in pain. It offers the city's biggest range of Canadian (mostly Ontario) craft beers, along with a few house-fermented beers (brewed by Bruce Halstead at the County Durham Brewing Company, including a hemp beer, a rye beer, and a coffee porter, none of which you see every day in most places). You get your choice of thirty-five almost entirely interesting taps, and the place even makes its own wines as well. There are usually five real ales available, and just writing about it makes me wish I were there right now. It's a pub that does beer tastings, wine tastings, port tastings, single malt tastings, and vodka tastings, plus a few tastings I've no doubt forgotten.

On the east side of Mount Pleasant, just south of Eglinton, you'll find the **Granite Brewery**, a local institution since 1991. I wrote about the Granite earlier, but some of it is worth repeating. This was not Toronto's first brewpub, but I believe it was the first to produce a dry-hopped, cask-conditioned ale, a beer that could hold its head up at the Great British Beer Festival. The two main rooms

Brrraaaaap!!!

with their large windows are bright and cheery by day, while the dining room in the back offers a view of the brewery. Owner Ron Keefe holds occasional beer-related events which you can learn about on his website.

Ron is an entirely genial man who keeps his staff a long time (always a good sign) and his customers even longer. It's a pleasure to give him your money. Brewpubs, by Ontario law (which is inevitably and bewilderingly inane), are forbidden to sell their beer off-premises, even at beer festivals, so Ron took advantage of a law change to become reclassified as a brewery with a tied pub, which means that he can now sell his beers to other pubs and operate a beer store on location. You can buy growlers or kegs of the Granite's fine beers, and I encourage you to do so. For a price, you can help Ron brew beer as part of his Brewer for a Day program. There's even free parking downstairs, but once you get comfortable at the Granite, you'll wish you'd left the car at home.

It was no surprise, back in 2005, when founder Paul Kellogg sold the **Victory Café**, 581 Markham Street, to three investors. Paul had been spending more time in Nova Scotia and had even returned from one of his visits with Nova Scotia plates on his car. But it didn't make his regulars happy. Regulars don't like change. A month or so into the new regime, I asked one of the long standing bartenders how he felt things were going, and he assured me that the new people seemed fine and that nothing scary appeared to be on the horizon.

Well, the new people made some changes. They took down the signed photograph of guitarist Liona Boyd, which was fine with me. Liona Boyd went to my high school, though I didn't really know her, and when she wrote her memoir I immediately looked to see what she had to say about her teen years. I didn't expect her to write about me, even if I had been her student council president when she was in grade eleven, but I also didn't count on seeing the following line: "The boys in Kipling Collegiate held minimal attraction for me." For starters, surely that "in" should be either "at" or "of," but apart from that I could name you several guys who were babe magnets, though sadly I had no reason to count myself in their number.

They also changed the range of draught beers, making it better and better and even eventually installing a beer engine for cask ale. They've turned a good neighbourhood pub into a destination pub, which has made it more difficult for some of us to find a decent spot, especially one where it's light enough to read. There's a mid-sized snug off to one side (when Paul Kellogg put it in, he told me that it wasn't an English snug or an Irish snug; it was a Canadian snug, which is true: it's quite cold in winter), and a room upstairs that gets used for private parties, musical events, literary readings, and as overflow when the main floor is packed.

**Caffe Volo**, 587 Yonge Street, has been around longer than some of these others, but it's been a destination for beer lovers only more recently. Owner Ralph Morana ran Volo as an Italian restaurant for some years before experiencing a kind of road-to-Damascus epiphany, becoming a beer enthusiast and turning his place into an Italian restaurant with an excellent beer list. (Don't worry—there's still wine as well, and very good wine too.) Ralph's enthusiasm led him first to a hand pump for real ale, then to instituting an annual cask beer festival, as well as the occasional smaller-scale cask ale "situation." Volo is technically more of a restaurant than a pub, but you'll usually find a claque of beer fans in the bar area, looking for something new and exciting. And Ralph seldom disappoints.

The newest entry in my top five is **beerbistro**, 18 King Street East. Opened in 2003 by beer writer Stephen Beaumont and chef Brian Morin, beerbistro is a relatively upmarket spot (you can tell by the lower case name) offering a mix of good local beers and interestingly chosen internationals, along with a very good menu of dishes prepared with beer. The frites are terrific. The space has a lively acoustic, so it can get a bit noisy when it's busy. The staff is efficient and knowledgeable and almost always very friendly. Beerbistro is the least pubby of all my choices, but they take beer seriously there and I never fail to enjoy myself. Beaumont remains a co-owner but has reduced his responsibilities and is seen on the premises less often these days.

## Downtown

**Smokeless Joe**, a small basement joint at 125 John Street, was a bizarre concept when it first appeared. It didn't open until 4 p.m. (still doesn't), so to heck with the lunch crowd, and it played only the blues. Although it had a sign outside announcing 250 FAMOUS BEERS (as if there really are 250 famous beers), it didn't sell most of the famous ones, specializing in beers that were almost pointedly not famous at all. The original Joe had an odd set of rules. The sight of a coat hanging on the back of a chair, for instance, seemed to drive him nuts. Coats were to be hung up. And, as the name suggests, there was a strict no-smoking policy. It seems to me that at first customers were allowed to smoke on the tiny patio out front, but Joe eventually banned that as well. Nowadays, of course, you can't smoke anywhere, so Smokeless Joe has lost its distinctiveness, as least on that score.

The original Joe has moved on, and things have relaxed. Feel free to hang your coat on the back of your chair; no one's going to stop you. You won't be asked your first name as soon as you walk in. And you don't hear the blues much any more. I'm not sure there are as many beers on offer as there used to be, but you'll still find something you can force down, perhaps with an order of fresh oysters. The draught beer choice is small but usually interesting. Which describes Smokeless Joe itself.

One of the huge success stories in Ontario brewing in recent years has been the Mill Street Brewery in the Distillery District. Open since only late 2002, and presumably backed by some fairly serious cash, Mill Street has made a dent in the local market with a couple of bland beers (Organic Lager and Stock Ale) and some very good brands (Tankhouse and Coffee Porter), and quickly outgrew its limited space and opened a separate brewery in Scarborough.

The original location in the Distillery District now houses a more modest brewery, making smaller batches of beer primarily for the **Mill Street Brewpub** at 55 Mill Street. It's worth visiting for the full range of Mill Street beers, but I wish I liked it more as a pub. On my first visit, I felt my chain-pub antennae twitching, and indeed the brewpub is owned and/or operated by something called F.A.B. Concepts Inc., which runs a growing number of pubs, mostly of the mock-Irish variety, around town. The staff uniforms, the predictable music, and the menu all seemed very familiar. It's okay, and I'm glad there's a pub there, and I'm happy to have a showcase for Mill Street beers, but . . .

Another corporate entertainment showcase is the **Esplanade Bier Markt**, next to Fionn McCool's way downtown. When it first opened, it hired Stephen Beaumont to oversee its beer list and train its staff in the ways of beer, a relationship that ended quite some time ago. It's a bit of an upmarket concept, pitched at young, well-dressed folk out on a spree. I note that the website says very little about beer, apart from the boast of more than a hundred beers from twenty-four countries. The dress code is "upscale casual," for what it's worth (and I believe it's the only place in this chapter with a stated dress code). The beer choices are good, but with C'est What and beerbistro in the neighbourhood, I don't get there often.

The **Rex Hotel**, by contrast, is not upmarket or corporate. It's an excellent example of an old taproom that has adjusted to changing times and turned itself into a distinctly non-hoity-toity jazz bar. I first went to the Rex in October 1972, when I was working around the corner. My boss at the time once darkly hinted that he'd fire anyone he thought lunched at the Rex. That's the sort of place it was, or at least he thought it was. It was a down-at-heels old taproom. Two down-at-heels taprooms, actually, because although the old Ladies and Escorts law had been repealed, the Rex maintained two separate rooms, and it was easy to see which had been which. In those days, the hotel rooms upstairs were being used primarily, as far as I could tell, on a very short-term basis. The people I saw going upstairs seemed to be consenting adults, and that was good enough for me. These days, it seems you can actually rent those rooms overnight, and the Rex's website claims they've been renovated.

Under the management of the ever-boyish Bob Ross, who took over from his father in 1965, the Rex has reinvented itself to keep pace with bustling Queen Street. Ross long ago took down the wall between the two rooms, improved the menu, brought in some okay-though-not-exciting beers, and turned the Rex into one of the city's prime live jazz venues. And he's done it all without changing the basic nature of the place. He's certainly done it without changing the men's toilet. By day, the Rex remains a friendly, unpretentious bar. By night, it hums with a constantly changing lineup of jazz bands of all sorts. There's a cover charge for the later shows; earlier on, the bands pass the hat. Dig deep, friends.

I love the Rex Hotel. It's a Toronto landmark with its own distinctive integrity. Chicago has Andy's Jazz Club: lucky them. We have the Rex: lucky us.

## North (or at least somewhat northish)

Yonge Street used to be something of a drinker's desert. Was there anything between the old Ports of Call and the Jolly Miller? Things have improved, I'm happy to say, though there still might not be as many watering holes as when Yonge Street was a major stagecoach route. I'm old enough that some days I think I actually remember those days.

That said, I don't get up the hill as often as I might. I live at the bottom of the hill, and the sight of the escarpment is a daunting one. In prehistoric times—back when the Leafs were competitive—most of what we now call Toronto was underwater, hidden beneath the waves of Lake Iroquois. There are many Canadians who are nostalgic for that era and wish it would return. To which I say, oh don't be like that. The shoreline of that ancient lake was at the top of the hill that makes the trek up Bathurst or Avenue Road such an ordeal. If Casa Loma had existed back then, it would have been a lakefront property.

There's a place just north of Davisville called the **Bow and Arrow**, 1954 Yonge Street, an early adopter of local brewing and local food. And they're still maintaining those worthy principles. There was a bit of a coup a few years ago, after which one of the stalwarts, Kieron Meaney, left the building. He opened his own place, the Blue Meaney, up the street, but alas it did not succeed. The Bow and Arrow carries on, though it is a trifle worrying how frequently they're out of stock of exactly what you want. Still, it remains an important purveyor of craft beers in this town, and if they're out of your first choice they'll have something that will make you happy. And their Sunday afternoon Celtic music sessions (no cover) are terrific.

Down at the bottom of the Yonge Street hill, a hundred feet or so under what was once Lake Iroquois, is the **Rebel House**, 1068 Yonge, on the fringes of Rosedale. What the Rosedalites are rebelling against escapes me, unless it's paying taxes, but they keep this pub busy much of the time. Now, I call it a pub, but it's more of a restaurant that looks like a pub. The distinction is worth making, because if you turn up expecting merely to drink, it's very likely you'll be restricted to the small yet amiable bar area at the front. I've seen some important people at that bar. I once sat very close to Pat Quinn shortly before he was fired as coach of the Toronto Maple Leafs. He seemed to think it was coming and had some interesting things to say about some of his players.

The rebels of the Rebel House are presumably the stroppy folk of 1837 who marched down Yonge Street from Montgomery's

Tavern, looking to correct an injustice or two. Some of them were hanged for their impertinence, possibly by the forebears of some of the regulars of the Rebel House. It's a pity the pub wasn't there in 1837; I could imagine the rebels dropping in for a break on the way downtown. Rather a long time later, in 1998, a large protest march retraced the steps of the original rebels, trying to discourage the attempts of Mike Harris to wreck our city. Anne and I found that by marching near the front of the demonstration we could nip into the Rebel House for a quick pint and rejoin the end of the column, having watched it all go by through the front window. As demonstrations go, it was a full pint in length.

It's not a big place, the Rebel House, though there's a nice patio out back, shielded in summer by an open parachute. Space on that patio is among the most cherished real estate in greater Rosedale. The beer is good, the food is interesting, the staff is friendly unless you want to sit somewhere off-limits, and the Rebel House is a place I'm fond of. They're apt to close for renovations on long weekends, so call first.

## East

I have been accused of selling the east end of Toronto short in the past, a charge I deny. Most Torontonians spend their lives on one side or another of Yonge Street. For better or worse, I came of age on the west side, so the east side has always seemed a bit exotic to me. And I'm guilty of exploring the east end insufficiently. But when I do, I find interesting places.

Cabbagetown, which isn't terribly far east, is still an interestingly mixed area. For a long time, public drinking in Cabbagetown was restricted to the Winchester and the sidewalks. For the most part, the Winchester is now a branch of Mr. Horton's empire. I fondly remember Mr. Horton as a Leaf defenceman and I bow to no one in my reverence of his memory, but turning a venerable taproom into a doughnut joint seems criminal.

There are now other places to drink in Cabbagetown, but the cream really seems to be the **House on Parliament**, 465 Parliament Street. It's run by a couple we used to know from the Duke of York on Prince Arthur Avenue, and it pulls in the punters most days and nights of the week. Quite rightly too. The beer choices could be better, but the place has a very nice feel to it. On my first visit, some years ago now, my excellent waiter (identified on my bill as Server 0020002, so possibly a highly developed cyborg) was as good as my liver and onions. And that was saying something.

Once you cross the mighty Don River, you have the immediate choices of **Allen's** and **Dora Keogh**, 143 and 141 Danforth Avenue, mentioned elsewhere in this book, which are hard to turn down. (There's also a place along that stretch of the Danforth called the Old Nick. A fine writer named Pete McCarthy, who was taken from us far too soon, had a number of inviolable travel rules, one of which was: never pass a bar that has your name on it. Easy for him. There are lots of bars called Pete's or McCarthy's. I've been to hundreds of watering holes in numerous countries, and the Old Nick is the only one I've seen that has my name on it.)

If you travel farther east, you'll encounter the Linsmore Tavern, described on pages 182 and 263. It's an excellent museum of drinking in Ontario before the 1970s, and I recommend it for that. But not much more than that.

Before you get there, however, there's the **Only Café**, 972 Danforth Avenue. This is the place I discovered on my Subway Game adventure eastward. It's a wonderfully quirky place, chock-a-block with images of counterculture heroes from Lennon to Marley, Castro to Guevara, and so on. The beer choice is good, there's a good array of bottled beers, and it's not like any chain pub you've ever seen. They also have a place in Peterborough.

As a west-ender, I refuse to be drawn into the debate over whether the part of eastern Toronto out past the old racetrack is the Beach or the Beaches. I don't care, quite honestly. I'm not sure I ever heard it called the Beach until sometime in the seventies, but I've never lived there, so I can't swear that the locals haven't been saying "Beach" since the dawn of time. I think I'll just call it "the B."

In appearance and temperament, the B is the part of Toronto most like Vancouver, and for a long time it shared Vancouver's shortage of watering holes. For ages, I can recall going out there and finding nowhere to drink but the old Orchard Park Tavern, a taproom that existed largely to refresh patrons of the now defunct Greenwood racetrack. The Orchard Park is now a Days Inn, but Queen Street East is now dotted with pubs and bars of all sorts. One of the more interesting of these is **Castro's Lounge** at 2116 Queen Street East. There must be something a bit bolshie about the east end, with their recurring tributes to the Cuban revolutionary.

Castro's is a fairly funky sort of place with a pretty good choice of beers from here and there. The B seems an odd mix of bohemianism and staid old Torontoism, and Castro's definitely appeals to the bohemian side. There are other bars that cater to the staid side.

On my most recent trek out that way, I stopped into a little place called Mullins, which was blessed with a feisty young bar-maid named Casey. When she heard where I was headed next, she said she had been in there only once, to drop off a résumé. She said she hadn't expected to hear from them, as she lacked the eti-quette for the **Feathers** (962 Kingston Road). I'd never thought of the Feathers in that light, but maybe it represents the staid part of B-town. Or perhaps the English side, as opposed to the Irish side represented by Mullins.

I was a bit apprehensive as I approached the Feathers. Had it turned into something I wouldn't recognize? Would I pass the dress code? Had the Feathers gone posh since my last visit? Not at all, but it's a different demographic: I wasn't the oldest person in this room. The Feathers is an unabashedly British-style pub with a football match on the telly, kippers on the menu, and literally hundreds of single malts on display (they claim 430; I didn't use valuable drink-ing time counting). It also, when I was there last, had Wellington County on a hand pump and Belhaven Twisted Thistle on tap, which I don't see every day, or practically any day.

The first time I went to the Feathers, I ran into my old friend Charlie Dougall. This was not surprising. I have run into Charlie at Pat McGinty's in Buffalo, so encountering him a few blocks from his home was almost inevitable. A product of the west end, Charlie has been living in what he calls the Beaches for a couple of decades. (He says there's more than one beach, so it's the Beaches. When he found me at the Feathers, I was well into a pint of the pub's no longer extant Beaches Best Bitter. Look, I'm just reporting what I see; I'm not judging.)

A bit surprised to find me drinking so far from home, out in the B, Charlie approved of my choice of venue. Up on Kingston Road, he told me, is where the geezers drink. We worked our way through many of the choices of the Feathers, then we made our way to Quigley's and Lion on the Beach (note singular) before Charlie was required elsewhere. At some point at Quigley's, he expressed regret that we baby boomers had not changed the world as we had promised to do. He was a bit hard on us, I thought, but you expect that when you drink with Charlie.

## West

You don't have to be a graduate student to drink at the **Graduate Students' Union Pub**, 16 Bancroft Avenue, but you have a better chance of finding it if you've done some post-grad work in geography. It's tucked away on the west side of the U of T downtown campus, behind a pharmacology building. If a circle had corners, it would be at the northeast corner of that circle that interrupts Spadina just north of College.

If you're guilty of being over, say, twenty-five, you might want to exercise caution in the evenings during the school year. It can get a bit noisy, you understand. Oh, and they're not open weekends and they shut for about two weeks over Christmas. Other than that, I can recommend the place enthusiastically. I described the two guys who run it in the chapter on bar staff, and I'm not about to do it again. The GSU has a decent beer choice, including Granite Best Bitter, and a nice patio outside in good weather.

What I like in a pub, apart from all the other things I like in a pub, is the sense that it isn't like most other pubs, that it's been assembled by somebody who actually drinks in pubs, that it reflects the personality of that person more than a quest for the bottom line. Welcome to **Kilgour's Bar Meets Grill**, 509 Bloor Street West, owned and operated by a pair of gout-riddled brothers, Andrew and Peter.

Kilgour's makes the list because one of the regulars egged Peter into adding Black Oak Pale Ale to the draught list, so there's something delicious to be had. It's a quirky place. A look behind the bar tells you that at least one of the brothers (Peter) has an interest in the Montreal Canadiens, Elvis, and Spam (the canned meat, not the email nuisance). It's not a sports bar, but in recent years Kilgour's has become known as a pub that shows all Habs games, often in the original French, and it can get a little raucous. It's worth checking the hockey schedule. Andrew is a keen Scrabble player and has turned Kilgour's into something of a Scrabble bar. These people are quieter than the hockey folk, but I don't think they drink anywhere near as much. At least, that's what the staff tell me.

The other reason Kilgour's makes this list relates to an evening in 2003, the occasion of the outdoor hockey game played in Edmonton. In a show of solidarity, the Kilgour boys put a television set out on the patio and opened for business. It was cold (not as cold as Edmonton, admittedly, but what is?), but the patio remained busy all evening.

I used to drink on Friday nights with a group of friends at the Duke of York. One of our number had been drinking there since the place opened, and his expenditures had probably single-handedly funded the growth of that pub from one smallish room in the basement to a full-blown three-floor entertainment centre. It was in the pub's interest to please Douglas, which was not always easy, so there was always a table reserved for him on Friday evenings. We just never knew where it would be, and all too often it was adjacent to the regular meeting of the Midtown Toronto Shouters' Society, which made conversation difficult.

I bow to no one in my high regard of the Duke's manager, a hard-working and charming woman named Kim Bartley, and I'm happy that she has achieved such success at the pub, but the beer choice was average at best and Fridays had become hard to bear. So we (or most of us, at least) moved to Kilgour's. And I think we're appreciated, though the music isn't always to our taste. A couple of times, a cheerfully refreshed Peter has thanked me for bringing our crowd to his pub, because we raise the tone. I don't think any publican has ever told me that before, so it gives you some idea of the normal tone at Kilgour's.

College Street is not renowned for its pub scene, but if you're walking westbound, approaching Bathurst, you might see a modest sign advertising a "nice little pub." If you check it out, you'll be inside a very small place called the **Cloak and Dagger**, 394 College Street. The many taps are a mix of micros and macros, with Arkell Best Bitter on a hand pump. If you're hungry there's a deep-fried Mars bar on the dessert menu, which I cannot personally vouch for. I am usually the oldest person in the joint, though I've never been around long enough for DJs or live music, which I understand occur with some regularity. Should you be interested in seeing actual hipsters in their natural habitat, check this place out. You'll feel hipper just for being there, and the beer's pretty good.

Bloor and Lansdowne is not perceived as the most salubrious corner in this city, unless you're in search of substances not provided by the LCBO, but it is where you'll find **Ciro's House of International Bier**, 1316 Bloor Street West. The name tells you that the thrust of the place is not geared toward fine domestic ales. There's no actual Ciro, but there is a guy called Frank, who told me that there's hardly anything domestic that really excites him (apparently even his wife is Greek), though when prodded he acknowledged that Denison's Weissbier sets itself apart.

He has a few taps and a lot of bottles, and is happy to bring things out to show you. He also usually has a few bottles that aren't on the menu, a little something for the discerning patron. Frank's an interesting fellow whose grandfather apparently opened the first Chinese restaurant in Toronto, possibly Canada. You see the things you learn in pubs?

Nearly due south of Ciro's you'll encounter the **Rhino Bar and Grill**, 1249 Queen Street West, in another part of town that is rapidly changing. The Rhino has been there for a while and is subtly adjusting to the new ways of Parkdale. According to its website, its fairly recent renovation was designed to create something that was a "neo-boho/post-hotel/supercrash of unconvention and artful transformation." I hope that's helpful.

It's a big place that seems ready to cater to its traditional not-unscruffy Queen Street market, plus the hip artists who flocked to Parkdale for the lower rents, as well as the incoming condo dwellers. Whether they get that last group, time will tell. Like Ciro's, the Rhino offers some good beers, both draught and bottled, at decent prices. They also had Durham's excellent Hop Head on cask when

I was last there, which is not at all to be sneezed at. Worth the trip to Parkdale if you're not already there? Hard to say, but you won't hate yourself for it.

Just about as far west as I'm prepared to go is **Whelan's Gate**, 1663 Bloor Street West. I wrote about it six chapters ago, and I stand by whatever I wrote then. Whenever I'm there, people seem to be happy, and isn't that what going to a pub is about? The beer choice is adequate, leaning toward the Irish—this being an Irish pub and all—and the place has a very pleasant look and feel to it. Of course they want to make money, but this is not one of those places where you feel they want to hang you upside down from the ankles till all the money in your pockets spills out.

I don't often get west of Whelan's Gate, but if you get to Burlington, you'll want to visit the Pepperwood Bistro. And if you persevere and make it all the way to Hamilton, you'll find, just behind the GO station, the Winking Judge on Augusta Street. Say hello from me.

# So This Fellow Walks into a Bar

This fellow walks into a bar in Red Deer, sits right at the end of the bar all by himself, and orders three pints. The bartender says he'd be happy to keep them coming, that there's no need to order them all at the same time, but the fellow says no, he'd like them all at once, thank you very much. He sits there quietly, drinks the three pints, and leaves. Same thing the next night. On the third night, the bartender's curiosity gets the better of him and he asks about the fellow's strange drinking habits.

"Oh that," says the fellow amicably. "When I lived in Vegreville, I used to meet my two brothers after work, and we'd have a pint together. Now that I'm in Red Deer, this makes me feel I'm still with my brothers."

The bartender is happy with this explanation, and he passes the word on to the other regulars, who had been finding it a bit odd themselves. And so it went through most of the winter.

Then, one evening in March, the fellow walks in and asks for two pints. The bar falls silent. The bartender pours the two pints and drops them in front of the fellow. A naturally empathetic man, like so many of his profession, the bartender wipes his hands on a towel and says, "Listen, it's none of my business, but I'd just like to say how sorry I am about your brother . . ."

The fellow looks up, a bit confused, then says, "Oh, I see what you're saying. No, my brothers are fine. I've just given up drinking for Lent."

***

A fellow walks into a bar in St. John's, takes a stool, and has a pint with a whisky chaser. After the second of these, he strikes up a conversation with the guy at the next stool. "You from around here?" he asks.

"Born and bred no more than a mile from here," the man replies.

"Get out," says the first fellow. "What school did you go to?"

"St. Michael's," is the reply. "How about you?"

"The very same," says the fellow. "What year did you graduate?"

"Sixty-two," the man responds.

"Extraordinary," says the fellow. "Same as me. What street did you live in?"

"Anderson Terrace," is the answer. "What about you?"

"Anderson Terrace myself," the fellow says, "just north of the bakery."

"Just north of the bakery!" exclaims the second man. "What are the odds against that?!"

At this point, another fellow walks into the bar, takes a stool, and says to the bartender, "So, anything happening around here today?"

"Naah," says the barkeep, "just the McGillivary twins getting drunk again."

A fellow walks into a bar in Williams Lake, carrying a small dog. The bartender tells him that dogs aren't allowed, to which the fellow replies that the dog won't be any trouble because he has no legs. Hearing this sad news, the bartender relents. "What's the dog's name?" he asks.

"Doesn't have one," says the fellow.

"Cute dog like this?" says the bartender. "Why don't you give him a name?"

"What's the use?" says the fellow. "Damn dog never comes when I call it."

This fellow walks into a bar in Toronto, actually the rooftop bar at the old Park Plaza Hotel. He sits at the bar, next to a guy in a suit. The other guy says to him, "How's it going? You from around here?"

"No," says the fellow. "I'm from Vancouver. I'm in town for the booksellers' convention."

"Ah," says the guy in the suit. "So you probably came up here to look at the literary stuff. You see the caricatures over here? Peggy Atwood, Bob Fulford . . ."

"Who's the guy with the funny ears?"

"Him? That's Doug Marshall."

"You don't say. No, that's not why I came up here."

"I see," says the guy in the suit. "You came up here because you heard about the unusual wind patterns around this place."

"Uh, no," says the fellow. "I never heard anything about that."

"Really?" says the guy in the suit. "This place is famous for it. You can jump off the balcony over there, and just before you hit the ground there's this incredible updraught that lands you soft as a feather on Bloor Street."

"Now *that* I don't believe," says the fellow, who wasn't born yesterday.

"Come over here," says the guy in the suit, leading him to the balcony. "If you jump from right here, you'll come to no harm. Give it a try."

"No way," says the fellow. "That's impossible."

"Impossible?" says the guy in the suit. "Hundred bucks says I can do it."

So the fellow pulls out a hundred bucks, and the guy in the suit jumps over the balcony. Sure enough, just before he hits the ground, he slows down and lands gracefully on his feet. He looks up, smiles at the fellow from Vancouver, and re-enters the building. A couple of minutes later, he steps off the elevator and, with a big smile, takes the fellow's hundred dollars. "Tell you what," he says. "I'll give you a chance to win back your money. Double or nothing if you do it yourself."

People in the book trade can't afford to lose that sort of money, so the fellow from Vancouver peels off his last hundred dollars, slaps it down on the bar, and walks back out onto the balcony. "Where's the right spot?" he asks.

"Right down there," says the guy in the suit. "Aim for that manhole cover. You'll be fine."

The fellow from Vancouver climbs over the ledge and jumps, aiming for the manhole cover. He hits it going a terrible speed. He'll never see the Yaletown Brewing Company again. The guy in the suit returns to the bar, picking up the late Vancouverite's money. Just then, Harold, possibly the best waiter in the world, walks by. "Jesus," says Harold. "Get a couple of drinks into you, Superman, and you turn into a real shit."

***

A fellow walks into a bar in Moncton and gets into conversation with another guy. They start talking about holidays they've had. The second guy mentions a holiday in the Gaspé.

"Jeez," says the first fellow. "Nothin' ever came out of the Gaspé except whores and hockey players."

"That so?" says the other guy. "My wife comes from the Gaspé."

"You don't say," says the fellow. "What team did she play for?"

***

A fellow walks into a bar in North Battleford with his golden retriever. The bartender says, "Sorry, pal, no dogs in here."

Thinking quickly, the fellow looks just slightly to one side of the bartender and says, "But this is my seeing-eye dog."

Abashed, the bartender apologizes, and serves the fellow a drink. When he's had his pint, the fellow leaves. Just outside, he encounters another fellow about to enter the bar with a chihuahua. "Watch your step," he tells the second fellow. "Seeing-eye dogs only in this place."

So the second guy walks in and is told by the bartender that dogs are not allowed in the bar. "But it's my seeing-eye dog," he replies.

"Seeing-eye dog?" says the bartender. "That's a chihuahua!"

"What?" says the fellow. "They gave me a chihuahua?!"

A fellow walks into a bar in Winnipeg and tells the bartender to set up one of each of his single malts. The barkeep pours them out, one by one, and sets them on the bar, all twenty-four of them. The fellow thanks him and starts downing them, one by one. The bartender watches, and within ten minutes most of the glasses are empty.

"You're in a hurry," says the bartender.

"You would be too," says the fellow, downing the last one, "if you had what I've got."

"Jeez," says the bartender. "What have you got?"

"About a dollar eighty."

A fellow walks into a bar in Victoria and sits down next to an attractive woman. He doesn't say anything to her, just starts checking his obviously high-tech watch. She watches for a bit and finally says, "That's a fancy watch you've got there."

"Fancy," he says. "That's an understatement. This watch does things no other watch can do. It tells me things that are going on around me. Like right now it's telling me I'm sitting next to the most beautiful woman in the place."

"Uh-huh," she says. "What else does it tell you?"

"Hang on a moment," he says. "It says you're not wearing any underwear."

"Not such a smart watch," she says. "I'm wearing underwear."

"Damn," he says. "The thing's running an hour fast."

A seal walks into a bar. The bartender says, "What'll you have?"

The seal says, "Anything but Canadian Club."

A fellow walks into a bar in Calgary. After he's had a beer he says to the bartender, "Listen, I know this great joke about Stephen Harper."

The bartender leans forward and says, "Look buster, you oughta know that I'm a supporter of Stephen Harper. That big guy sitting next to you, he's a major fundraiser for Stephen Harper. The huge guy standing behind you with the tattoos, he's our local Stephen Harper candidate. You still sure you want to tell this joke?"

"Hell no," says the fellow. "Not if I'm going to have to explain it three times."

⁂

Three brewers walk into a pub during the Guelph Beer Festival, and the bartender asks them what they'll have. The fellow from Molson orders a pint of Golden. The fellow from Labatt thinks for a moment and orders a pint of Blue. Ken Woods, from the Black Oak Brewery, pauses and asks for an orange juice. "Hell," he says, "if these guys aren't going to have a beer, I won't either."

⁂

So this dyslexic walks into a bra.

⁂

A fellow from Quebec walks into a bar in Toronto and finds there's a competition going on. The bartender explains that anyone who can drink twenty pints of Molson Canadian not only gets it for free but wins a hundred bucks as well. "Well, I don't know," says the guy from Quebec, who then walks out.

The competition goes on, with no winner in sight. Finally, the guy from Quebec comes back in and says, "Okay, let's go."

The twenty pints are put in front of him and he makes his way through them, finishing the last pint after about twenty-five minutes. He gets a round of applause and five crisp twenty-dollar bills. "Congratulations," says the bartender. "But I have to know why you disappeared for twenty minutes before you came back and won the contest."

"Oh, dat," says the guy from Quebec, who only now has put on an accent, "I 'ad to go to the place next door first to see if I could do it."

A fellow walks into a bar and says to the bartender, "Quick, give me a pint before the trouble starts."

The bartender serves him a pint, which goes down pretty quickly. The historic comic rule of three applies, so we know that the same thing is going to happen a second time—a pint before the trouble starts—without comment, and finally a third time. Having served this fellow his third pint, the barkeep asks if the fellow is considering paying for these beers.

"Uh-oh," says the fellow. "Here's where the trouble starts."

Three fellows walk into a bar in New Liskeard. They each order a pint of beer, and—wouldn't you know it?—each pint has a fly paddling like crazy in the foam. The fellow from Vancouver puts his beer to one side and orders a fresh one. The fellow from Halifax deftly pulls the fly out of his glass and drinks the beer. The fellow from Toronto takes the fly out of his glass and squeezes it over his beer, crying, "Spit it out, you little bastard!"

A fellow walks into a bar on Granville Island, sits down, and from a bag takes out a small wooden box. He opens the box and out steps a little man in a tiny tuxedo, who runs down the length of the bar and jumps over to the piano, where he plays a few warm-up scales before dazzling the bar with a Bach fugue and a Scott Joplin rag. A guy sitting next to the fellow with the little wooden box is impressed, and he says so.

"Oh, you see a lot of surprising things in here," says the fellow. "You see that old lamp down at the end of the bar? There's a genie in that lamp, and he'll give you a wish, but you want to be careful."

Without another word, the guy approaches the lamp and rubs it a bit, and out comes the genie. The fellow with the little wooden box watches as the guy speaks softly to the genie. "Speak up!" cries the fellow with the little wooden box, but it's too late. A moment later the bar is filled with ducks.

The guy returns to his seat, fighting his way past all these ducks. "Man," he says, "that genie is deaf. I asked for a million bucks, but I got a million ducks."

"Tell me about it," says the fellow with the little wooden box. "You think I asked for a twelve-inch pianist?"

Superman walks into a bar. It's the sort of bar that superheroes go to when they've had a long day of fighting evil. Rubberman is already at the bar, and he can see that Superman is not at his best. His tights are scuffed and there's a rip in his cape. "What happened to you?" asks Rubberman.

"What a day," says the bedraggled superhero. "There wasn't much going on today, and I was just flying around, keeping an eye on things. Anyway, I found myself flying over that building that Wonder Woman lives in. You know the place?"

"Sure," says Rubberman. "I been to a couple of parties at her place."

"So you know she's got that terrace outside. Well, I'm flying overhead at about eight thousand feet, and I look down and there's Wonder Woman out on her terrace and she's got nothing on."

"Wow," says Rubberman. "Wish I could fly."

"So I bank left, decelerate, reduce altitude, go over again at about four thousand feet, and I can see she's definitely naked. And she seems to be writhing."

"Oh man," says Rubberman. "What did you do then?"

"Bank left again, decelerate further, reduce altitude again, so I'm flying immediately overhead. All previous conclusions verified. Wonder Woman is clearly in a state of sexual excitement."

"So what the hell did you do, Supe?" asks Rubberman, who is by now in a bit of a state himself.

"Do?" asks Superman. "What could I do? I'm only superhuman, after all. I swooped."

"You swooped?"

"I swooped straight down on Wonder Woman."

Rubberman pauses to visualize the moment. "I bet Wonder Woman was surprised."

Superman rubs his powerful chin. "She was surprised, all right. But not half as surprised as the Invisible Man."

A grasshopper goes into a bar in Saskatoon and orders a beer. The bartender says, "Say, did you know we've got a drink named after you?"

The surprised grasshopper replies, "Really? You've got a drink called Bob?"

The original animal-walks-into-a-bar joke: This alligator (1) walks into a bar and orders a beer (2). The bartender pours the beer (3) and says to the alligator, "That'll be $13.50." (4) The alligator pays up and drinks the beer, then prepares to leave. "Say," says the bartender, "we don't get a lot of alligators in here."

"At these prices," replies the alligator, "I'm not surprised." (5)

(1) This joke has encompassed practically the entire animal kingdom over the years. Sometimes it's a bear, an emu, various breeds of dog, you name it. I use the alligator myself, because it's the way I first heard it, and I like the visual image.

(2) It is a given of the animal-walks-into-a-bar joke that the animal can both speak and comprehend English.

(3) It is also a given that the bartender is of the I've-seen-everything school and will serve the animal without asking for ID or checking the local bylaws.

(4) The joke—feeble as it is—hinges upon the animal being overcharged for its beer. It has never been clear to me if this is simply an expensive bar or if the bartender is deliberately bilking the animal, assuming that an alligator, say, will not know the going price of a beer. If the latter, it reflects poorly on the bartender.

(5) The punchline is one you can see coming a mile away, but it becomes clear why this has to be an animal. See the definitive study by Smithers and Smithers (University of Oshawa Press, 1984) on the comic incongruity of animals in bars. It wouldn't work if it were, say, a Nova Scotian or a Jehovah's Witness or a priest or a rabbi.

# A Wee Bibliography

**B**ooks and pubs go together like port and Stilton; they're terrific on their own but sensational together. You could make an argument for matching authors and beers, much as wine (and beer) writers match beverages to particular foods. If you're reading, say, early Evelyn Waugh, you might want a beer with a biting hop character. A spunky American IPA would do the trick. Carol Shields might call for something with an air of surprise to it—something made a bit perky through the addition of cherries or raspberries, for instance. The Russians, on the other hand, need a beer that's big and solemn, a beer to get you through a Moscow winter: a big Belgian knock-you-down kind of beer.

Or you could simply read books about drinking. Ray Oldenburg's *The Great Good Place*—mentioned in my introduction—makes an eloquent plea for a place that is neither home nor the workplace, a democratic third place where men and women can gather as equals and speak freely. In most cultures, the third place is some sort of bar or pub; elsewhere, it might exist to serve coffee. I know which I prefer.

I have taken much inspiration from *The Faber Book of Drink, Drinkers and Drinking*, an eclectic collection of drink-related poetry and prose edited by Simon Rae. (A barkeep of my acquaintance asked me what I was reading one day, and I told him the title. "It combines all my interests," I told him.) This invaluable compilation draws on such writers as Shakespeare, Marco Polo, Dorothy Parker, and Homer—a quartet that would make up an admirable dinner party.

Anything by Michael Jackson (and I mean the bearded Englishman, not the eccentric American entertainer) is worthy of your attention. The man who made writing about beer respectable and downright honourable, Jackson was all-wise and all-knowing. As well as excellent beer guides, Jackson regularly produced eye-catching coffee-table books filled with wonderful, thirst-inducing images.

Jackson's Canadian equivalent is Stephen Beaumont, author of *A Taste for Beer* (1995) and *Premium Beer Drinker's Guide* (2000). His *Great Canadian Beer Guide* (2nd edition, 2001) is compulsory reading for anyone who even considers drinking a beer in this country and is long overdue for an update. It is not for nothing that the Campaign for Real Ale updates its outstanding *Good Beer Guide* annually for the pleasure and edification of beer lovers in the UK. I wouldn't go to Britain without it, though I often take *The Quiet Pint* and *The Good Pub Guide* as well.

Literate drinking folk in my neck of the woods can learn plenty from *Tavern in the Town: Early Inns and Taverns of Ontario* by Margaret McBurney and Mary Byers, published by University of

Toronto Press. It's out of print, but the resourceful reader can track one down on abebooks.com.

*Brewed in Canada* by Allen Winn Sneath (2001) is a very good history of beer hereabouts, and I'd also recommend Craig Heron's *Booze: A Distilled History* (2003), which is a first-rate history of all manner of drinking in Canada.

An offbeat book about beer is *Fermenting Revolution: How to Drink Beer and Save the World* (2006) by Christopher Mark O'Brien, a simultaneously breezy and earnest book about, well, drinking beer and saving the world. And you thought you were misbehaving all these years.

At once a cautionary tale and an eloquent memoir about growing up practically in a pub, *The Tender Bar* (2005) by J.R. Moehringer is a beautiful and often funny book.

Finally, if you've always wondered what drinking and hanging about in pubs is like but have been too timid to try it yourself, read practically anything by Kingsley Amis. Amis is the most frequently cited contributor to Simon Rae's aforementioned collection, and for good reason. He knew whereof he wrote.

# Acknowledgements

**D**iane and Peter Waldock plied me with intoxicating beverages and made me write this book in the first place, so the lion's share of the blame must rest on their shoulders. Lloyd Kelly of Collins Canada seemed to find merit in its pages and thought there was life left in it, so he's hardly innocent. My great friends Charlie Owen and Linda Jenetti, on some otherwise unremembered birthday in the seventies, gave me a second-hand typewriter, an instrument that started me on the slippery slope that led to this book, so some of the blame accrues to them as well.

In fact, there are few innocent parties in this sorry tale. Anyone I have passed time with in a pub is in some small way guilty of aiding and abetting, and it's a very long list. I must single out John Jackson as a singularly egregious influence. (To his long-suffering wife, Mary, I can simply apologize for having allowed John to burn down their kitchen one memorable evening. I had no idea that macramé was so dramatically inflammable, and I bet John didn't either.)

Drinkers tend to travel in packs, and I'm happy to acknowl-
edge members of the Sunday afternoon baseball/Artful Dodger
crowd, the estimable Morrissey Tavern set, and the august denizens of the Duke of York and Kilgour's, not to mention habitués at
various times of the Embassy Tavern, the Chez Moi, the Rex Hotel,
the Sticky Wicket, the GSU, and other such palaces of pleasure.
Veterans of the Walk to the Ballpark are worthy of attention, if
only for their ability to drink and walk on the same day, sometimes
at the same time.

I thank Kevin Harper and his colleagues at North 49 Books for
their initial support for this project, and the team at Collins Canada
for their subsequent enthusiasm. And as a writer and bookseller,
I know how much I owe to my fellow booksellers, hard-working,
underpaid purveyors of the written word. Support your local pub
and your local bookseller.

Thank you, Patrick Kennedy, for the Subway Game. When I
told Patrick I was stealing his idea, he bought me a pint. Surely this
should have been the other way around, and I really mean to rec-
tify this oversight. Thanks also to Glen "I'll have wings with that"
Sutherland, who bravely came along on a couple of fact-finding
missions to pubs unknown. I am grateful to Bill Bryson, that wonderfully funny and insightful writer, for graciously contributing his
foreword. There can be no nicer guy on or off the bestseller lists.
I must also grovel to my former workmates at the University of
Toronto Bookstore for enduring me at the best of times, let alone
when I was attempting to write a book in my spare time. Now that
I toil sporadically at Nicholas Hoare, down on Front Street, I'll
grovel to those colleagues as well.

I salute the quality brewers of the world, those men and women who persist in making good beer when it's cheaper and clearly more profitable to make bad beer, and those publicans who bring their own distinct verve to their establishments, valuing character over formula.

There's a song in *Les Miserables* about empty chairs and empty tables, and as we get older we lose some of our companions. I could wish for another pint with the likes of Michael Lee, Winston Nelson, Tom Monohan, Sky Jones, Douglas Marshall, and John Pashley, all taken from us far too soon.

Finally, at the head of the Without Whom column is my wife, Anne, the Evergreen Bride, whose loving support continues to dazzle me. During the writing of this book, she awarded me more than one Compassionate Litter Leave, cleaning up after cats even when it wasn't her turn, and she behaved with remarkable forbearance even when I came home late, stinking of research. To her, countless thanks.

# The Last Word

**A** writer goes into a bar and orders a beer. The bartender, drawing the pint, says, "You seem pretty chipper tonight."

"Indeed I am," replies the writer. "I just finished my book."

"Hey, me too," says the bartender, handing over the beverage.

"Really?" says the writer.

"Yeah," says the bartender, "just before I started my shift. You can borrow it if you like. It's by Tom Clancy."